Singing Was the Easy Part

Singing Was the Easy Part

VIC DAMONE

with

David Chanoff

Foreword by

Larry King

ST. MARTIN'S PRESS NEW YORK

 Printed in the United States of America. For information, address St. Martin's Press, 175 Fifth Avenue, New York, N.Y. 10010.

www.stmartins.com

Library of Congress Cataloging-in-Publication Data

Damone, Vic.
Singing was the easy part / Vic Damone with David Chanoff. — 1st ed.
p. cm.

ISBN 978-0-312-57026-2

1. Damone, Vic. 2. Singers—United States—Biography. I. Chanoff, David. II. Title.
ML420.D1423A3 2009
782.42164'092—dc22
[B] 2008046330

First Edition: June 2009

P1

I dedicate this book with love to my wonderful wife, Rena,
who has been my inspiration in so many things,
not least in helping me decide to write my story.

Also to my sisters, Pia, Teresa, Elaine, and Sandra;
to my children, Perry, Victoria, Maria, and Daniela,
and to the beautiful grandchildren they have blessed me with.

Contents

Acknowledgments

While I was writing this book, several of my dearest friends read at least parts of the manuscript and told me what they thought: Lee Iococca, Larry King, Steve Lawrence, Frank Chirkinian. They know how grateful I am for their feedback, but far more, for their friendship.

There are others I need to thank in a different way. My mom and dad had five children, four girls and me. I loved my sisters, but I always missed having a brother. I used to think about that all the time: how great it would be to have a brother.

As things worked out, over the years I have had the great good fortune to find a group of friends who have been as close to me as brothers, guys who would do anything for me, as I would do anything for them. I consider them the brothers I have chosen rather than brothers I was given. It's a pretty long list, but I've been around a pretty long time, and I have been blessed with friends who have stuck with me. Some are from the music world, some from boxing, some from the movies, some from golf. A few are old pals from when I was growing up in Brooklyn. Others are more recent.

These brothers of mine are the people I have had in my mind while I was writing the story of my life. A storyteller is like a singer;

he needs an audience. Otherwise it just doesn't work. Whether they knew it or not, they have been my audience. For that I have to thank them: Charlie Cumela, Lou Cammarata, Al Silvani, John Dennis, Bill Armanino, John Loiacono, Bill Fugazy, Pat Mazzarulli, Jack Hoffman, Tommy Lasorda, Tony La Russa, Johnny Lujack, Jim McGuigan, Joe Phillips, Sid Mark, Nick Sevano, John Guarino, Joe Favali, Joe Cinque, Ray Cohen, Daniel Sullivan, Al Evans, Father Leo, Norman Geller, Jim Hanna, Tony Martin (ninety-five years old, but still singing, a great, great singer), Rocco Masseli, Rocco Marcello, Jim Palmer, Carroll Shelby, Nelson Sardelli, John Scarpa, Sid Taylor, Donald Trump, Dominic Visconsi, Andy Williams, John Williams, Gary Quinlan, Al Vargo, Steve Wynn.

Then there is David Chanoff, whom I met while he was helping my wife, Rena, write her book—*On the Wings of Love,* which is, by the way, one of the most interesting books I've ever come across, and one of the best reads. While he was working on her book, we would all go out and have dinner together and share stories from our lives. When David heard about some of my experiences, he said that maybe I should write a book, too. And when my wife said I should think seriously about it, I did. *Singing Was the Easy Part* is the result. After a year of working closely together, David, too, has turned out to be a great friend and another brother.

My list of those to whom I owe a debt of gratitude would not be complete without Ann Titus. Over many decades now, she has been my most loyal fan. She has collected articles, photos, letters, records—a veritable archive of material, which she has shared unstintingly with me, together with her constant support. Every entertainer should be so fortunate.

Finally, I would like to thank my agents, Helen and Lorin Rees, for their enthusiasm and support, and my editor at St. Martin's, Michael Flamini. How lucky was I, an Italian kid from Brooklyn, to find a fellow *paisan* who understood what I was talking about.

Foreword
by
Larry King

Vic Damone is a national treasure. His extraordinary voice has been unmatched in American popular music, so much so that on one of the occasions when I interviewed Frank Sinatra and asked his opinion of various singers, when I got to Vic his response was immediate: "I wish I had his pipes. No one sounds better. He is *the* essential baritone."

In this absolutely wonderful book Vic traces his career back to the days in Brooklyn, New York—where we shared the same high school, Lafayette. In fact, I sat at the desk that Vic had sat at three years before. He had carved his name into the top of the desk—"Vito Farinola" (it was wisely changed some time later).

When Vic began to get hits in his early years, we in the neighborhood would listen, enthralled and appreciative that one of us had made it. Vic Damone was a star.

Vic was a headliner throughout his entire career, but he never obtained superstardom. Not because of a lack of talent, though. With a little better luck Vic would have been classed right with Frank Sinatra. At that, he is probably regarded one rung below, but it is a very short rung.

Vic entertained at the very first Larry King Cardiac Foundation gala. Marvin Hamlish played piano, Don Rickles (another friend of Vic's) provided the humor, and Vic Damone closed the show with an array of songs that really set that charity off and running. It is now in its twenty-first year, and we never forget that Vic started it all.

You'll enjoy hearing his multitude of stories, some self-deprecating, many humorous, stories of his romances, and of his various stage exploits throughout the years, including his early movie career. Vic Damone is a wonderful friend, a great guy. He has overcome illness to keep on keeping on. You will enjoy this book as much as I did. I call him a national treasure. You will, with no doubt whatsoever, treasure this book.

Singing Was the Easy Part

1

Stardust on His Shoulders

I've had a couple of angels in my life. One was Frank Sinatra, who was my idol when I was a teenager just learning how to sing and was my friend from the moment he forgave me in Madison Square Garden for the disrespect I showed him not once but twice in an embarrassing case of mistaken identity. Frank saved my life once, but I'll tell you about that later. First I want to tell you how we met. That's probably as good a place as any to begin my story, since it happened in Brooklyn, where I'm from. Brooklyn, as in Bensonhurst, 288 Bay Fourteenth Street. A neighborhood full of Italians when I was born there in 1928, and still full of Italians seventeen years later when WHN asked me to sing for *The Gloom Dodgers*.

WHN was the Brooklyn Dodgers' radio network—they broadcast all the games. And every morning at nine A.M. during the baseball season the *Gloom Dodgers* show would come on. *The Gloom Dodgers* was pure entertainment, jokes and music meant to chase away the gloom after the Dodgers lost another one, as they regularly did in those pre–Jackie Robinson days. Morey Amsterdam was a funny, talented guy, and when I won the audition to sing on the show he said, "You know, the name Vito Farinola just isn't going to work. I think you have to change it."

I could see that, even if I was only seventeen. "Yeah," I said, "I agree. We've got to change it. But since it's my name, I'll tell you what the new name will be. Vito . . . Vito . . . How about Vic?"

"Yeah," he said. "Vic. I like it."

"No," I said, "*I* like it." I was a pugnacious little street kid, and anyway, it was my name we were changing. "Now, how about the second name, something American, like . . . Drake? Vic Drake."

"No," he said, "I don't like it."

"Good," I said. "Neither do I. Let's see, Farinola. Maybe Farin. No, that doesn't sound right. Hey, my mom's maiden name was Damone. How about Damone? Vic Damone?"

"Terrific," Morey Amsterdam said. "Vic Damone! I like it."

"Me too," I said. "My father won't he happy, but my mom will love it."

And from that moment on, as far as performing went, I stopped being Vito Farinola and became Vic Damone.

After I had been singing on *Gloom Dodgers* for a while the program director said he'd like to try something different. Sometimes during the Dodgers' games there would be rain delays. Whenever that happened Red Barber, the famous Dodgers announcer, would have to fill in with patter. But WHN had an orchestra, and the program director thought that if I were to sing with the orchestra during rain delays it might help keep the audience tuned in.

"Let's give it a try," he said. "We'll put together maybe fifteen minutes of music. Then, when there's a rain delay, we'll put you on live. But we won't tell them you're live. All we'll say is "And now here's Vic Damone to entertain you."

That sounded okay with me. I sang with the orchestra on *Gloom Dodgers,* so I knew them well. "What I'd like to do," I said, "is get hold of some of Frank Sinatra's arrangements. I love Frank Sinatra. We can learn his arrangements, and I'll try to sing them exactly the way he does. It'll be like a tribute to him." I'd been listening to Sinatra on the radio every chance I got since I was about thirteen and I had tried hard to imitate his sound. I knew I had the timbre of my voice just about right, that I had his phrasing down, that I could really make myself sound like him. As far as I was concerned, Frank Sinatra was it, *the* model for how I wanted to be able to sound.

We did manage to get hold of five or six copies of the original Alex Stordahl arrangements of Sinatra's songs, but the first night I went to the studio there was no rain. So we rehearsed. We rehearsed the second and third nights, too. We had those arrangements down pat. Then the fourth night it did rain, and the game was delayed. "Five minutes," said the producer. "You're on in five minutes." We were ready, the orchestra, the conductor, and me, all of us cramped into WHN's little studio. We were going to do the numbers one after another, no pauses, no announcements, no applause, since there was no audience; it would sound just like a record, one cut followed by the next followed by the next.

Five minutes later Red Barber announced, "Tonight, ladies and gentlemen, during the rain delay we're going to have some entertainment. Here, for your listening pleasure, is Vic Damone." At that the producer signaled us from the control booth, and we launched into "Somewhere in the Night There Must Be Someone for Me." I thought I was sounding just like Frank.

At exactly that moment in an apartment at the Waldorf Astoria in Manhattan a bunch of guys were sitting around playing poker. In the background the radio was on. They had been listening to the Dodgers game, but now that there was a rain delay, they had turned it down and were concentrating on their hands and their kibbitzing. The guys sitting around the table were Jule Styne, Sammy Cahn, and Jimmy Van Heusen, all famous songwriters. Also Bullets Durgom, a talent manager, and Frank Sinatra. It was Frank's apartment. The guys hadn't heard Red Barber say that Vic Damone was singing, but they recognized the music, even if it was soft in the background. Sammy Cahn cocked his ear and said, "Frank, listen. Those are your records?" And Frank said, "Yeah, there's a rain delay, so they're playing my songs."

They listened for a bit, to one song, then another. I was singing my heart out, mimicking Frank Sinatra for all I was worth. And finally Red Barber came back on. "Ladies and gentlemen, the rain has let up and it looks like we're going to resume play. That was Vic Damone singing for your enjoyment."

And Frank said, "What? Who?" He threw his arms up in the air. "Who did he say? That was *me* singing! Vic *who*?"

Back in the studio we were off the air and congratulating each other. "Hey, great band. Good work. Great, yes, thank you." Just then the phone rang in the control booth and the engineer pushed the button to talk into the studio. "Hey, Vic, there's a guy on the phone says he wants to talk to you. It's Frank Sinatra."

"Yeah, right," I said. "Frank Sinatra's calling me. Right." I knew who it was, and for sure it wasn't Frank Sinatra. It was the guys in Brooklyn, my buddies. They all knew I loved Frank, that I practiced singing like Frank, that I was trying to be Frank. And of course they were listening to the game. Who in Brooklyn wasn't? So I took my time getting to the control booth, and while I was going there I was doing in my head what Danny Thomas used to call the "Jack story." The Jack story is about the guy who buys a beautiful new car that conks out on a deserted road. He's frustrated, angry. He just bought the car. As soon as he gets out to walk to the nearest service station, it starts to rain. Now he's really angry. The whole way to the service station he's talking to himself. They're going to charge him a fortune to fix the car, they're going to charge him even more, the bastards, for having to go get the car. Then, when they see it's a new car, they're going to jack up the price even more than that! The bastards are going to leave him penniless. By the time he gets to the service station, he hates the mechanic heart and soul. "Don't you tell me how much you're going to charge!" he yells at the startled mechanic, who hasn't the vaguest idea what he's talking about. That's the Jack story; you build something up in your mind that's completely disconnected from reality.

On my way to the control booth I was doing the Jack story. The Bay Fourteenth Street guys are calling me, pretending to be Frank Sinatra. Just to break my balls. Bastards don't like that I can sing like Frank, huh? Think it's funny, huh? Have to call me here at work where I'm trying to make a few bucks, lazy bastards! Frank Sinatra on the phone. Right!

By the time I picked up the phone I was fuming.

"Hello?"

"Yeah," comes this voice, "I wanna talk to Vic Damone. Is he there?"

"Yeah, who is this?"

"Frank Sinatra!"

"Yeah, right. And I'm the pope!" Slam! I hang up.

"Hey," said the engineer, "you just hung up on Frank Sinatra."

"That wasn't Frank Sinatra," I said. "That was my buddies from Brooklyn. Frank Sinatra's not gonna call me. What're you, crazy?"

Just then the phone rang again. I was still standing next to it, so I picked it up.

"Hello."

"Listen, I want to talk to Vic Damone. This is Frank Sinatra and—"

"Yeah, and I'm still the pope." Slam!

Eight months later I had recorded a song, "I Have But One Heart," that had gone straight up the pop charts. At that point I was a one-hit wonder; no one knew if I could do it again, including me. But at least people recognized my name. So much so that Ed Sullivan invited me to sing at a Madison Square Garden charity fund-raiser as part of a star-studded lineup that included some of the biggest names in the business. I was going to sing in front of thousands of people, at Madison Square Garden. I was in awe.

On the day of the concert I was standing backstage with my manager, Lou Capone, and Jack Kelly, my piano player, watching the stars arrive. All of a sudden I see Frank Sinatra coming in the middle of his retinue, with his bow tie hanging down, the way he used to wear it then. "Oh my God," I whispered to Lou Capone. "Look, it's Frank. Aw Jesus, it's Frank Sinatra." I was absolutely star-struck. I was going to sing on the same stage as Frank Sinatra. I couldn't believe it.

All of a sudden Frank's eyes caught mine—he must have sensed I was staring at him—and somebody said, "That's Vic Damone." Now he was looking straight at me. "Jesus, Lou," I whispered, "I think he's looking at us."

"No, he's not," said Lou. "He's looking at *you*."

"Wh . . . wh . . . wh . . . why is he looking at *me*?"

And then Frank Sinatra points at me and says, "You!"

And I say, "Me?"

"You! Come here!"

"He wants to see us," I whisper to Lou.

"No, he wants to see *you*."

So I go over, with Lou and Jack Kelly, my piano player, trailing behind. And Frank Sinatra sticks his finger in my chest.

"Who do you think you are," he says, "hanging up on me?"

"What?"

"Who do you think you are?" He's jabbing me in the chest with his finger. "I called you after that show. The Dodgers game? I heard you singing. You sang great. And I called you. And you hung up on me" Jabbing.

"Whoa," I said. "Was that really you?"

"What do you mean, was it me? I said it was Frank Sinatra!"

"Yeah, but I didn't know it was you. I wouldn't hang up on you. You're the greatest. I try to copy you in every way. "

"What?"

"I thought it was my pals in Brooklyn putting me on. Why would Frank Sinatra ever call *me*?"

"Well, I did call you. And you hung up on me. Twice!"

"But I didn't know. I'd never . . . I thought it was my pals in Brooklyn."

"Kid." He's looking at me. "Is that really what happened?"

"Yeah, yes. I'd never hang up on you. You're like God to me."

And Frank Sinatra grabbed me around the neck, and hugged me and kissed me on the cheek, and said, "Kid, okay. Now I understand."

Then he went over to Ed Sullivan, who was also greeting people backstage. "Ed," he says, "this is Vic Damone. I want him to follow me, and I want to introduce him."

"Sure," said Ed Sullivan. "Whatever you say, Frank."

A little later Sinatra was onstage singing a couple of his songs, and when he finished, and the screaming and yelling had died down, he said, "Folks, I'm going to bring a kid out here. And this kid can sing. He's got a hit record and he's doing great. This kid has stardust on his shoulders. Vic Damone!"

Frank and I kept a close relationship until he died. He always had a certain thing about me, a little as if I was his younger brother. They say that imitation is the sincerest form of flattery, and at the beginning of my career, before I matured and developed my own style, I did do my absolute best to copy him. I think he was touched by that. He also appreciated my voice, which, of course, meant a lot to me. Respect is a big thing for Italians, and to get respect from Frank Sinatra meant the world, especially for a young singer. But, of course, he knew how much I reciprocated his feelings, and it was the reciprocity that kept us tight for all those years. The fact was, I owed him a lot. He saved my life once. I'm not saying that lightly. He *really* saved my life.

I was married to Anna Maria Pierangeli at the time, a beautiful Italian movie star who was making movies in Hollywood. Anna Maria had been going out with James Dean when we met, but when the dust settled it was me that she ended up marrying. We had been together for four years or so, and we had a son, Perry, who was three years old when these events happened.

My career was really in high gear then. I had developed a fan base in Europe as well as in the United States, and I had gone off on a European tour for a couple of weeks. Everything had been more or less fine between us when I left. Normal. No big fights, no jealousies, nothing. But when I got back Anna Maria told me she wanted a divorce. No reason given. She just wanted one.

I was shocked. I couldn't imagine what had happened. But after I calmed down a little I moved out of the house to give her some space to think about it. At the same time, I had my suspicions. What would make her suddenly want a divorce? The only thing I could think of was that maybe there was some other guy. With that in mind, I hired a private detective to watch and see whether there was something going on, somebody I didn't know about.

My agent at that time was Fred Apollo, and every morning at ten-thirty I would go over to his office in the William Morris Building to see what developments might be happening with my career. And every morning while I was there I would call the private detective for an update. "Anything happen last night?" I'd ask. And for the first three or four nights he was on the job, the answer was, "Nothing.

She never left the house." Then one morning I asked and he said, "Yes." "Okay," I said, "let me hear it." So he gave me the report.

"On or about eleven-thirty last night your wife got into her car and drove off. We followed her to Bel Air, the west gate. She pulled up at a house and rang the doorbell. A man opened the door and kissed her. Then they went inside."

"When did she leave?"

"She left at three A.M."

"Do you know whose house it was?"

"The house belongs to Al Hart."

"Al Hart?" I think I screamed this into the phone. "That son of a bitch! I'm going to kill that son of a bitch right now!" I slammed the phone down. Freddy Apollo was staring at me. His mouth was working, but nothing was coming out. I was beside myself. Al Hart, that weasily little son of a bitch! That weasily little soon-to-be-dead son of a bitch! I kept a gun in the glove compartment of my car. We lived up on Moraga Drive in an out-of-the-way area, which is why I had it. Well, now I was going to use it. I'm going to drive over to that son of a bitch's office and shoot him right between the eyes—that was the one thought I had in my head. I was going to kill the lying little prick. I was so enraged I could hardly see.

Al Hart! A so-called friend. Al Hart was a rich man; he owned the City National Bank in Los Angeles. He was a member at the exclusive Hillcrest Country Club, which was saying something. Hillcrest was known for its championship golf course and its spectacular Sunday brunches. Hillcrest's brunches were the talk of the town, they were so lavish. And Al Hart used to invite us for brunch, after which he'd say, "Vic, why don't you play some golf while you're here?" I was already semi-obsessed with golf, and the Hillcrest course was beautiful. We'd eat and he'd say, "Go ahead play nine holes. Don't worry about Anna Maria, I'll take care of her." So I got used to playing at Hillcrest on Sundays while Al "took care" of my wife. Which I now knew what he meant.

I was out the door and on my way down the stairs before Freddy could say anything. I was going to drive over to the main bank where Hart had his office. I was seeing this in my head as I hurried across El Camino to the parking lot. Hart wouldn't be expecting me. I'd say, Hi, I need to see Mr. Hart. It's Vic Damone. Very nice. I knew he'd invite me in. And once I was in I'd take out the gun, put it right between his eyes, and blow his fucking brains out.

I got in my car, a special Dual-Ghia sports model, and checked the glove compartment. There it was, the snub-nose .38. I started the engine and went to pull out of the lot. But suddenly there was Poochie standing right in front of the car, blocking me. Pucci. Pooch. Frank Sinatra's bodyguard. A huge former football player who weighed in at around three hundred pounds. Stronger than an ox. I knew Pooch. We all knew Pooch. Anyone who hung out with Frank knew him.

"Pooch, get out of the way. I gotta go."

Pooch stood there. The man was like a mountain. "Get out of the car!" he said.

"Pooch, I gotta go do something. Get out of the way."

"I said, get out of the car. Mr. Sinatra wants to see you."

"Well, I can't go see him now. I gotta do something."

"Listen. You don't get out of the car, I'm gonna pick it up and throw it."

This Dual-Ghia was one of the great cars of all time. There were only four of this special model in the country. I had one, Peter Lawford had one, Frank had one, and someone else we didn't know had one. The front of it looked like a jet. Poochie dwarfed the thing. The guy was definitely big enough to do it.

"No, no, no," I said. "Don't touch the car."

I got out. "All right. What?"

"Come with me." Pooch put his arm around my shoulder. Very heavy. "Mr. Sinatra wants you."

Sonofabitch. "I'll be right back," I said to the parking attendant. "Leave the car right where it is."

I was walking with Pooch back across El Camino to the William Morris Building, where Frank had his office, too. But my mind was still on Al Hart and how I had to kill him.

"Pooch," I said, "what does he want?"

"He wants to talk to you." His arm still around my shoulder.

"I wonder what he wants to talk to me about. Only for him. He's the only guy. I gotta go do something."

"I know. That's what he wants to talk to you about."

I was still puzzling this out as we rode the elevator up to Frank's floor. How did Frank know? We got out of the elevator, and there was Frank standing in the hallway, his arms folded.

"Frank," I said. "What is it? What do you want?"

"C'mon, kid," he said. He put his arm on my shoulders and guided me into his office. When we got in he turned around and locked the door behind us, leaving Pooch outside. In case I should escape or something.

"You know what?" he said.

"What?

"Wait. First, you want a drink?"

I didn't drink, but this time I could really use one.

"Yeah. Yeah, I do want a drink. Anything."

Frank poured a Jack Daniels for himself and one for me.

"You know what?" he said. "Instead of killing *him,* why don't you kill *her*?"

I'm thinking, Freddy Apollo called him. That was the only way. Fred knew me. He knew I had a temper, and if I said I was going to do something, I was going to do it. If I said, "I'm going to kill that son of a bitch Al Hart," Fred knew that that was what I was going to do. So then what? Fred's stunned, except suddenly he thinks, Frank Sinatra. Frank Sinatra can stop me. And Frank's office is in the same building. So he calls. "Vic Damone is on his way to kill Al Hart. He's got a gun in his car. You better stop him." So Frank tells Pooch, "Go down and get him. He's going to kill somebody. Stop him and bring him up here." That was how.

"Don't kill *him,*" he says, "you ought to kill *her.* Him you should send roses to."

Send roses to him? What was he talking about? And suddenly I snapped out of it. It was as if someone had poured a bucket of cold water over me.

"Roses? What are you saying?"

"Dago, listen." He called me Dago. "You want to find out how the fuck this guy ever did it. I mean, just how did he do it? You're a good-looking guy, you have a kid with her. And look at him. Jesus. How in the world did a guy like that manage it? I want to know. I want to learn how he got her away from you. Send him roses. Talk to him. 'You son of a bitch, how did you do it? What did you say to her?' And if you're going to kill someone, kill her. But you know what? She's not worth it."

And I thought, Oh my God, he's right. Why should I kill him? And *her*? She's not to be trusted. She has no character. For her to do that to me, and us with a child? She's not worth a cent. I felt as if I had awakened from the blind rage I was in. I was thinking again. And what if I had gone to the bank and shot him? They would have killed me. The bank guards wouldn't have waited for the police. They would have stormed in and gunned me down. And if it hadn't been for Frank, that's exactly what would have happened.

The way I got out to Hollywood in the first place was that after I had a couple of hit records William Morris booked me at the Mocambo on Sunset Boulevard, one of the two big Los Angeles clubs. My PR people there, Henry Rogers and Warren Cowan, did a great job at getting the word out, and celebrities began coming out to my shows, including Joe Pasternak, a famous MGM producer. Pasternak had made various hits, including *Destry Rides Again* with James Stewart and Marlene Dietrich and *Anchors Aweigh,* with Frank Sinatra and Gene Kelly. He was now in the planning stages for another one, and when he saw me at the Mocambo he asked me to come in and do a screen test. I did that, and suddenly I found myself under contract with MGM.

My maiden voyage there was *Rich Young and Pretty,* in which I played Jane Powell's love interest. Pasternak's next movie was going to be *Golden Boy,* a remake of a 1930s William Holden movie about a boxer. Something told him that I might be right for the boxer's role, and when we sat down to talk about it, one of the first things he asked was if I knew how to fight. "Sure," I said. "I'm from Brooklyn. Of course I can fight—dirty."

"No," Pasternak said, "I mean box. You have to know how to box. If you can't, I suggest you get yourself a professional trainer and learn. You'll need it."

That was how I met Al Silvani. Al was a famous boxing trainer Sinatra had hired to teach him how to defend himself. Silvani was a legend. He trained Jake LaMotta, Rocky Graziano, Henry Armstrong, Carmen Basilio, and Ingemar Johansson. By the time he retired he had trained twenty world champions, including Floyd Patterson, Alexis Arquello, and Eddie Machen. He was also a stuntman and technical adviser to the movie industry. If you remember Sylvester Stallone's corner man in the original *Rocky,* the guy with the Q-Tip in his mouth? That was Al Silvani. Al knew everybody. If he hadn't trained them, he was friends with them.

So Al agreed to teach me how to fight clean—I mean, to box. He started me with calisthenics, put me to work on the speed bag, the heavy bag, taught me to bob and weave, the whole works. I took to it like a duck to water. *Golden Boy,* the movie, was never made, for reasons I don't know. But Al and I got along great, and he stayed with me for a year and a half, working out almost every day, even when I was on the road. Later I got interested in kung fu and spent a lot of time training with Bruce Lee. But that's another story.

Hanging out with Al Silvani, I got to know most of the big fighters, including Sugar Ray Robinson, a sweet man who was maybe the greatest fighter of all time, and Giacobbe LaMotta, that is, Jake LaMotta, the Raging Bull, who might have been the toughest fighter of all time. Al and I would go to the boxing matches together, then get together with the fighters afterward. When I began performing all over the country I got to see lots of fights. I'd sing, Al and I would work out, then we'd go see whatever fights were going on.

That's what I was doing in Miami in the winter of 1950. I was singing at the Beachcomber Hotel there, a mob-owned place, on a bill with Cab Calloway and the Ritz Brothers. Cab was famous from his stint at the Cotton Club, and the Ritz Brothers, Al, Jim, and Harry, were a big song, dance, and comedy act, like a cross between the Nicholas Brothers and the Marx Brothers. On opening night I went on first and Cab went after me, with the Ritz Brothers headlining and going last. We were doing two shows a night.

After the opening, though, the mob manager decided to change the order. I was onstage in a tuxedo doing beautiful songs, and Cab following me with his hi-di-hi-di-ho routine just didn't work, they said. So they told me, "Tomorrow Cab Calloway's going on first and you go second. He can't follow you." I said, "Okay, but I think it's going pretty well as is."

"What?" the manager said. The way he looked at me, he didn't have to say anything else.

I knew this wasn't going to sit well with Cab, and it didn't. It pissed him off that he had to open the show. But who's he going to be pissed at, the mob? So instead he was pissed at me. Really pissed. A couple of nights later, between acts, he saw Al Silvani with me backstage, and he recognized Al.

"You're a boxing trainer, aren't you?" he said. "What are you doing with the singer?"

"Well," says Al, "he's doing a movie and I'm teaching him how to fight."

"You're teaching him how to fight?" Cab says. "How to box? Good! Why doesn't he box me?"

"What do you mean, box you?" says Al.

But now Cab was looking at me. "Come over here," he says. "Al's teaching you how to fight?"

"Yeah, he's getting me in shape for a movie."

"Good," he says. "Put up your dukes." And he throws up his hands.

"Cab," I say. "What are you talking about? What are you doing?"

"Come on," he says. "Let's see what he taught you."

Cab Calloway was a burly guy, strong, and also completely nuts. "Come on," he says. "Put up your dukes."

"Cab," says Al. "C'mon. Cut it out. Why are you doing this?"

"I'm going to see how good he is," says Cab. "Come on, put 'em up." I hadn't realized how truly pissed off he was.

"Why?" says Al. "What for?"

And *bam,* Cab hit me right in the face. Not hard, but hard enough.

"Hey," I said. "Don't do that!" But before I could do anything Al had grabbed him and pulled him off to the side. "Don't you get cute with him," he says. "You get cute with him, I'm gonna get cute with you. You want to show how tough you are? You want to go? You want to fight somebody? How about me? You want to pull some shit with me?"

Al was a tough son of a bitch, intimidating.

"Okay," says, Cab. "Okay, I got it."

"Don't fuck with him," says Al. "You fuck with him, you're gonna fuck with me. He's a nice kid. What'd he ever do to you?"

"Okay," Cab says. "I got it. I got it."

Meanwhile, every day Al and I were going to the gym. He'd have me working on the speed bag, the heavy bag. In the ring he'd put on two catcher's mitts and move them around while I hit and ducked, hit and ducked, left hook, right cross, *bam, bam, bam*. I loved it. I felt great. One day we were in the gym, and there was Sugar Ray Robinson and his manager, George Gainford. They were friends of Al's, of course, and when he introduced me, Sugar Ray said, "You sing, man, right? You sing so pretty. I love the way you sing. What are you doing here?"

"Thanks, Sugar Ray," I said. "I'm doing shows at the Beachcomber."

"I've gotta do this fight tonight," he said. "An exhibition. You gonna come and see me?"

"I hadn't planned on it."

"But would you like to come?"

"Are you kidding? I'd love to see you fight."

"George," he says to Gainford, "set it up. And let me know when he gets there."

This was just great. I was going to see Sugar Ray Robinson fight. "Ray," I said, I've got to do a show, but I'll come right over afterward."

"I'll tell you what," he said. "In case the fight starts before you get there, come to my corner and let them know you're here. Don't worry about it, it's just an exhibition. Make sure you come over to my corner, so I know you've arrived."

"Okay," I said. "We'll get there just as soon as we can."

When we got back to the Beachcomber, I talked to Cab—I figured our little episode was behind us. "Cab," I said, "could you do me a favor? Sugar Ray Robinson's fighting tonight. I saw him today at the gym, and he asked me to come see him. I'd like to get there as soon as I can. Would you mind shortening your act a little? Then I could shorten mine and get to the fight on time."

"Sure, kid," he said. "No problem. You got it."

As you might have guessed already, that night he stayed on an extra twelve minutes. I was staring at my watch the whole time. "That son of a bitch," said Al. "We ask him to do us a favor."

"Get a cab ready," I told Al, "so when I finish we can hop right in and get over there." I cut my own act ten minutes and practically ran off the stage without even taking a bow. But by the time we got to the fight, it was already the fourth round. We went immediately down to Sugar Ray's corner to tell him, and when the round was over I could see he was mad.

"We just got here," I said. "I'm sorry it took so long."

"Where you been, man?" Ray said. "I want to put this bum away. I've been waiting for you. Where you sitting?"

"Right over there," I said, pointing. George Gainford had gotten us ringside seats, second row.

"Okay," said Ray, "I'm gonna put him right in your lap."

When the round started I could see Sugar Ray looking for where Al and I were sitting. I could also see that the guy he was fighting felt cocky. He was moving around and putting on a little show. The great Sugar Ray Robinson had done nothing over four rounds, and he figured maybe he could even put him away in the fifth. But it only took a minute before Sugar Ray had danced him into position near the ropes on our side, just feet in front of us. Then suddenly, boom, boom, boom; left jab, right hook, right cross, and the guy went down like a tree, right in front of us. Ray stood there for a moment and smiled. It was beautiful.

Afterward we went to Ray's dressing room and watched while

they took pictures of him giving a check to Walter Winchell, who accepted it for the Damon Runyon Cancer Fund. The fight had been a benefit for them. "Hey," he said, "wait for me while I take a shower, then we'll go over and see your show." The second show at the Beachcomber went on a little later in the night.

So Al and I waited, and we walked out of the dressing room with Ray, George Gainford, and another of Ray's boxing friends. On the way out Ray said, "Man, I'm thirsty. I haven't had a drink." We had just passed the arena soft drink stand, which was still open. "Let's stop at the stand," I said. "I'll get you a Coke."

"No, no," he said. "It's all right. I'll get something later." He knew something I didn't. This was segregationist Florida in 1950, and it didn't even occur to me. So I said, "No, let me," and I walked over to the stand. "I'll have five Cokes," I said to the guy, thinking Al, me, Ray, Gainford, and Ray's other friend.

"You can have two," the guy said.

"No, no, there's five of us. I want five."

"I don't serve niggers," he said.

"What?" I couldn't believe it. I thought he was joking. "Niggers? That's Sugar Ray Robinson!"

"I don't give a shit," the guy said. "I'm not serving him."

"Sugar Ray Robinson," I said. "You know who he is?"

"I told you, I don't give a shit."

"You don't give a shit? You made your money tonight because of him. You're not going to serve him a drink?"

"That's right. I'm not."

I was so angry I just dove over the counter and grabbed the guy by the collar and started shaking him. I'm shaking him. I'm ready to choke the son of a bitch to death when I hear Ray and the others laughing. And while they were laughing Al grabbed me from the back and pulled me off the guy. They're laughing and laughing. "I can't believe it," said Ray. "You fancy-Dan singer. You doing that for me? Forget about it. I'm used to this shit. C'mon, I want to see your show."

At that moment I was embarrassed to be white. Can you imagine, the great Sugar Ray Robinson not able to get a Coke? But I saw the humor in it too, why they were all laughing. There I was with these four very tough guys, and I was the one who went over the counter. They thought that was hilarious. I saw Ray many times after that, and he never forgot it. "Hey, tough guy," he'd say. "How you doin', tough guy?"

After the show that night I introduced Ray to Cab Calloway, although I think they probably knew each other from before. And Ray told him what had happened. "You know what this crazy son of a bitch did for me tonight? He was going to fight this white pecker who wouldn't give us a Coke. Called us niggers. He went over the counter. Can you believe that? The singer!"

Cab listened. When Ray Robinson talked, everybody listened. But Cab never forgave me for taking his spot. And I had nothing to do with it.

Jake LaMotta was another fighter I became friends with through Al. Jake was from the Bronx; I think they called him the Bronx Bull before they called him the Raging Bull. He was middleweight champion for a while and had six fights with Ray Robinson, only one of which he won. But he was so tough even Robinson couldn't knock him out. The referee stopped their last fight in the thirteenth round, after Robinson had hurt Jake so badly he couldn't raise his arms to defend himself anymore. Robinson was beating the hell out of him, but the man just refused to go down. I got to know Jake well, and also his pal Rocky Graziano, another killer in the ring. Strangely enough, they were both funny guys. Graziano even became a stand-up comedian after he retired, which Jake also tried for a while.

Al trained Jake at some point, and was his cut man too, so the fact that he was training me put me in a kind of elite circle. I got so interested in self-defense that I started doing kung fu in addition to boxing, and through Jay Sebring I met Bruce Lee. Jay Sebring was close friends with Sharon Tate and was at her house along with other friends when the Charles Manson family arrived and murdered everyone there. Jay had been a great hairstylist, and hugely successful. He cut a lot of celebrities' hair—Steve McQueen, Warren Beatty, Kirk Douglas. Kirk Douglas even hired him to do all the hairstyling for the movie *Spartacus*. Jay cut my hair also, and I sent all my friends to him. I even helped finance his Hollywood salon.

Among other things, Jay practiced kung fu and worked out with Bruce Lee, and I started working with him, too. From Bruce I learned how to stun someone if he came after you, and how to cripple him if he still came after you. Bruce taught these techniques in steps, the final one being how to break a person's neck if he was really nuts and kept coming at you. Bruce said that fighting is not something you look for, but something that looks for you. That might be, though I didn't find it to be true in my case. I actually kept waiting for someone to try something with me, but whatever confrontations I did have never descended to that level. I was ready, though. Maybe not anxiously waiting, but waiting, anyway.

I thought my time had arrived one night when I was singing at Basin Street East in New York. I was in the middle of a soft ballad when I heard a bullhorn voice from the back somewhere go, "Sing it, you Italian faggot!"

I couldn't believe my ears. I stopped singing. My conductor, Joe Parnello, was looking at me; he had heard it, too, and he didn't know what to do. I had stopped singing. Should the band keep playing, or what?

"Stop the music," I told him. "I just heard someone say something to me that wasn't very polite." I said this into the mike, to the audience. "And I don't know if I heard it right."

Just then it came again. "I said, Sing it, you Italian faggot!"

"Okay, now I definitely heard it," I said.

Oh my God. I'd been just waiting for something like this. I had trained, boxed with Al, done martial arts with Bruce. All the time just waiting for some wise guy to say something like this. And here it was. Oh man, was I ready.

"Will you turn up the houselights, please?" I said. "I want to see who said that. Would that person please stand up?" And someone stood up in the back and yelled, "It's me, you schmuck. It's Jake LaMotta."

"Jake LaMotta, you son of a bitch." The audience was absolutely on edge until Jake and I both started to laugh. Then they broke out laughing, utterly relieved, I'm sure. "Ladies and gentlemen," I said, "of all the people in the world. I've been learning how to take care of myself, waiting for some crazy bastard to come along so I could whack his head off. And of all people, it's Jake LaMotta, the world's toughest man. Come up onstage, you crazy son of a bitch." Which he did, and started to tell funny stories. I practically had to push him off so I could get on with the show.

2

Frank Costello Put His Thumb Up and Said . . . He Lives!

This story's still a little sensitive, even after fifty years, which is why I'm going to use a couple of made-up names here. You'll see why in a minute. But other than those couple of names, every detail is God's truth.

I had my first hit record at seventeen, so my career took off early: I recorded, went to Hollywood, began singing at clubs all around the country. And, of course, at these clubs I met all sorts of people, by which I mean mob people—they owned or controlled many of the venues, so there was hardly any way not to. The fact is, if you were an entertainer in those days, you automatically performed at mob-owned places; there weren't that many other clubs for you to go to.

Among the people I met, though I can't remember precisely where, was Johnny D'Angelo, who controlled upstate New York and parts of Ohio. And through Johnny I met his daughter, Francesca—Franny. Franny D'Angelo was just a year or two younger than me, which would have made her about eighteen or nineteen when we met. She was a stunner, a total knockout. Exquisite features. Skin as delicate as a porcelain doll. So dainty that when she picked up a glass she held it with both hands, as if she were afraid that it might break, or maybe that holding your drink in one hand was too uncouth.

I had never met anyone like her. I was mesmerized by her looks. I couldn't take my eyes off her. Her hair was always done perfectly, her nails were manicured, her figure was simply gorgeous. Everything about her added to how delectable she seemed. I can't say exactly what she saw in me, since she hardly knew me, except that I was a young, decent-looking Italian guy on a fast upward trajectory. But that was apparently plenty for Johnny, and for his daughter, too.

Now, Franny D'Angelo was not the kind of girl who did any work, certainly no housework or after-school job, or anything like that. She never had to do anything, except maybe go to the beauty parlor. She was perfect, a delicate princess whom her father loved fiercely and protected from anything that might be harsh or upsetting to her, his only child. But we were obviously attracted to each other, and Johnny and Mrs. D'Angelo liked me, and next thing I knew, Franny and I were engaged to be married. It was a whirlwind, as if it had been destined somehow.

When we got engaged the D'Angelos threw a huge party at their house in Ohio. I flew up there with George Wood, my agent at William Morris. George was more than the usual kind of agent. George was the bridge between the mob and the entertainers, the clubs and the talent. In those days of mob control he was the one indispensable man, the liaison. Everybody needed him.

George helped me pick out a beautiful ring, then he went up with me to the party. It was quite a night. The party was in Johnny D'Angelo's big yard, more like a mini-estate, and everybody was there, all his associates. And they all seemed absolutely delighted with the match between Franny and me. At one point I was talking to Johnny—Mr. D'Angelo—near some trees, when I heard a phone ringing. This was many decades before cell phones. "I think I hear a phone ringing," I said, wondering. One of the big guys standing nearby went over to a tree, opened a little door in the trunk, and took out a phone. Then Johnny went over and talked into it, after which he put it back in the trunk and closed the door. You'd never know anything was there. I don't know how they did that, but there it was.

It was a strange relationship, Franny D'Angelo and me. We never went on a date; I don't think her mother, and especially Johnny, would have permitted her to go out alone with some guy. They weren't going to allow her to put herself in harm's way like that, even if Johnny was enough to scare the crap out of any potential boyfriend who might possibly think he'd like to get fresh with her, or just about anybody else for that matter. He was a very scary guy. Instead of dates, we went to dinner together, all four of us, Mom and Dad D'Angelo, Franny, and me. When we said good night I'd give her a kiss on the cheek. Once Johnny even invited me to go to Florida with them for a couple of days; this was after we were engaged. "I'd love to come," I said. "I'll get a room.

"No," said Johnny, "it's all right. You'll stay with me."

"Sure," I said. "Whatever you say," thinking he'd get some kind of big suite with separate bedrooms. When I got down there he had gotten us a suite all right, but with only two bedrooms. Franny and her mom slept in one, while Johnny and I slept in the other. It was very strange. But then, the whole relationship was strange. It was a relationship, yet it wasn't. I felt as if this was something happening to me, like a movie someone else was directing: VIC DAMONE MARRIES THE PRINCESS.

At the time I was living in a little house I had bought for my mom and dad in Bay Ridge. One day when I was between gigs the doorbell rang, and when I opened it, there was Franny. A surprise visit.

"Franny," I said, "what are you doing here? It's so good to see you. Come on in. Where's your mom and dad?"

"Well, they're in New York. I came in with them."

"That's great. I've got nothing happening tonight. Let's have dinner. We can eat here. My mom can cook. Mom!" She was in the kitchen. Other than us no one was home. My pop was at work; my sisters were out somewhere. "Mom, look, Franny's here," I said. "Let's have a celebration. Could you make a lasagna tonight?"

"Oh, sure," Mom said. "Very nice to see you"—that to Franny. "Sure, I'd love to. But I don't have the ingredients."

"Let me go," I said. "I'll go shopping while you two stay and talk."

So I got in my car and went off, leaving them to get to know each other a little better. I bought lasagna noodles, I bought the meat, the other ingredients, then I drove back and pulled into the driveway. I was coming through the back door into the kitchen when I heard sounds from the living room, Franny's voice, loud. "Don't tell me, you bitch! I don't cook. I don't cook for anybody. Don't tell me I have to cook!"

She's shouting, and I could hear my mom crying. "All I said was . . . your husband . . . you're going to get married . . . I want to tell you what he likes . . . I'll teach you the recipes."

"I don't cook, you bitch. Not for anyone!"

I couldn't believe my ears. I walked in. "Whoa, what's going on here?"

"Your mother's trying to tell me I have to cook for you. Who does she think I am? I don't cook for anybody."

"But if he's your husband . . ." This from my mom. "You gotta cook for your husband."

"Don't you tell me, you bitch! I'm not cooking for him or anyone else!"

"Whoa, that's my mother. You don't call my mother a bitch. Please. Franny, apologize."

"I don't apologize to anybody!"

"Listen, Franny, it's my mother. She's a nice Italian lady. You are not gonna call her a bitch! You have to apologize."

"Not on your life! I'm not going to!"

"I'm going to ask you one more time. You don't call my mother a bitch. She was just trying to help. Now apologize."

"No!" she says.

"Okay, then." Needless to say, I had never seen this side of her before, or anything even close to it. I still to this day don't know what might have gotten into her; it was so unlike the girl I had been seeing. But whatever the reason, I was hot. I had shown her and her mother and father nothing but respect, and they had reciprocated. And now this? "Okay, you show me disrespect," I said. "I don't need this. And I don't want this. I'll tell you what, I don't think we should get married. The wedding's off. I'm not going to marry you. If you don't show respect to my mom, how could I marry you? I know your father might be upset, but I can't. That's it!"

"You know my father!"

"I'm not marrying your father. I was marrying you. You're not going to show my mother disrespect. I would never show your mother disrespect. All I asked you to do is apologize to her."

"I'm not apologizing."

"Okay, it's off. You can tell your father the wedding's off. I'm going to go to New York, to the William Morris office. I'll be there with George Wood. Tell your dad that if he wants to talk to me he can get me there. At George Wood's. Now, please leave my house."

"What?"

"I said, Please leave my house now."

She slammed the door on her way out. And meanwhile my mother was crying, "What did I do? Vito, what did I do?"

"Ma, don't worry about it. She showed you disrespect, and she's not going to do that. Not in front of me. Not ever. So don't worry about it. Stop crying. Please, stop."

Twenty minutes later I was at William Morris. I walked into George's office. "George," I said, "I have to talk to you."

"Hey, Vito. What's going on?"

So I told George what happened.

"You've got to be kidding me," he said. "She called your mother a bitch?"

"Yeah. I asked her to please apologize. My mom was just trying to help, you know, telling her my son likes this kind of sauce, I'll teach you to make the lasagna, the manicotti. All the things my mom knows I like. And she says, 'I don't cook for anybody.' And my mom says, 'He's your husband, you're going to marry him.' And she says, 'I don't cook for anyone. Don't tell me, you bitch.'"

"Oh my God," said George.

"Yeah. I told her to please apologize, not to me—to my mom. If you don't respect my mom, how can you respect me? Then I told her to tell her father the wedding's off, and if he wants to talk I'll be here with you."

"Oh my God," said George.

Just then the phone rang. The secretary picked it up. "Mr. Wood, it's Mr. D'Angelo on the line."

"It's him," says George. "Oh God." He put it on speaker. "Hey, Johnny, what's going on? Everything okay?"

"Listen," said the voice. "Is the singer there?"

"Yeah, he's here."

"Good. I wanna talk to him."

George took it off speaker and handed the phone to me.

"Hello?"

"Hey, what happened? What's goin' on? What is this?"

"Johnny, it's Franny. I don't know what got into her. I come in and my mother's trying to tell her about cooking for me, and she says she doesn't cook for anybody, and my mother says, if you're going to be married, these are the things he likes. And Franny says, 'I don't cook for anybody, and don't tell me, you bitch.'"

"Ahhh," says Johnny, "she's a kid. Forget about it."

"Johnny, I told her to apologize. Nicely. I asked her three times to apologize to my mom. My *mother.* I told her, You don't call my mother a bitch."

"Listen, I said forget about it. She's just a kid."

"Johnny, I'm sorry. No disrespect."

"Look," said Johnny, "I can't talk now. I'm in a meeting. Meet me at the Edison Hotel, room 1410."

"Okay," I said, and hung up the phone.

"What did he say?" said George.

"He wants to see me."

"When?"

"Now."

"Where?"

"At the Edison Hotel."

"The Edison Hotel? They don't stay at the Edison Hotel, they stay at the Waldorf."

"I don't know. He wants to see me at the Edison. He gave me the room number."

"I'm coming with you," said George.

"No, don't. You don't have to."

"No, no, no. I've got to come with you."

George Wood knew Johnny D'Angelo just like he knew all the mob guys. He spent a lot of time with them. He was in their world.

So I went, and George came with me. George was not a big guy, and he had a funny way of walking. He was hunched over slightly, and kind of shuffled. But he had clout. He was their guy in what was an important business for them. He was close to Joe Adonis, Frank Costello, Albert Anastasia, Meyer Lansky. He got them Sinatra, Milton Berle, Jimmy Durante, Danny Thomas, Sophie Tucker—well, practically everyone. He had the biggest roster in show business. He was the man. He made them a lot of money.

We got to the hotel and found the room, 1410. I knocked on the door.

"Who's there?" It was Johnny's voice.

"It's Vic."

The door opened. I took a step in, and as I did Johnny D'Angelo grabbed me and rushed me toward what I now saw was a wide open window on the other side of the room. In a second we were at the window, and he was shoving me out. I was hanging over the edge, fourteen stories up, panicked. Johnny was snarling at me, pushing. My rear end was over the edge already. But I had my legs hooked over the sill, and I grabbed his tie, which was loosely made with the knot over to the side, with a little tie clip up near the top. I grabbed with both hands. I had a death grip on that tie, thinking, If I'm going over, you're going over with me. But I didn't want to go over. I was trying to pull myself back up on that tie, like it was a lifeline. I'm pulling and Johnny's shoving. I am not letting go of that fucking tie. And at that moment, while I'm dangling upside down out of the window, George Wood comes into the room. This whole struggle had taken just moments, and shuffling along like he did, he had just gotten there. Walking in just in time to see Johnny shoving me out the window, and me with only my legs in the room, bent over the windowsill, trying to keep some kind of a grip.

"Noooo!" yelled George, and he grabbed Johnny in a bear hug and wrestled him back, which was hard to believe, since George was not exactly a physical specimen. But I think adrenaline must have given him a shot of superhuman strength, because a moment later we were all sprawled on the floor, inside the room, me still holding Johnny's tie. George yelled, "Get the hell out of here." Johnny was trying to push George away and get at me again, but George was holding him, and I squirmed away and got out the door, slamming it behind me and sliding down with my back against the wall in the hallway into a sitting position, my breath coming in huge heaves and my body shaking all over, and I'm trying to get some air into my lungs, which don't seem to be working right for some reason. I'm still hearing the horns and street noises I heard while I was out the window, and I can't stop shaking.

After a while, I have no idea how long, the door opened, and George stuck his head out. "Okay," he said. "Come in here."

I stood up and walked in. Johnny D'Angelo was sitting on the bed, his face white as a sheet. Staring at me with murder in his eyes.

"Johnny," George says, "we're going to do this the right way. You want to kill him, we got to have a meet and vote on it. We'll do it right. If he's going to die, we're going to vote it. He doesn't belong to you. This ain't Buffalo. He's part of the family here."

Johnny was looking at me like I'm dead already, a look that's stayed with me for half a century. George said, "Tonight at the 14 Hotel." Then he and I walked out of the room and into the hallway. We closed the door behind us. "Jesus Christ," George said. "Now I gotta set up that meeting."

Of course, the William Morris Agency knew what kinds of things went on in George's office, what kinds of relationships he had, and who he talked to—not that they wanted to give those things too much consideration. And who he was talking to once we got back there, setting up the meeting, was everybody, all the New York big guys.

The 14 Hotel was right above the Copacabana; the mob owned the club and the hotel both. When George and I got there that evening, the room was already full. Johnny D'Angelo was there, but he had a lot of company, including Joe Adonis, Tommy and Johnny Dio, Vincent "Jimmy Blue-Eyes" Alo, and Phil "Cock-eyed Benny" Lombardo—not that anybody ever called him Cock-eyed Benny to his face.

Shortly after we got there and sat down, Frank Costello walked into the room. Frank Costello was the most powerful boss in New York, the head of the Lucky Luciano crime family. He had been a top guy under Luciano, but Luciano had been deported to Italy and Costello had taken over. The man exuded power; people called him "the Prime Minister."

After Costello sat down, Jimmy Blue-Eyes started the proceedings. He was my lawyer for the meeting, a good talker. He once told a Senate investigating committee, "To the best of my recollection, I can't remember," which left them speechless for a minute. George Wood and I had told him the whole story.

"Look, Johnny," Jimmy Blue-Eyes said, "your daughter and Vito, they're engaged to get married. You have to understand, this is Vito's mother we're talking about. Her son's going to get married. He's marrying an Italian girl. So his mother is trying to tell her son's future wife all the dishes and all the meals he likes. She's going to teach your daughter, his future wife, all the recipes to cook for him. That's what mothers do for their sons, right? So she's gonna be his wife, she should know all the dishes he likes. Right?"

"Aaaaah, I don't know," said Johnny. "My daughter doesn't cook. She's just a kid."

"No," said Jimmy Blue-Eyes, "no, you don't understand. When a girl gets married, she's not a child anymore. She's a married woman. She should know certain things about husbands and wives. So when your daughter called his mother a bitch—'Don't tell me, you bitch. I'm not cookin' for anybody'—what is that? What does that mean? If you get married, you gotta know that if this is your husband, you cook for him. Or at least, if you're not gonna cook, so you give the recipe to someone else who *is* gonna cook for him. This is a marriage. This is an Italian marriage."

But Johnny didn't seem to get it. It was as if he had a completely one-track mind on this subject.

"No, no, no," he said, "*you* don't understand. She doesn't cook!"

"No, but she *should* cook. She should learn how to cook. At least know his dishes. Listen, how about you and your wife before you were married? Supposing the same thing happened to your wife, where your mother wants to tell her what to cook for you?"

"Aaaaah, that's different."

"Why is that different?"

"Hey, my wife is my wife and my daughter's my daughter."

"No, no, no, I mean when you were going to marry this woman who's now your wife, and you're going to have a child with this woman, and your mother said, 'These are the dishes Johnny likes.'"

"No, but that's different. My daughter doesn't cook."

"But your daughter called his mother a bitch."

"Yeah, but she's a kid."

"No, she's not a kid. If she's going to get married, she's not a kid. And you don't call your future mother-in-law a bitch. Supposing *your* wife called *your* mother a bitch?"

"That's different. What are you, kidding?"

"Well, it's the same thing. Your mother is your mother and his mother is his mother. Why is it your wife can't call your mother a bitch, but your daughter can call his mother a bitch?"

"Well, she's a kid."

"You keep saying she's a kid, but if she's engaged to be married she's gotta grow up. And she's gotta show respect. No, she's wrong. He lives!"

Now everybody looked at Frank Costello. Costello waited a moment, then he put his fist out, looked around the room, and stuck his thumb up. And the rest of them, Joe Adonis, Tommy Dio, Johnny Dio, Cock-eyed Benny, Jimmy Blue-Eyes, they all stuck their thumbs up.

"So here we are," Costello said to Johnny D'Angelo. "He's gonna live. Don't touch him. He's part of our family. What's right is right.

We're here talking, we hear the whole story. And we say he lives. That's it."

But this was not the end of the story. My breaking that engagement stuck in Johnny D'Angelo's craw. I can understand that; sometimes things stick in my craw, too. It can be hard to forgive and forget. Johnny D'Angelo was a violent man, but he was not a stupid man. It wasn't that he didn't understand what Jimmy Blue-Eyes was saying; it was that he felt deeply offended by my calling the wedding off; he felt that I had shamed him. And that feeling, the anger of it, the *agita,* wasn't going to go away just because Frank Costello stuck his thumb in the air. He wasn't allowed to kill me. All right, he had to listen to that. But that didn't keep it from eating at him inside.

A year later I was opening at the Town Casino in Buffalo, New York, a Saturday night. Al Silvani was still training me at the time, and traveling with me. If it was possible, we'd get to a gym during the day, but if not we'd do a routine of calisthenics in the afternoon, then another one late at night after my second show. We were in Buffalo, Johnny D'Angelo's town, but a year had passed since the meeting at the 14 Hotel, and I hadn't heard a peep about anything since. So I was not expecting anything special when I walked out onstage. But as I got into my first song, and my eyes got accustomed to the lights, I saw them. Right in front of the stage, sitting at a long table, were Johnny D'Angelo, Mrs. D'Angelo, Franny, and about ten other people, some of whom I recognized from the engagement party.

When I finished the first song, I thanked the crowd for coming, and I acknowledged the D'Angelos. "Mr. and Mrs Johnny D'Angelo. Johnny, Mrs. D'Angelo, how are you? Franny. Great to see you here." Then I went into the rest of my set. I was trying to stay cool and relaxed, but a river of sweat was running down my back. When the show was over I told Al Silvani backstage that they were there. Al knew all the mob guys, and he knew the story. He had seen them out there.

"I have to go and say hello to them," I said.

"Come on," said Al. "I'll go out with you."

So I went out to pay my respects, which I did, very carefully. "I hope you enjoyed the show. It's great to see you, Franny. You look beautiful. Mrs. D'Angelo, hello, you look great. Johnny, thanks for coming. I hope everyone enjoyed the show."

No one said anything; they just sat there.

"Okay," I said. "Bye now. Thanks again."

I went upstairs to my dressing room, thinking, Oh God, what a thing that was. Thank God it's over. I had a little something to eat, washed up, rested some, and got ready for the second show, feeling vastly relieved.

The second show started at midnight, about an hour and a half after the end of the first. I walked out onstage, ready to sing—and there they were, all of them, sitting at the same table. They hadn't moved. "You're here," I said, trying to keep the anxiety out of my voice. "Ladies and gentlemen"—this to the audience—"I'm honored to have Mr. and Mrs. Johnny D'Angelo and their daughter, Franny, with us tonight. They were here for the first show and they've stayed. I hope you like my music." And I launched into the first song.

After I took my bows I went up to the dressing room to change out of my tux, more than a little nervous about what, if anything, was going to happen next. Then there was a knock on my door, a waiter from downstairs. "Mr. Damone? Mr. D'Angelo would like for you to join them."

"Okay," I said. I looked at Al. "Al?"

"I'm right with you," he said.

The second show went on at twelve, so this had to be one-thirty, quarter to two in the morning. Al and I went down and sat at the table with them. We're sitting there talking about nothing. How's the weather? How do I like Buffalo? How's my hotel? Is the food good? This and that. Nothing. I'm sitting on one side of Johnny and Franny's sitting on the other. And time is going by, slowly, but it's going. It's three, four. We're still talking about nothing, and people are starting to leave, the guys they had with them and their wives. And finally it was just the five of us, Johnny, Mrs. D'Angelo, Franny, me, and Al. We're just sitting. I'm not going to get up. I can't get up. They have to get up first, then I'll walk out with them and say good night. The waiters and the busboys are cleaning up and putting the chairs up on the tables around the whole room, except for our table. I look at my watch. It's six A.M. The waiters and busboys are standing around, trying not to be obvious, but waiting for us to leave. Not that anyone is going to say anything. Johnny D'Angelo is the boss of the town, the don. He ran everything there. So they're waiting. And finally Mrs. D'Angelo says, "It's after six. You know, we can go to church from here."

"Yeah," says Johnny, "that's a good idea."

So we all got up and walked together through the deserted streets of downtown Buffalo at six o'clock in the morning, still talking about nothing, until we found the church, where we all said good night. Al and I headed off to the Statler Hotel, where we were staying, and as soon as we were out of earshot I said, "Al? What was that?"

"Hey," he said, "you were very nice. Courteous. You showed respect. Don't worry about it."

When we got up to our suite neither of us felt like sleeping. The thing had been just too nerve-racking.

"Why don't you get ready?" said Al. "We might as well work out. I'll just go down and get the papers. I'll be right back."

While Al was gone I got into my pajama bottoms, my usual workout outfit, thinking, We'll do the calisthenics, I'll stretch out, then take a shower, and get to sleep. I started a few stretches, waiting for Al to come back. He always got the papers in the morning; he usually read a couple of them. But he didn't come. I'm waiting, but he's not coming. You buy the papers, it takes a minute, and you come back—but ten minutes go by and there's no Al. Fifteen minutes, then twenty minutes. I'm beginning to get very worried, when suddenly there was a knock on the door.

I opened it and there was Al, with Johnny D'Angelo.

"Johnny!"

He looked at me in my pajama bottoms. "What are you," he said, "showing off your muscles?"

"No. What do you mean? What are you doing here? I thought we said good-bye, good night?"

"Come on, Johnny," said Al. Johnny was staring at me. "Come on, don't do this. Shake hands with him, for chrissake."

The moment seemed like it was frozen. Then Johnny stuck out his hand, but when I took it, it was like a cold dead fish "I'll see you later," he said, which sounded ominous. Then he turned around and left.

Al put down his newspapers. "Jesus Christ," I said, "what happened to you?"

"Yeah," he said. "What happened? Well, I went down to get the newspapers; the stand's right next to the elevator. So I buy the papers and go to get back on, and here comes Johnny with two guys with baseball bats."

"Baseball bats?"

"Yeah. So I said, 'Where are you going, Johnny?' And he says, 'I'm going to go up there and fix that son of a bitch. I'm going to break his fucking arms and legs. We'll fix it so he'll never walk again.' And I told him, 'Johnny, you want to do that, you're gonna have to go over my body. Anyway, what do you want to do this for? Baseball bats? For chrissake, what did the kid ever do to you? Come on. He was courteous to you tonight, respectful. He sat with you. He sang his heart out for you. Don't do this. Be a man, come up and shake his hand. You don't need this. Come up with me and shake his hand. Not like this.'

"Vic, he wants to do this, but he's not sure if it's worth it. And, finally, he tells those guys to get lost and take the bats with them. And he comes up. I'm telling you, I don't know what goes on inside this guy's head."

That happened a year after Franny D'Angelo and I broke up, which might have been in 1948 or '49. But even that wasn't the end of the story. In 1960, Jack Kennedy ran for president. I was well established by then. I had a restaurant and a six-hundred-acre cattle ranch in Fresno. I had good friends in Hollywood. Frank was there, and Joey Bishop, Sammy Davis, Dean Martin, Peter Lawford, and Peter's wife, Pat Kennedy, who was JFK's sister. I knew Peter and Pat well; we'd go over to each other's house on occasion. I supported Jack and did a fund-raiser or two, when I sang myself and brought in some other performers. And then Jack was elected, and he appointed his brother Bobby as attorney general.

One day I got a call from Peter Lawford inviting me and my wife over for lunch. Bobby was going to be there, he said, and Bobby wanted to meet me in particular. So I said, Sure, we'd be more than happy to come.

When we got there lunch was just about ready, so we all sat down around the Lawfords' big table, about ten of us, and Bobby said, "Vic, please, sit here, next to me."

"Sure, Bobby," I said. I hadn't met him before and he was the attorney general, so maybe I should have called him Mr. Kennedy, I don't know. But anyhow, "Bobby" seemed more natural.

So I sat down, and as they were bringing the salads out, before anybody had taken a bite, Bobby said to me, "Now listen, Vic. I want you to tell me about Johnny D'Angelo."

"What?" I said. And immediately, it went through my mind: Bobby was going after the Mafia. It was in all the papers.

"Johnny D'Angelo, from Ohio, you know."

"Who?" I said. "It doesn't sound familiar."

"Johnny D'Angelo. You know the story. Remembah"—Bobby had a high voice, with a sharp Boston accent—"remembah when he wanted to throw you out the window? Remembah that? He wanted to throw you out the window in that hotel in New York?"

"Uh, who was that again?"

"He wanted to throw you out the window. Remembah that? Remembah that?"

"Bobby, gee, I don't know what you're talking about. Where'd you ever hear a story like that?"

"Johnny D'Angelo! You know Johnny D'Angelo! You know who he is! He tried to kill you!"

The whole table was just staring, kind of in a state of shock. Bobby was practically shouting at me by now. "You remembah! I know you remembah!"

"I'm sorry, Bobby. Could you spell the name?"

"D'Angelo, for Christ's sake! Johnny D'Angelo! Youngstown! Buffalo!"

"I'm sorry. I don't know him. Maybe I met him. I meet a lot of those guys at the clubs. But I don't know who he is, and I don't know what story you're talking about."

"Don't tell me that!" he said. I thought he was going to burst a blood vessel. "You know you know! I want you to tell me the whole story of how he tried to kill you!"

"Bobby, I don't know what you're talking about. I don't know Johnny D'Angelo, and I don't know what you're saying. Is this why I'm here?" I looked at Peter Lawford.

"You have to tell me! You have to tell me the truth! *I WANT THE TRUTH!*"

"Jesus. I don't know what you're talking about."

He was so angry that he just got up and left the table. I don't know where he went, into another room, I guess. But he never came back. I looked at Peter Lawford, and at Pat. Peter was so embarrassed he had his head down. He wouldn't look at me. Pat looked mortified. It was obvious that they had had no idea that Bobby was going to do this. Afterward Peter felt so badly he could hardly talk to me for a while, though Pat apologized for the two of them. They just hadn't known.

That was a bad scene, but it had consequences. The fact is that they never did get Johnny D'Angelo on anything. I'm pretty sure he stayed out of prison and died a natural death. But some years after this incident, I was working in Buffalo again, with Danny Thomas this time. I was, of course, on the usual performer's schedule. That is, we did two shows, the second one at midnight, so nobody ever went to bed before two or three. Which meant I would get up around noon. That's when the hotel gave me my daily wake-up call, and before that they wouldn't allow any other calls through.

But one morning the phone started ringing early and dragged me out of a deep sleep.

"Mr. Damone," the voice said. "This is the hotel manager. I'm sorry to wake you, I know we're not supposed to call until twelve, but—"

"Yes?" I interrupted him. "What? What's happened?"

"I apologize, Mr. Damone, but there's a Mr. D'Angelo downstairs. He's sitting at the bar and he wants to talk to you. He's waiting for you there."

Oh, for God's sake, I thought. Here we go again. I can't believe it. This guy just never gives up. But there was no alternative. I had to go. I pulled my clothes on and left the room.

Downstairs, the hotel bar was closed and dark at this hour. But there was one light throwing a puddle of illumination on the bar. Sitting on the bar in this puddle of light were two snifter glasses, and there he was, Johnny D'Angelo, sitting on a stool, leaning with his elbows on the bar, smoking his cigar.

"Johnny?" I said.

He took his right hand off the bar, held it out to me, and looked me dead in the eye. I took his hand. His grip was hard this time, firm. "It's over," he said. "Take a drink."

I picked up a snifter. He picked up the other. "*Salud,*" he said, and we drank. Then he picked up his cigar and walked out.

It's over, I thought. Twenty-plus years later, and now it's over. He had finally gotten the vendetta out of his system. But I think, I'm pretty sure, that what did it was my little encounter with Bobby Kennedy, which he had to have heard about. And even after that it had taken him years. Italians, I thought. Italians just do not forget.

3

You Gotta Vocalize

When I was three years old, my mother had pleurisy and had to go into the hospital. My father took me to visit, but first he taught me a song I could sing for her: "You're Driving Me Crazy." "You're driving me crazy," the song went. "What did I do? What did I do?" My father had a sweet voice and accompanied his singing on the guitar. He had come from Bari, Italy, when he was twenty-two to marry my mother, whose sister Carmela was already married to my father's brother Mike, who had come over earlier. Having arrived on these shores as an adult, my father spoke broken English with a heavy Italian accent. And so, naturally, that's how I learned the song, with his accent. And that's how I sang it to my mom: "You're drivin' me-a crazy. What did-a I doo? What did-a I doo?"

I'm sure my mom loved it—how cute it must have been. She herself had been born in Brooklyn, although her parents had immigrated from Bari, so even though she was pure Baresi, she spoke native English. But aside from the pleasure I like to imagine she got from my song, she also apparently heard something in my three-year-old voice, something she liked. And she knew her music. In our small apartment we had a piano. She was a talented pianist, and she gave lessons, bringing in a few extra dollars a week to supplement my father's salary as an electrician.

So, as soon as she came home from the hospital and was back on her feet, she started making me "vocalize," as she put it. I'd stand next to the piano, and we'd do scales together. She'd play the notes and I'd sing them. Up the scale, down the scale, "Do re mi fa so la ti do . . . Do ti la so fa mi re do . . ." "Half a step up now, here we go, Vito." "Do re mi fa so la ti do . . ." I'm a tiny kid, not much more than a toddler, and there I am standing next to her at our upright singing scales and doing vocal exercises: "Meh meh meh meh meh meh, ma ma ma ma ma ma, mi mi mi mi mi mi." And then we'd sing a song from the lead sheets she used to teach her students, one of the hit songs of the day. Maybe something by Irving Berlin, like "Blue Skies."

Strangely, all this playing and singing sounded somehow familiar to me. And why not? I'd been hearing her play and teach from the time I was born, actually, from before I was born. She was on that piano bench giving lessons to her students while I was nestled down there in her womb. Teaching her students scales or playing popular music for my father or herself, Hoagy Carmichael's "Stardust" or Berlin's "Change Partners." So when I started singing at the age of three and doing the scales, they sounded very natural to me.

When I got older, I wasn't so happy with all this vocalizing, though. Singing might have come naturally to me, but I didn't like being forced. I didn't want to stand at the piano going, "Mi mi mi"; I wanted to play baseball. I loved baseball. I loved the Dodgers, Pee Wee Reese and Pete Reiser, and my all-time favorite, first baseman Dolph Camilli, who always seemed to either strike out or hit a home run. And when my father figured out a way to buy me a little secondhand mitt, all I wanted to do was be outside with my friends on the sandlot that ran down to Gravesend Bay next to our house. All the kids came from families like mine, poor as church mice, many of the parents immigrants. But somehow those fathers, all of them working themselves to the bone, managed to scrape up money for mitts for their kids, and uniform shirts with BAYSIDES scrawled across the front in dark red letters.

That was us, the Baysides. As one of the youngest, I was the Baysides' right fielder, practicing almost every afternoon until that horrible, inevitable moment would arrive when I'd see my mother coming out of the house. Sometimes someone else would see her first, and I'd hear, "Jeez. Here she comes again." Then all the guys would see her. Oh God, I knew it would start, and it did. The dreaded chant: "Here comes your mo-ther, here comes your mo-ther, here comes your mo-ther." It only took her a moment—the field was right next to the house—so sometimes I didn't even have a chance to run before she'd catch me by the ear. Other times I did, and she'd have to chase me.

"Maaaa. Come on, Ma, don't do this to me. Please don't do this to me."

"No, Vito, you're coming inside. You gotta vocalize."

"Ma, please. I'm playin' baseball here."

"Vito, no! It's time to sing." Pulling me toward the house by the ear, some of the guys laughing, some of them just staring in awe as I was hauled off.

"But Ma, I wanna play ball."

"No!" She had that iron two-fingered grip on my ear. "You are going to vocalize now."

Vocalize—had any of my pals ever even heard the word? But there I was a moment later, standing next to the piano, vocalizing. Still with my glove on, pounding my fist into the pocket while I'm going, "Mi mi mi mi mi meh meh meh meh," until an eternity later, the half hour was up, and I'd be released to go racing out of the house, back to the field.

Needless to say, my public singing career started early. At St. Finbar's, our parish church, I was in the choir. I was an altar boy too. *Dominus vobiscum,* the priest would chant at Mass. *Et cum spirito tuo,* we altar boys would chant back. I think Father Doneghan liked my chanting; I was as clear as a bell. He and St. Finbar's other priest, Father Landy, also liked it when I filled the chalice for Holy Communion. Some of the boys would pour just a little, but I'd fill it to the brim. "We want Vito to pour the wine," they'd laugh.

I sang at church functions, too, in the Bingo Hall: church breakfasts, game nights, fund-raisers, performances with the choir. Sometimes I'd be given a solo, which I'd do even though I really wished they'd let me just stay in the choir, where nobody would notice me. It got to the point that people started calling me the Bobby Breen of Brooklyn, Bobby Breen being a child singing star who was just a year or two older than me but was already famous for his appearances on radio and in the movies. My mother would teach me the songs he sang in his films, and people would hear this local kid who could sing just like the one out in Hollywood.

How my mother found out about *Rainbow House* I don't know. *Rainbow House* was a kids' music show on WOR radio hosted by "Big Brother" Bob Emery. I had never heard it, but one day she took me to Manhattan—"New York" to us—on the train, telling me to watch carefully which trains we were taking and which stops we got off at, because this was the only time she was going to come with me. Next thing I knew, we were at the WOR studios on Broadway, and I was auditioning for the show's chorus, which I made. So, starting that Saturday there I was, one of Bob Emery's singing kids, which I loved, especially since I didn't have to do any solos. Phil Senna did those. He was a couple of years older, and he was the star, the lead singer. All I had to do was have fun with the other kids in the chorus.

So off I'd go every Saturday, with two dimes and two nickels in my pocket, the dimes for the BMT subway up and back and the nickels for lunch at the Horn and Hardart Automat across the street from the station. You put a nickel in the slot and got your sandwich out of the little glass receptacle. Another nickel got you your drink.

Everything was going just great on *Rainbow House.* Bob Emery was a decent musician himself and had already had a long radio career handling kids, so he knew how to make sure everyone had a good time. My whole family, my parents and sisters, along with all my aunts and uncles and cousins, used to tune in the show every Saturday morning to listen to me sing, which they couldn't really, since I was just a voice in the chorus. But it didn't matter. They were proud of me anyway. Until one morning when disaster struck.

That fateful morning, Bob Emery looked at me and said, "Vito, you're going to sing a solo today."

"No, no," I said. "Please, I really don't want to."

"Vito, listen, I want you to sing. You're going to sing, okay? Don't tell me no."

I could see there was going to be no arguing about this. I didn't like it, but I didn't see any way of getting out of it, either.

"Okay," I mumbled. "What song do you want me to sing?"

"You pick a song," said Bob. "Any song."

A popular song I liked just then was called "You'll Never Know," by Harry Warren. My mother had the lead sheets to it, and played it on the piano, so I had sung it at home. I knew the song cold. But now I was going to have to sing it on radio, a whole different thing. And when Bob Emery announced that Vito Farinola was going to do a solo, I started thinking, Oh my God, all my relatives are listening, and I began to feel shaky. But then the piano started—Emery had a wonderful piano player named Bill Werges—and suddenly I was singing.

You'll never know just how much I miss you . . .
And if I tried, I still couldn't hide . . .

And as I sang "hide" my throat closed on me. "Couldn't" was fine, "hide" was nowhere, not a sound came out. Something had happened; I couldn't sing a note. And everyone in the studio knew it. An instant later Bob brought in the chorus, and they took the song from there.

Now, what that probably sounded like on the radio was me starting off the song and the chorus coming in to join me, as if it was an arrangement. But I didn't think of that. I was too mortified to think of anything except how royally I had screwed up, with my entire family listening to me, including my uncle Mike, whose house we were living in then, as we sometimes did when times got too hard for us to pay our rent. Uncle Mike, who used to belittle me regularly anyway, telling me I couldn't play ball, why was I even trying; I couldn't sing, what was the point; I couldn't seem to do anything right, what was wrong with me, anyway? And now I was going to have to go back to Uncle Mike in Brooklyn, where he was just going to ridicule me mercilessly.

I was thirteen years old—this was in 1941—and I couldn't stand the thought of it. With a screw-up like that, how could I go home and face anybody, let alone him? So I didn't go home. Instead, I went to my uncle Tom and aunt Millie's place on Eighty-sixth Street. To hide. I stayed there all day, and, of course, they thought at first that my parents knew I was coming over, so they didn't bother calling them. Meanwhile, my mother was frantic. I always came home after the show. I'd eat my lunch at H and H, then I'd get on the train and come home. So where was I? And who knew what kind of awful things might happen to a boy by himself in Manhattan? But finally, Aunt Millie got to the bottom of why I was acting so strangely, and she called.

"He's here," she said. "He's so embarrassed he doesn't want to come home."

"Embarrassed?" my mother said. "What's he embarrassed about?

He was on the show like always. Everything's fine." So Uncle Tom had to take me home, to my mom and dad, and to Uncle Mike, who didn't miss a beat. "See, what did I tell you? He's got no talent. He's got nothing."

"Ma," I said the next week, "I don't want to go back."

But she wouldn't hear of it. "You're going back. You have to face the music, Vito. You've got to go back there and sing with the chorus again."

"Ma, they don't want me to sing anymore. I goofed up. I can't—"

"You're gonna do it!"

"But jeesh, Ma . . ."

"Go on! You just do what I tell you, and go back there."

So I went back, shamefaced. But Bob Emery was as sunny as always, as if nothing had happened. Except he said, "Listen, I want you to learn a new song."

"No," I said, "I can't. I can't do any solos. I'm not going to."

"Vito," he said, "I don't know when you're going to do the song. All I want you to do now is learn it. Eventually you'll do it, but we'll figure out when later. I'd just like you to learn it, okay?"

The song was called "Can't I Just Pretend." Bill Werges, the piano player, had written it. So I worked on it with him before the show, and I learned it. But I was suspicious. I just knew Bob Emery was going to call me up to sing it, and I could feel myself tightening up.

The show started, and things were going along as usual. Phil Senna's doing the solos, and I'm singing with the chorus, but I'm waiting and waiting and he's not calling me to sing. Now it's three minutes to the end of the show. And I said to myself, That's it, I'm not going to sing! And I felt so good. I'm not going to sing, I'm home free. And right then Bob Emery said, "By the way, folks, remember Vito Farinola, who sang a little for us last week? Vito! Come here, get up here. You know that new song you've been learning? Sing it for us, would you?" And before I knew it, I had the music in my hand, and next thing I was singing it. I didn't have any time to get nervous about singing, I just sang. And I finished the song. It was great. All the kids were so happy for me that I got through it, but not as happy as I was. And Bob Emery was the one who had done it, who knew how to get me back on the horse after I had fallen off. I wonder if I ever would have sung a solo again if he hadn't done that. I doubt it. Looking back, I think he saved my career, which could easily have gone down the tubes when I was thirteen, before it even got started.

Of course, at age thirteen I had no idea about any kind of career. But the fact was that I was just at the point of getting enthralled with singing. I had gotten over being aggravated and vexed about my mother forcing me to sing, and I really liked being part of Bob Emery's chorus and the St. Finbar choir—as long as I didn't have to stand out there in front and do solos. But then I had a moment that changed everything, that just turned my head all the way around. This might have been a year after my near-debacle on *Rainbow House*. One minute I was a kid who liked to sing but wasn't completely comfortable with it, and the next minute I was on my way to being obsessed.

It was a Sunday afternoon and we were all sitting around the table having our usual big Sunday family meal: my mother, my father, my three sisters—Pearl, Theresa, and Elaine—and me. Sandy, my youngest sister, hadn't been born yet. And as usual everyone was talking at the same time, especially the girls. Meanwhile, somewhere in the background the radio was on, tuned into *The Battle of the Baritones* on WINS, which I had gotten into the habit of listening to. *The Battle of the Baritones* played the great popular singers of the day, Bing Crosby, Dick Haymes, Tony Martin—all of them—and listeners would vote for their favorite. Then, at the end of every year, people would vote for whomever they thought was best, with the winner being named "King of the Baritones."

With all the noise around the table I couldn't hear the radio very well, but at some point something in one of the radio voices caught my attention, something that made me want to listen closely to it. So I got up from my chair and bent down in front of the radio so I could put my ear right up next to the speaker. The voice was singing a song called "I Can't Get Started."

I've flown around the world in a plane,
I've settled revolutions in Spain

I'm there with my ear up against the speaker, and I'm thinking, That's so pretty. My God, he's singing so beautifully. Who *is* that? And then they announced the singer, and it was Frank Sinatra.

I also thought something else while I was listening to him singing. I thought, I can do that. I can copy that. My voice was already more or less mature. And I thought, I'll bet I can make myself sound just like Frank Sinatra, who was already a star, an idol.

I asked my mom if she could get me the music to that song, which she did, and I started learning it. Sinatra had other great songs, too: "Everything Happens to Me," "I'll Never Smile Again," "Stardust." I got the sheet music for those, too, and I learned them, listening to Sinatra on the radio every chance I got and imitating him. I'd try to tune myself to him to get the timbre just right, but it was more than just his sound; it was his phrasing. When I sang, I just sang lyrics, words. But as young as I was I could tell he was doing something different. This voice on the radio wasn't just singing words; it was telling a story. Maybe I didn't know what the story was about: "I'll never smile again, until I smile at you." What did that mean? But it meant something, something about longing, or sadness, or somebody losing somebody. But whatever the words meant, the man singing that song understood it perfectly. He was heartbroken. He was telling a sad story with a beautiful melody, in a beautiful voice.

Listening to Sinatra, the whole singing business began to make sense. I didn't know the story yet, I was too young for that, but at least I was learning that a song *was* a story: "I'll never love again, I'm so in love with you." That was somebody singing to somebody, from his heart. That's how you had to sing these things. And actually, I already did have some inkling of feelings like that. My wonderful Italian father was a romantic to his toes. He played the guitar, and he would play and sing in his lilting light baritone to my mother, sitting on her piano bench, songs from the old country, songs of love and romance. *Ma n'atu sole* ("But another sun"), *cchiu' bello, oi ne'* ("that's brighter still"), *'o sole mio* ("It's my own sun"), *sta 'nfronte a te!* ("I see in your face!"). And she would play for him, too, or they'd do American popular songs together, which he'd sing in his broken English while we kids sat on the floor and listened.

And now that I was listening to Sinatra and Haymes and the rest, I mean really listening, I began hearing other things, too. I'd sing these songs with my mom playing the piano. But Sinatra was singing with Tommy Dorsey's orchestra and Dick Haymes with Harry James and Benny Goodman. I'd listen to the arrangements and the tempos, and I'd think, Oh, so *that's* the way it sounds. *That's* the way it's supposed to go.

And there was something else. Frank Sinatra was the heartthrob of every teenage girl in the country. You'd hear stories about girls screaming so loud for him that they fainted in the aisles and had to be carted off. So after I had gotten my imitation down pat, I began singing to the girls at school. I'd say, "Listen, I heard a really great song," and I'd launch into "Night and Day (You Are the One)." The girls loved it. And I loved it that they loved it, even if I didn't have time to actually do anything about it, like ask someone for a date. By the time I was old enough for that I was working much too hard to be a teenager in love.

I got my first job when I was eight or nine. I knew we needed money. My father was making twenty-seven dollars a week, raising a family—three girls and me, then when Sandy was born, four girls—putting food on the table and paying the rent. And even with my mother's few dollars from teaching, sometimes it wasn't enough and we'd have to move in with Uncle Mike and Aunt Carmela, who had five children of their own. Under those circumstances it didn't take a genius to realize that anything I could bring in would be helpful.

Also, though I never said this to anybody, I wanted to get out of the house. Our apartments were always small, and there were a lot of us. The apartment we lived in longest had a living room, where my mom's piano was, a small dining room, my parents' bedroom, my sisters' bedroom, where the oldest three slept in one bed, a kitchen, and a kind of little storage room in back of the kitchen where I slept on an army cot. So it was crowded, in addition to which, as the only son in an Italian family, my mother doted on me constantly, when I would have been happier with a little less attention. Having a job would mean at least a little money to help my mom and dad. It would also mean being able to get away from everything for a while. So I went looking. And the first place I looked hired me, which was the grocery store on the street level of our building, directly under our apartment.

The grocery store smelled great. It carried all the Italian specialties—cheeses, pancetta, prosciutto, salamis, pastas, big barrels of olives and pickles. I worked there after school and all day Saturday, stocking shelves, checking which items needed to be replaced and carrying new ones from the storeroom in back. On Saturday I'd be so excited when lunchtime came because the owner would make me a sandwich. He'd cut a piece off an Italian bread and lay it open. Then he'd fill the bread with prosciutto that he'd slice paper thin, salami, lettuce, tomatoes, cheese, peppers, and the final touch, a sprinkling of olive oil and vinegar. And a bottle of Pepsi to wash it down. I'd be famished from working since early in the morning, and the thought of the sandwich he was going to make for me for lunch would practically make me faint with anticipation. "Don't worry, Mrs. Farinola," the owner would tell my mother, "we'll feed him. He's a good kid, he works hard. When he's hungry, I'll feed him." I thought I was in heaven. Besides which, the owner gave me a couple of bucks a week, which I'd instantly turn over to my mother, feeling extremely proud of myself.

Then I saw a way to make even more money. There was a bigger food store a few blocks away, where women bought entire bags of food, not just a few items like they did in the grocery store. And they had to carry their heavy bags of food home, which might mean a walk of two or three or four or five blocks, with no one to help them. Now, there was a neighborhood kid a few years older than me who used to ride around on a bright red bike, which just seemed like the most desirable thing in the world to me. I used to watch him and admire that bike, with its handlebars that looked like they'd just been shined and its big balloon tires. What a great bike, I thought. I'm sure the kid used to see me watching him, and one day he pulled to a stop next to me and said, "I've got to sell it. You want to buy it?"

"You want to sell it? How much?"

"I don't know, three or four bucks."

Three or four bucks? Where was I going to get three or four bucks? Then I thought, With a bike like that I could put a basket on the front and help the women home from the food store with their bags. I could probably make a fortune. So I went to my mom.

"Ma, there's a bike I could buy from this kid for four dollars. I could deliver orders from the food store. I'm sure I could make a lot of money." And my mom gave me the four dollars. So now I had my own bike. What a thrill that was, just owning the bike! Then I got a basket somewhere, which my father helped me attach. I was ready for business.

The manager of the food store hired me immediately. He taught me to wrap oranges and apples in paper by twisting the paper at the bottom, which made it easier to build them up into a big pyramid. And he let me ask the women who were checking out, "Can I help you with your bags?" And most often they'd say, "Okay, okay. Go ahead." So I'd put their bags in the big basket and follow them home, then carry the bags up two or three flights into the kitchens of their railroad flats, the same kind we lived in. And they'd always give me a tip, sometimes just a few pennies, but more often a nickel or a dime, and once in a while even a quarter. On Saturdays, my long work day, my pockets would be jingling with change. When I came home after work I'd empty them out on the kitchen table and count it up, then hand my mom a little pile of coins. And once, after a particularly good day, my mom gave *me* four quarters. "Vito, you've been working so hard. Here, you take these. Buy yourself some candy or an ice cream. Whatever you want."

I didn't do it, though. Instead, I took the quarters back to my little sleeping room, feeling dizzy at having this kind of money for myself. I sat next to my bed, which I always made tight, the way my father had taught me. "It should be so tight," he told me, "that you can bounce a quarter off the blanket." Now I could see if you really could do that. And I could. For the next hour or so I sat there and bounced quarters, feeling great, although in the end I gave them back to my mom. I thought she needed the money more than I did. Besides, what really made me feel good was being able to help out, which I could do with the money and also with the two big bags full of fruit and vegetables the manager gave me every Sunday, instead of actually paying me anything. I had my tip money, and we could use the food, too. That was my contribution.

When I was twelve I left the food store and got a job as an usher at the Deluxe Theater on Bath Avenue. By that age I was dying to see movies, but I never had money to go. As an usher I could see them for free and bring in a few dollars at the same time. Then, after I had been at the Deluxe for a while, I got to thinking that I could upgrade, get a job at a fancier theater that showed more first-run movies. With that in mind I went to work at Lowes Oriental on Eighty-sixth. Then, feeling really cocky, I applied for a job at the RKO Albee, which was even bigger and fancier. I could hardly believe how great this ushering business was. You show people to their seats, then you watch the movie. I'd change the billboards, too, helping the manager put up the big posters announcing upcoming shows, but there wasn't really anything else to it. It was mainly just watching movies. I'd see Clark Gable, Abbot and Costello, Betty Grable, Lana Turner, Humphrey Bogart, and sometimes a movie with the Count Basie or Tommy Dorsey orchestras, which I really loved.

By this time I was singing on Bob Emery's *Rainbow House,* which was broadcast out of WOR Mutual on Broadway near West Fortieth. One Saturday all the kids from the show took a walk up Broadway, through Times Square. In a couple of blocks we passed the Paramount Theater, which played all of Paramount's new movie releases, but also presented stage shows featuring the biggest bands of the era. Wow, I thought. The Paramount Theater! I stopped to look at the billboards. Tommy Dorsey was going to be playing, and Artie

Shaw, and Duke Ellington, bands I had been listening to religiously for a few years already on Martin Block's *Make Believe Ballroom* radio show on WNEW. Perry Como was scheduled to sing, and Peggy Lee and Dick Haymes, too. And there—I could hardly believe it—there was a poster advertising Benny Goodman and Frank Sinatra. The thought just exploded in my head: What if I could be an usher here? Man, this is the place to work! So the next Saturday, after *Rainbow House,* I went and applied. You had to be sixteen to usher at the Paramount and I was only fourteen, so I lied about my age. And I got the job!

4

They All Played the Paramount

The Paramount Theater presented big-band stage shows and movies fresh out of the Paramount studio. The audience would come in, and we'd check their tickets, and show them to their seats in our red ushers' jackets with the brass buttons. When everyone was settled the lights would go down, and from somewhere, you weren't sure where, you'd hear music, which if you were a big-band fan you would recognize as the theme song of the orchestra that was headlining that week. Then the side lights would come on, illuminating the pit stage, which was rising up on a hydraulic mechanism of some sort until it was flush with the regular stage. And as the pit stage was rising the lights would get brighter, and you'd see the band arrayed on it playing their music. It was always dramatic, even after you'd seen it a hundred times. There would be nothing there, then music in the darkness, then suddenly the band would be rising up there right before you with the famous bandleader, Harry James or Tommy Dorsey or Count Basie or whoever, out in front. The audience was thrilled.

Right after school I'd get on the BMT with my books, which I'd open immediately and start doing my homework. I'd work the late afternoon and evening shows, then get back on the train and finish off my assignments on the forty-five-minute ride home. I didn't have a moment for anything else, not hanging on the street corners with my buddies or dating girls or anything. But I loved it. I couldn't get enough. I'd get people to their seats, then just stare: at the band, the singer, the lights, the whole show business world that was opened up right there in front of my eyes.

I knew almost all the bands even before I got to the Paramount; I'd been listening to them on radio for a couple of years already. As badly as I wanted to buy some 78 records to play, I just didn't have the money. The only records we did have were Caruso, Gigli, and Di Stefano, my father's favorite opera stars, whom I loved, too. The whole family used to sit and listen when he put the big vinyl disks on. But though Sinatra and Tommy Dorsey or Benny Goodman and Perry Como and others were selling records like mad, I had to make do with the radio shows.

Radio was great, but it was a far cry from seeing and hearing them play right there in front of you. There were the saxophones lined up, and the trumpet section and the trombones, the drummer, the pianist, and sometimes a guitar, like in Basie's band, that would get the rhythm going with that offbeat *jing jing jing,* not pounding in your head, but insistent, beautiful, the way it set everybody else off, cutting right through the harmonies of the other players.

These weren't just bands; they were the world's greatest bands with the world's greatest musicians. Duke Ellington playing piano; Lionel Hampton on vibes; King of Swing Benny Goodman, with his clarinet; Tommy Dorsey, with his unbelievably smooth trombone and Buddy Rich playing drums for him; Charlie Spivak blowing the sweetest trumpet you ever heard—Les Elgart was in his band, and Nelson Riddle. One name after another, show after show after show.

Each band had its own personality, its own flavor and style. Johnnie Long, the left-handed violinist, had a great band; they'd all stand up in the middle of a piece and sing. It was such a showstopper that other bands started doing it, too. Claude Thornhill had six or seven clarinets and a tuba in his lineup, and played music that was more like cool jazz than swing. Most of the bands were white, but some were black—Ellington, Basie, Dizzy Gillepsie, Billy Eckstine—while Benny Goodman integrated his band, bringing in Lionel Hampton to play with him. He might have been the first to do that. But to me it was all just music, white, black, it made no difference. All of them were such masters of what they did. And there I was, standing at the top of the aisles on the main floor—my favorite place—taking in those great sounds, soaking it all up.

I saw things I could hardly believe. Frank Sinatra's appearance with Benny Goodman almost sent the whole usher crew into shock. The mobs of teenage girls were uncontrollable. The din they made, the shrieking and crying, turned the theater into a screaming madhouse. The Beatles had nothing on what happened when Sinatra came out to sing.

But Sinatra's performance was only one memorable event. The first time I saw Harry James play, he almost fell off the stage. The pit stage started rising, as usual, and there was James in front of the band with his trumpet. And when the stage lights came on he looked down at the audience and began to sway back and forth. He was so dizzy he couldn't play; it was all he could do to keep from toppling over. We heard later that he had a bad case of vertigo. For the second show that day he came on standing on the second riser, with the piano behind him and the drummer to his right. He conducted from there and never left the spot.

My favorite, all the ushers' favorite, was Peggy Lee, who was Benny Goodman's girl singer. Goodman would say, "And here she is, Peggy Lee." A few of us would be standing together, as close to the front as we could get, because we knew what was coming. "Here she is," we'd whisper to each other. "Look, she's coming. How tight is it going to be this time?" And Peggy Lee would walk out onto the stage in a dress that was so tight she could only take tiny steps in it, moving her body left, right; left, right; left, right. It would take her a full minute to walk to the microphone. We were like cartoon characters with our eyes popping out of our heads, watching every little motion inside that dress. But it wasn't only us. The audience would be going absolutely nuts as she made her slow entrance, so provocatively you wondered if it was legal. She'd walk to the front center of the stage, where the mike was protruding straight up, at the very edge, with the audience sitting right below her. She had the whole place eating out of her palm before she ever opened her mouth. And once she did start singing she just carried you away. What a great dramatic singer she was, in her way a little like Sinatra. She didn't just sing, she told a story. She lost herself in the song. When she sang, you believed her, utterly.

At first I was entranced by the music, by the sound of the instruments blending together and playing off each other. But before long I began noticing the other elements that went into a performance. Playing wasn't just playing and singing wasn't just singing, no matter what kind of virtuosos the musicians and singers might have been. Part of their greatness was in their overall presentations. You could see how professional the leaders were, how calm. They had complete control of everything—their instruments, the orchestra, the pace of the show, how each number would create a mood, and how they swung the moods in one direction, then another. I heard how the bands would vary their tempos, their volume, from pianissimo to fortissimo, and how the changes affected the audience. I got a feeling for how the lights were used to heighten a mood or sadden it. I watched the star singers. I stood there and studied them, what they did with their hands, how they held the microphone when, on occasion, the Paramount would provide a regular floor mike instead of the rigid mike that jutted out of the stage lip, how they leaned into it or swung it down toward their side, or cradled it in both hands. I saw how they dressed and how they presented themselves to the audience: Peggy Lee with her sexuality; Perry Como with his gentleness and politeness, smooth as silk. I wasn't even aware I was learning all of this, but I was watching like a hawk, absorbing it all, picking up the tools I was going to need in the future I still had no idea I was going to have. Whatever I might have been learning at Lafayette High School, at the Paramount Theater I was getting a graduate education in musical performance.

But actually, at Lafayette I was already putting some little bits and pieces of my new knowledge to work. I had started off there by singing to some of the high school girls, showing off my Frank Sinatra imitation. But then I became the singer for a swing band one of the older kids had started, Sid Dweck, who played the drums. We had trumpets, saxophones, trombones. We had a bass player and a pianist. And I was the vocalist. We performed in the auditorium or the gym, where they'd hold the high school dances. The publishers used to give out the original arrangements, and a thousand or maybe ten thousand little high school bands all across the country would play the same arrangements as the radio hits. I'd go up to sing a couple of songs with the band, kids would be dancing and having a great time. What a reaction we'd get, especially when we'd launch into a Sinatra number, where I could really shine.

One day a former student at the school was invited in to sing at a school assembly: Aldo Sigismondi, who later changed his name to Alan Dale and had a number of hit songs, including "Cherry Pink and Apple Blossom White." He had graduated a couple of years earlier and was already making it as a singer with the Carmen Cavallaro Band. Sid Dweck's group played, then they called me up to sing a song with them, then they were going to introduce Aldo. While I was singing I glimpsed him poking his head out of the side curtains to see who was singing like that, which gave me a shot of pride—a professional singer taking notice of me like that.

I also had a chance now and then to pick up a little gig outside of school. When I was fifteen there was a piano player who lived around the corner from us, George Fera. He played in a little group led by Ted Mack, before Mack took over *The Amateur Hour.* The guys on the street knew I sang, and they knew George played piano for a group. So somebody said to George, "You know, Vito sings. You ought to hear him." And one day George saw me on the street and said, "Hey, I hear you sing. Why don't you come over. We can do a few things together."

So I went to his apartment and met his wife and children, who seemed very nice. Then George sat down at his piano.

"What should we do?" I asked.

"How about 'Begin the Beguine'?"

"No, I hate that song."

"What do you mean, you hate that song? Why?"

"I don't want to sing that song."

"Why not? It's a good song. It's Cole Porter, for chrissake."

The reason I hated "Begin the Beguine" was that a few years earlier my mother had insisted on taking me to audition for the *Major Bowes Amateur Hour,* not once but repeatedly. And every time we went I'd sing "Begin the Beguine." My mother would play the piano, and I'd sing the damned song. This happened every two or three weeks—and I never got past the audition. After I lost the first time, the only way she could get me to go was that they had a Nedicks across the street, where you could get a hot dog and a special Nedicks orange drink. I'd say, "No, Ma, I'm not going." And she'd say, "I'll get you a Nedicks." And I'd say, "Okay, I'll go." The singing was a small price to pay for a Nedicks. Forget about the singing, I was going to get a Nedicks.

I knew I was never going to sing on that show. The men in the control booth at *Major Bowes* would see us coming, the second time, the third time, the fourth time. I'm sure they were saying to themselves, Jesus, here those people are again. My mom would sit down, and I'd start off, "When they begin the beguine, it brings back the sound of music so tender." I just knew they were turning the sound off in the control booth. I was always singing the same thing, and they had already made up their minds. They listened the first time and decided that this wasn't for them, so why would they listen now? I could tell, because every time I'd look in the booth they'd be talking to each other. Talking and laughing. If they were listening, they wouldn't be talking, right? And when I was finished singing, the voice would come out, "Thank you very much. We'll call you. Don't call us, we'll call you." And I'd say to Ma, "Okay, let's go get the Nedicks." I hated that song.

But anyway, George and I did a few other numbers together, and afterward he said, "C'mon, Vic, sing with us. I'll get you ten bucks."

So that was how I got to perform with Ted Mack's band at a USO dance, singing the popular songs I had learned with my mom: "Embraceable You," "Change Partners," "Must You Dance." I sang all night, thinking how great it was to be doing this. And then to get paid afterward? Ten bucks was a lot of money.

After the show, as the band was packing up, Ted Mack came over to me. "Vito, here," he said, and he put a five-dollar bill in my hand. I looked at it.

"Mr. Mack, I thought it was supposed to be ten dollars."

"No, no. I keep five dollars of your ten."

"But I thought I was singing for ten dollars."

"No, I keep five dollars of it. It's my band. I book everybody. That's my booking commission."

"But, but, you're the leader."

"Yeah," he said, "but see, I'm also the agent."

That extra five dollars would have helped at the time, our money situation was always so tight. But it wasn't too long afterward that we found ourselves in truly desperate circumstances. My father was installing equipment in the basement of one of Manhattan's skyscrapers when a large machine tipped over and pinned him against a wall, breaking both his collarbones and several ribs, as well as doing other damage. At the hospital they put him in a full body cast. It started from his hips and went up into a plaster vest that left his arms free, and then extended to the top of his head, with an opening for his face so he could breathe and eat and see. He came home encased in that thing and lived in it for a year. He slept sitting. It was agony seeing him like that; I can only imagine what it was like for him to be living in it.

Of course, he couldn't work, so that left my mom's few dollars from teaching and whatever I could bring in. It was obvious as soon as it happened what I had to do. A week later I quit school and buckled down to work at the Paramount—full time. I was sixteen years old. My father was heartbroken that I had to quit. But I said, "Pop, I'm the only one. I have to do it." We all knew there was no choice.

As a part-time usher, what I mainly did was show people to their seats, but full-time ushers, senior ushers—which I now was—got paid a little more, and we got to do overtime, too, if we wanted it. I wanted it. I'd work a shift and a half or even two shifts if I could. We also found ways to up our incomes a little that weren't completely kosher. Whenever we had a really hot show or movie, the lines to get into the balcony seats would snake all along the hallway and move like molasses. For a quarter we'd let people at the end of the line go in through another entrance. A guy with his girlfriend would usually say, "Sure, here's a quarter." "Great," we'd say, and in they'd go through the back entrance. So there was another couple of bucks for my mother. If a big movie played for two weeks we would make out like bandits. I remember Betty Hutton's *The Miracle of Morgan's Creek.* It was huge, the biggest smash of the year. The lines were going around the hallways and up and down the stairs. We loved those blockbusters.

I felt guilty about it, though. I always confessed it at church on Sunday before taking Communion. "Forgive me, Father, I have sinned. I charged people a quarter to cut the line."

"Why did you do that, my son?"

"Well, see, Father, my mom needed the money for food."

"I see, my son. Say five additional Hail Marys and two Our Fathers."

As a senior usher I also got to work backstage, which meant seeing the stars really close up, maybe even talking to them a little. One of my jobs back there was to run the elevator, an old manually operated type that was used to take the musicians from their dressing rooms down to the stage for rehearsals and shows and back afterward. The stars' rooms were on the fifth floor; the rest of the musicians were on three and six. Since the bands usually played two-week gigs at the Paramount, I'd spend two weeks bringing everybody up and down many times a day. Of course, I got to hear them all talking with each other, and I got to see a little of their personalities.

Some of them had tempers, like Benny Goodman and Tommy Dorsey. Others were more easygoing. Perry Como came across as a true gentleman. He was always kind and polite, not just to his musicians, but to me. To some of the stars I was invisible, just another stagehand, but to him I was more than a piece of furniture, I was somebody to say hello to, and even exchange a few words with. During one of his star turns I felt comfortable enough with him that I even got up the nerve to talk to him about singing.

"Mr. Como," I said—this was after one of the shows, and I was taking him up to the fifth floor—"Mr. Como, my mother and dad think I can sing. I'm taking singing lessons. And we can't afford it." Even in our dire straits my mom had insisted I take singing lessons, and elocution lessons, also.

"Well," he said, "how much are they?"

"A dollar."

"A dollar?"

"Yes, sir, a dollar a lesson. Like I said, we can't afford it. I'd love to sing a couple notes for you, if it'd be okay, and you could just tell me if you think I have any talent, because I don't want to waste my father and my mother's money. I'd love it if I could sing to you, and you could tell me whether the lessons are worth it, or what."

And he said, "Sure, kid, sure. Let me hear you sing."

"You mean here in the elevator?"

"Yeah. In the elevator. Why not?"

So I stopped the elevator between floors and sang the first line of one of his big hits: "There must be a way to help me forget that we're through . . ."

"Why are you stopping?" he said.

"Well, I don't know. I didn't want to bother you too much."

"No," he said. "Sing it. Go ahead and sing it."

So I sang.

There must be a star in the sky,
that doesn't reflect in your eye.

And I stopped again. I was feeling like this was very brazen, singing for Perry Como. But he said, "Will you please finish the song!" And I said, "Okay, I will." So I did.

"Oh no, kid," he said, "you gotta sing. You got something. You got a beautiful voice. Hold it, stop on the fifth floor. Wait for me."

This was after a show, and the musicians, the Jerry Wall Orchestra, were down on the stage level, waiting for me to pick them up.

They were Perry Como's backup band for this gig. "But the musicians are waiting," I said.

"It's okay," he said. "Let them wait a little." So I went to the staircase and yelled down, "I'll be right there!"

"Listen," Perry Como said, "you know who Johnny Long is?"

"Yes, I do." Johnny Long was the left-handed violinist whose band stood up to sing. I knew his shows by heart.

"He's working at the New Yorker Hotel," Perry Como said, "and he's looking for a singer. So you go and audition for him." He scribbled out a note to Johnny Long and gave it to me.

"Thanks, Mr. Como. When do you think I should go?"

"Go there right now."

I went down fast and took the musicians up to their dressing rooms, then I ran and found Mr. Lapp, my boss.

"Mr. Lapp," I said, "I have a chance to sing for the Johnny Long Orchestra, but it's right now, at the New Yorker. Do you think I could leave to go audition?"

"Sure," he said. "Don't worry about it, Vito. Go ahead."

I changed my clothes as fast as I could and ran from Forty-third Street and Broadway, where the Paramount was, to Thirty-fourth Street and Eighth Avenue, where the New Yorker Hotel still is, clutching Perry Como's note, which said—I had peeked at it while I was dressing—"This kid can sing. Listen to him. I think he's got something." Signed "Perry Como." I was holding onto that note for dear life.

In the lobby of the New Yorker Hotel I told the bell captain I was looking for Johnny Long. Where could I find him?

"He just went into the room where he works at night," the bell captain said. "He's in there." But as I walked into the room, Johnny Long walked out, with some guy I didn't recognize trailing behind him.

"Mr. Long?" I said, still half out of breath.

"Yeah, kid? What?"

"I have a note here. It's from Perry Como."

"From Perry? What's up?"

"Well, I sang for him and . . . could you read his note?"

So Johnny Long read it. "Oh man," he said. "You're not going to believe this. I just hired this guy here, Bob Houston"—the man who had been trailing behind. "But listen, you must be a pretty good singer for Perry to write me this note. So whatever you do, keep working at it."

"Thank you very much," I said. "I appreciate it. Thank you for seeing me."

When I took Perry Como up in the elevator later, I told him Johnny Long had just hired someone named Bob Houston. "Oh yes?" he said. "He's a pretty good singer. But you keep right at it. Don't you give up."

Tommy Dorsey always started his show with "The Star Spangled Banner." Not too long after Perry Como's gig, Dorsey was headlining, and opening the way he always did. He and the band would rise up on the pit stage, he'd introduce his singer at the time, Teddy Walters, and Walters would sing the national anthem. It happened like that for a week. Then one day something different happened. I was seating people that day, and I happened to be right up front as the show started. The lights went down, the stage rose, Dorsey introduced Walters. Everything normal. Then, all of a sudden, people were arguing onstage. I looked up and Dorsey and Walters were going back and forth with each other, right in front of the audience. I couldn't believe it. First, that they were arguing onstage, but even more that Walters would ever do something like that. Tommy Dorsey was the boss. You didn't argue with Tommy Dorsey. The singer was just the singer.

"No," Dorsey was saying, "you're going to sing it, and you'll do it the way I tell you to do it." And Walters was saying, "No, I want to sing it my way." And the audience was listening to all this. Walters wanted a different tempo, and he wanted the guitar to do something, which I didn't catch. Finally Dorsey said, "You're going to do it my way. I'm telling you, you sing it my way or that's it!" And Walters said, "No no no, I'm singing it my way." And Dorsey said, "Really? You're fired! Get the hell off my stage!"

And I'm standing there right below them, thinking, Wait. Wait a minute. He just fired him? Wait, I know all the arrangements. I'd been listening to the show four or five times a day for a week now. I knew every song Dorsey's singer sang, the words, the music, the arrangements, everything. I had the whole show by heart.

I walked up the aisle to where Mr. Lapp was standing in back, my boss. "Mr. Lapp, did you hear that? He just fired him onstage. I'm going to go back and try out." By now I guess Lapp was getting used to this kind of thing from me.

"Go ahead, Vito," he said. "Go on back there."

So I ran backstage looking for Nick Sevano, Tommy Dorsey's road manager, whom I knew to talk to after taking him and everyone else up and down on the elevator for the week. I found Sevano in the back somewhere.

"Mr. Sevano, Mr. Sevano."

"Yeah? Hi. How ya doin'?"

"Mr. Sevano, I'd like to try out for the vocalist job."

"What do you mean? What are you talking about?"

"Mr. Dorsey just fired Teddy Walters onstage. I'd like to try out for the job. I sing. I know all the songs."

"What? Get outta here. Tommy's not going to fire him onstage! Are you crazy?"

"I'm telling you, Mr. Sevano, he just fired him."

"You gotta be kidding me."

"No, no. I'd like to sing for him. I'd like to audition for him."

Sevano was digesting all this. "Listen to me," he said. "First of all, I have to check into the firing. Now, Mr. Dorsey"—he was talking to me like, what business did I have, an usher for chrissake, even approaching him with such a thing—"Mr. Dorsey doesn't listen to anybody sing in person. No one auditions for him. You have to record. Make a recording. There's a studio called Nola Studios. It's just down the street. I'll give you the address. Go there and do an audition record."

"How much does that cost?" I asked.

"About five bucks. There's a guy who plays piano, and for five bucks you go and record."

I didn't have five dollars. Every penny I was making was going to the family. So I said, "Okay. Thank you." And I never did get to audition for Dorsey.

A year and a half later I met Nick Sevano again. I had had my hit record by then, and I was working all over. I had sung in Madison Square Garden with Sinatra. The radio DJs were playing my songs. My name was out there. One evening I was having dinner at the Pennsylvania Hotel with my date, and Tommy Dorsey's band was playing the room. I asked the maître d' if he knew Mr. Sevano, and if he did, did he know where he was.

"Sure," he said. "Mr. Sevano's back in one of the dressing rooms."

"Well, could you please ask him to come out? Tell him Vic Damone would like to say hello."

So the maître d' went back, and a couple of minutes later he came out with Nick Sevano, pointed in my direction, and said, "Over there."

"Hey," I said when he came to the table. "How are you?"

"Good, good," he said. "I'm glad to meet you. I love your records. They're doing great."

"Thanks," I said. "Would you like a drink, Nick?"

"Sure."

They brought his drink and I said, "So, how are you, Nick?"

"Good," he says. "I'm good." He can't figure out why I'm being so familiar, as if we knew each other.

"Look at me," I said. "Do you recognize me at all?"

"No, I don't. Do I know you from somewhere?"

"Remember the usher at the Paramount who wanted to sing for Mr. Dorsey, the one who told you he had fired Teddy Walters onstage?"

"Was that you?"

"Yes. It's me. I wanted to sing for Mr. Dorsey, but you wouldn't let me. I just wanted you to know, I'm doin' okay."

"You son of a bitch," he says. "Oh my God. Doin' okay? You're doin' great. You gotta come backstage with me and meet Tommy."

During the break we went backstage and Sevano introduced me. "Tommy, here's a kid I want you to meet. What's your real name?"—that to me.

"Vito Farinola."

"Yeah, Tommy, I want you to meet Vito Farinola—Vic Damone."

"Hey, Vic, man! You've got a hit record! Good to meet you."

"Mr. Dorsey," I said, "you have no idea what a great honor this is to meet you. But you don't recognize me, either."

"Should I recognize you?"

"I used to run the elevator at the Paramount Theater, and I used to take you up and down, many times, every time you played there."

"You know, I never really looked at you."

"I was ushering there when you fired that guy onstage, Teddy Walters."

"Teddy Walters? That son of a bitch! That son of a bitch was arguing with me onstage."

"I know. I saw it."

"What do you mean you saw it? Were you in the audience?"

"No, like I said, I was an usher."

"You were?"

"Yeah. I was there when he wanted to sing it his way. And you kept telling him, 'No, you do it my way.'"

"That's right! The son of a bitch!"

"I heard that whole thing. Everybody did. And you fired him onstage."

"My God."

"I went backstage, and I wanted to sing for you. I knew all the arrangements. I had been listening to you four or five shows a day. But Mr. Sevano said no, you don't listen to anybody in person."

"Yes, that's right. I really don't. But hey, I would have listened to you."

"You would have? Why?"

"I don't know, I just would have."

"Mr. Sevano told me I had to make a recording, but I didn't have the five bucks."

At which Dorsey looked daggers at Nick Sevano. "You son of a bitch. You should have at least had him sing a couple of notes for you. Oh, my God, Vic. Wouldn't that have been something if you came up from the audience in your usher's uniform and sang with my band!"

Dorsey and I got to be good friends after that, as did Nick Sevano and I. Years later I even got Nick to work for me as a road manager for a time.

Dorsey probably thought a bit about what might have happened if he had hired me as his singer. I wondered about it myself. It was one of those big "what ifs" that happen in life. Of course, Sinatra had been his singer for several years, and Sinatra always said he had learned a huge amount from Dorsey, about phrasing, articulation, pacing, and especially breathing. Dorsey was a magician at everything that had to do with putting on a performance. He was also a virtuoso trombonist who had an unusual ability to elongate phrases without seeming to breathe.

Sinatra wondered about that. When he wasn't singing he was sitting right there in front of the band—Dorsey's singers didn't come onstage and go off, they sat in front of the band for the whole performance. And when Dorsey turned around to face the audience and play, Sinatra was behind him, studying his back to see when he breathed, and it almost seemed as if he didn't.

Eventually Dorsey showed Sinatra what he was doing, taking almost imperceptible breaths out of the corner of his mouth that were actually deep and full. In Sinatra's old movies, like *Higher and Higher* or *Step Widely,* if you watch carefully you can see him doing exactly that. He's singing, and it seems as if he has a tiny twitch at the corner of his mouth. That's him breathing. His breath control allowed him to phrase lyrics with tremendous feeling, giving meaning to full lines instead of having to stop for a breath, as most singers do. He learned that from Dorsey.

One day during the time I was working at the Paramount I went out to Long Island to see my uncle, Gerry Foglia, and my aunt, Jojo—Josephine—my father's sister. Uncle Gerry was one of the two doctors in our family, my father's younger brother, also Jerry, with a J, being the other one. We all used to go to one or the other for our checkups. I was out at Uncle Gerry's house that day getting examined, and it so happened Uncle Jerry's sister Tina was visiting with her husband, whose name was Lou—Tina and Lou Capone, whom I called Aunt Tina and Uncle Lou, even though they weren't my blood relatives. They lived in Brooklyn, only five or six blocks from where we did. After my examination I was going to take the train back, but Aunt Jojo said, "Lou, you going back to Brooklyn? Why don't you take Vito? Why should he take the train?"

So I drove back with Tina and Lou, sitting in the backseat of their car. While we were on the Belt Parkway, Tina turned to me and said, "Vito, you still sing?" I'm sure she used to listen to me on *Rainbow House* when I was thirteen. And I said, "Well . . . yeah. I still sing." So she said, "Why don't you sing us a song?"

When she said this—"Why don't you sing us a song?"—I glanced in the rearview mirror and noticed Uncle Lou's face. He was making a face that said, Oh for Christ's sake, now I have to listen to this kid sing? Uncle Lou was an olive oil salesman, but on weekends he played drums in a dance band, so he had heard actual professional singers. And now he was going to have to listen to his pissant kid nephew squawk out a song.

I don't know if I would have sung for Aunt Tina, sitting there in the back of the car. It was kind of silly. But when I saw Lou's disgusted face I said, "Sure, Aunt Tina. Why not?" And I launched into "There Must be a Way": "There must be a way to stop me from thinking of you." Of course, now I wasn't thirteen anymore. I had sung with Sid Dweck in high school. I had sung for Ted Mack and Perry Como. I think there's a good chance Johnny Long would have hired me, and who knows, maybe even Tommy Dorsey. I had a little higher register than I did later in life, but my voice was already pretty much what it was going to be. When I started singing, Lou Capone stared at me in the rearview mirror. I think he would have turned around completely, except we were going fifty miles an hour on the Belt Parkway. And when I was finished, he said, "Sing another one."

By the time we got to Brooklyn, Lou Capone was going to be my manager. "If you sign a contract with me," he said, "I'll pay you a hundred fifty dollars a week." By this time my father was out of the cast and back at work, making the same as he had been making before his accident—maybe a hundred dollars a week by that time. And Uncle Lou was going to pay me a hundred fifty? I could hardly imagine that much money. So I said, "Okay." Of course.

"That's great," Lou said. "I'll be your manager. You're going to be terrific. We're gonna do it together."

When we got to my house I ran in to tell my mother. "Ma, Uncle Louie is here, and Aunt Tina, and he heard me singing, and he wants to manage me." And Lou said to my mother, "I love Vito. Vito's great. I'm going to manage him, and I'll give you a hundred fifty dollars a week. My father and I will handle him together." And my mother said, "A hundred and fifty dollars a week?!"

"Yeah," said Lou. "We'll sign a seven-year contract. When Rocco gets back from work, I'll come over with the contract and I'll give you the first hundred fifty."

When my father came home I was so excited I could hardly get the story out. "Pop, Pop, we're gonna sign a contract tonight with Lou Capone and his father, and they're going to pay us a hundred fifty dollars."

"A hundred fifty dollars?" My father was incredulous. "To do what?"

"I don't know. He's going to get me some singing jobs."

"That's an awful lot of money. You sure about that?"

But shortly afterward, there were Aunt Tina and Uncle Lou at the house, and Uncle Lou had a contract with him that said he would be my manager for seven years. I signed it, and my father signed it. Then Lou handed me a check for one hundred fifty dollars. I turned around and said, "Pop, here's one hundred fifty bucks." I don't know which of us was in a bigger state of shock.

5

I Have But One Heart

Uncle Lou was going to get me some singing jobs—that's what I told my father. But the whole notion was a little hazy to me. He was my manager, but what, exactly, did that mean? Just how was he planning to get me those jobs?

Lou made his living as an olive oil salesman, so he didn't really know much more about managing than I did. But he did play drums in a band, and his wife's family, the Navarres, were all musicians. Ted Navarre was a pianist, and Ted's brother Georgie played alto sax at the El Morocco. So the next thing I knew I was over at the Capones' house every day vocalizing with Ted Navarre. I did scales and exercises, just like I had been doing all those years with my mother, and I learned some songs: "You Came to Me Out of Nowhere," which Bing Crosby had made famous; "Babalu," a Latin song Desi Arnaz had recorded right then, which later became his trademark on *I Love Lucy;* "Temptation (You Came, I Was Alone)," one of Perry Como's big hits at the time, and a couple of others.

Once I had gotten a few numbers down, we rented a studio and I recorded a demo, two songs on a 78 rpm, "Babalu" and "Temptation." I can still hear myself warbling "Babaluuu! Babalu, babalu, babaluuu!" To go with the demo, we took pictures. "They'll hear you, but they also got to see you," said Lou, and he loaned me one of his suits for the photo session, since I didn't have one myself, also a shirt and tie. It was a striped suit, and it hung on me a little, but fortunately he wasn't a big guy, so wearing it wasn't a total embarrassment.

If I listened to that demo now it might make me a little uncomfortable, but it obviously made some kind of impression. Lou took it around to any place he could think of, mainly radio stations, and the next thing I knew, I was singing on WHN's *Gloom Dodgers* at nine A.M. every morning, which meant getting up at six. There was Morey Amsterdam bantering and telling jokes, trying to make people feel better the morning after Dodgers' games. Then he'd say, "Here he is, the original kid from Brooklyn." And there I was, rubbing sleep out of my eyes and doing my best to sound like Frank Sinatra.

Somehow Lou also got me an audition on *Arthur Godfrey's Talent Scouts,* although I can't remember how that happened; Godfrey usually had his friends, his "talent scouts," bring in the aspiring performers. I knew being on *Arthur Godfrey* was a big deal. He was a radio personality whose voice everyone in the country knew. He had an easy, informal way of speaking that put people at ease, as if they were just listening to a friend talking to them. His *Talent Scouts* show was huge, sponsored by "brisk" Lipton Tea. It would be hard to count the number of stars who got their start on that show: Rosemary Clooney, Steve Lawrence, Al Martino, Connie Francis, Jonathan Winters, Eddie Fisher, Patsy Cline. The list goes on and on. At the time I probably couldn't have actually named anybody that Godfrey discovered, but I knew this was an unbelievable opportunity. I was so nervous I felt I was in a kind of trance.

The song I prepared was "Prisoner of Love," a number-one Perry Como hit.

Alone from night to night you find me,
Too weak to break the chains that bind me.

Apparently my nervousness didn't affect my voice too terribly, because I did well in the audition, which meant I was chosen to compete.

The night of the show I was doing the dress rehearsal, again in Lou Capone's suit. Godfrey was sitting onstage listening, and while I was singing someone else came in to say hello to him, though I didn't look to see who it was. When I was finished this voice said, "Hey, kid." And standing there was Milton Berle. "Hey, kid," he said. He had been listening. "Let me tell you something. If you win tonight, I'll help you with your career. You'll be with me."

"Mr. Berle. Oh my God."

"You hear what I said, kid?"

"Yes, who should I call?"

"Call me! Call me tomorrow—if you win." And he gave his number to Lou Capone, who was standing there, I'm sure as awestruck as I was.

That night I sang "Prisoner of Love." This was in front of a large studio audience. On *Talent Scouts,* the audience applauded after each performer and the volume was recorded on an applause meter. Then, at the end of the show, the contestants lined up, and the audience applauded for each one in turn. The one whose applause registered loudest won. My applause meter went right up there. But so did the meter for a young comedian who looked like Edward G. Robinson. Godfrey called it a tie. But a tie was good enough.

After he announced the winners, Godfrey talked to me, trying to get me to open up and tell the audience a little about myself. He couldn't have been nicer or more gentle. I'm sure he was used to talking to young people who were scared out of their wits. I was, he said, a very talented young man. Where was I from? Brooklyn. And where did I go to high school? Lafayette. I actually have a recording of that show. I hear someone giving Godfrey one-word answers in a voice so shy you can hardly hear it. It sounds to me like the voice of pure innocence. The audience applauds again, and then Godfrey asks if I would sing another song. And I hear myself say, "Mr. Godfrey, I don't have another song." I know how scared I must have been to have said that. Of course I knew other songs. But at that particular moment, in that place, I couldn't think of a single one.

So Godfrey said, "Then how about singing the same song again? Would you do that for me?' The audience laughed and applauded, and I launched into "Prisoner of Love" a second time. I think that his talking to me must have put me a little more at ease, because the second time through I was more relaxed. I can hear it in my voice. The first time I sang it well enough to win. But the second time around I really nailed it.

The next day we called Berle and met him at the William Morris office. Berle took me to his agent at the time, Ted Ashley. Ashley was a top show business agent who not long afterward went on to found his own agency, Ashley-Famous, and later became studio chief at Warner Brothers. Berle came right to the point. He looked at Ashley and said, "Sign this kid." So Ashley signed me. I didn't know anything about what was going on there, except I could see that the William Morris Agency was a pretty impressive place. But it didn't matter. I was with Mr. Milton Berle. I was seventeen years old, and the day before yesterday I had been wearing a red usher's jacket at the Paramount. And now I had a manager and an agent both.

After that Berle took me under his wing. He was doing a lot of benefits at the time, fund-raisers for Jewish causes all around the city. He took me with him to these events, introducing me and having me sing a song or two. Looking back, I wonder if many of those benefits had something to do with the Holocaust and the Jewish efforts to help refugees. I wasn't aware of any of that, but it was just about that time. What I did know was that Berle was my leader, and that he was introducing me to what seemed like all of New York. And singing to those live audiences, little by little, I became more sure of myself.

Ted Ashley wasn't idle either. Maybe he didn't feel I was ready for the club circuit yet, I don't know. The name Vic Damone certainly wasn't going to draw in any crowds. But my voice was about as strong as it was ever going to get. So, what medium needed singers but didn't need a name and didn't need a face? Ashley's answer was: Muzak. Elevator music. Background music. Piped into offices and public spaces, and, of course, elevators. Meant to be beautiful and warm and comforting. Ballads, love songs, "up" tunes—standards. Originally, I think, it was invented to keep people calm in skyscraper elevators. And the next thing I knew, I had a contract as a Muzak singer.

Here's how Muzak worked. They would send me a list of songs they wanted me to record. I'd rehearse them with Ted Navarre, so that I knew the lyrics and melodies. Ted and I would pick the keys for each song and let the Muzak people know what they were. Then Muzak would select a top arranger to write an arrangement and conduct.

On recording day I'd go into the studio together with an orchestra that was invariably made up of the best musicians in New York. That would be the first time I'd hear the arrangements—it was also the first time the musicians would have them. Muzak kept us on a strict time schedule. We'd have three hours exactly to record ten songs, which was next to impossible. To do it we'd only have time for one run-through per song, unless it was really off, in which case we'd do two. We'd rehearse a song, record it, rehearse another, record it, rehearse the next and record that. "Rehearsing" meant we'd go through it once. The rehearsing was for us, of course, but it was also for the engineer, who would get to hear what I was going to do with the song, which I hardly knew myself, since I was hearing the arrangement for the first time. The engineer would also be able to give me pointers about using the mike, how differently the mike would pick up, depending on whether I sang loudly or softly, how to move back a little or turn my head a bit to the right or left, so my voice wasn't going smack-on into it—the little tricks recording artists know. We went fast, but the musicians were great. I did eight sessions, which means eighty songs. I think my voice must have been in the heads of almost everyone who rode an elevator. Without them knowing it was me, of course.

After I had gone around with Milton Berle for a while, he thought I was ready for club singing, and he told Ted Ashley that it was time to get me a date, which he did, at La Martinique on Fifty-seventh Street. La Martinique wasn't the Copa, but it was an exciting place anyway, a real nightclub, with a house band, entertainers, a floor show—a perfect place to start out. I was booked for a two-week stay.

This wasn't radio and it wasn't Muzak. It wasn't even singing at benefits with Milton Berle. This was being a nightclub performer. It was live. It was adult. There were showgirls. This was something I had to look good for. So Lou Capone broke down and bought me my own suit, dark blue, so I could at least appear a little more elegant onstage.

My first night at La Martinique, Berle came with me. I could hardly believe my luck. He did all the preparation at rehearsal. He set the lights, he did the sound check, he worked with the band, and he told the manager he would introduce me. I was going to do a set, then the girls would come on and finish the show.

La Martinique had only one dressing room, which was reserved for the showgirls. The male entertainers used the men's bathroom.

That night, and on all the succeeding nights, I went into the men's room with Lou Capone, carrying my new suit in a bag. Since there was no place to hang it up, Capone would hold the suit while I got undressed. I'd take off my street clothes, hand them to him, and put my suit on, moving aside for people who were coming in to use the facilities. Later on, when my stay was extended and there were other male performers on the bill, we'd crowd in there together among the urinals and stalls, trying to keep our balance while we put our pants on.

That first night went great. People loved the music, especially when I did Kurt Weill's wonderful "September Song." When I sang about how it was when I was a young man courting the girls, and how the days grow short when you reach December, everyone in the place smiled. Between shows people asked me to come out and talk to them at their tables. This happened the first night and every night afterward. "We enjoyed it so much," they'd say. "Please sit down with us for a minute."

"I'd love to," I'd mumble. "But I can't."

"Why not?"

"Well, I can't wrinkle my suit"—which I'm sure must have sounded insane. But it was true. I was being as careful as I could to stand straight and not bend my elbows if I could possibly help it. I had a couple of shirts, so my mom could wash and iron a fresh one for each night. But that one suit was it.

I was booked at La Martinique for two weeks, but it went so well that they asked me to stay on. I was there for thirteen weeks all told, part of the time sharing the bill with Phil Foster, who years later played Penny Marshall's father on *Laverne and Shirley.* I loved it probably more than I had ever loved anything. Every night was a shot of adrenaline, in addition to which I was surrounded by all those skimpily clad showgirls. This was definitely not *Arthur Godfrey's Talent Scouts.* Working as much as I did, I had had a stunted romantic life in high school. I had never, ever seen anything like the cornucopia of nearly naked bodies on display at La Martinique. Seventeen years old and I was swimming in a sea of desire, not that I ever asked any of them for a date. But boy, did I look.

Meanwhile, people at Mercury Records had somehow heard my Muzak recordings. I don't know if some Mercury person had been in an elevator and had looked into whose voice it was, or if maybe Ted Ashley had approached them. But however it happened, Lou Capone got a call asking if I might be interested in signing with them. I don't think it took a minute to make up our minds about that. And suddenly I had a recording contract with Mercury, a new label, but one that was growing fast, a three-to-five-year deal, with royalties.

For my first recording date, Art Talmadge, one of Mercury's founders, suggested I do four songs: "Ivy," "You Do (Who Knows How Much I Love You?)," and one more, which I've forgotten. But it was the last song, "I Have But One Heart," that really got to me. "I Have But One Heart" was an old Neapolitan song that someone had put English lyrics to and arranged, a beautiful melody that I had known since I was a kid listening to my father play and sing it to my mother. "*Dicimo o mare,*" the Italian went, "*facimu l'amore.*" "Let's tell the sea that we are making love."

I knew "I Have But One Heart" in the original, or at least in my father's Baresi-accented rendition of the original. I can't say that my own Italian was perfect, or even that it was actually Italian. What it was was Barese dialect, "Bares," as we said. Bares has its own distinctive pronunciation, more nasal and very different from standard Italian. Because it wasn't standard "school" Italian, my father never wanted to teach it to us. But in the usual way these things happened, all of us kids learned it anyway. We heard it all the time when Dad's friends or brothers and sisters came over. Then on Sundays after Mass, he and I and my sisters would go visiting while my mother stayed home preparing our big Sunday meal. We'd go to see his friends; he was so proud of us, he loved to take us around to all his *paisans,* all of whom would be gabbing away in Bares, so of course we picked it up, despite his idea that if we were going to learn Italian, we should only learn proper Italian, with a proper Italian accent. *Per piacere,* he would tell us, enunciating every syllable distinctly. "Here's how you say it. *P-e-r pia-ce-re.* You got it? *P-e-r pia-ce-re.*

"I Have But One Heart" was arranged so that I sang it in English and Italian. I recorded it, and Mercury released it early in 1947. I didn't know how they were marketing or distributing it. I was happy just to have a contract with them, and being able to record a song with so many associations was like icing on the cake. But then Mercury called us and said the record was doing great; it was headed straight up the pop charts. All the disc jockeys were playing it, and many of them wanted to have me on for interviews. "I Have But One Heart" was going to be a smash hit.

One of my first radio dates was an early morning show on a New York station that included news and weather reports along with music. The DJ and I talked some, then, when it was time for the weather, he asked if I would read the report. I said, "Okay, I guess," and he handed me the read-out. I started off with the current conditions, the temperature, the highs, the lows, but then I got to a place where the report mentioned the barometer, which was falling. And I read, "The barometer is falling," except I said "barometer" like "barrow-meter." The DJ said, "What? What was that?" and I said, "I don't know, barrow-meter."

"Let me look at that," he said—this was all on the air. "That's 'barometer,'" he said, "not 'barrow-meter.'" "Oh," I said. "Excuse me, I'm so sorry. You know, I didn't graduate high school." This is sixty-plus years ago, and I still remember my ears burning. But I never said "barrow-meter" again, and sales of the record continued to skyrocket, in New York as well as in all the other big markets. And in the middle of the excitement Ted Ashley called and said he had booked me. I'd be singing with the Stan Kenton band. At New York's Paramount Theater!

Eight months earlier I had been working at the Paramount as an usher. And now I was headlining. Stan Kenton was a big star, but I was headlining. "I Have But One Heart" had put me right in the middle of the limelight. My world had turned around 180 degrees. That first show, Stan Kenton and the band rose up there on the pit stage, playing their theme song, then after a couple more numbers they announced, "And now—here's Vic Damone." And I walked out on that stage, which may not have been an actual sacred place, but wasn't far from it in my estimation. When I looked down, there were all my buddies in their usher's outfits. "You know," I said to the audience, "I used to work here." Then, I couldn't help it, I waved at the guys. "Hey, Charlie. Hey, Joe. How you doin'? Jesus, can you guys believe this? I'm singing up here!"

"Hey, Vic. Great to see you up there."

"Yeah, Vic. Way to go."

I was talking to them from the stage, maybe partly to relieve my fright at being up there in front of that huge house. I was so nervous that first day that I asked if someone else could close the show—something the star usually did. But by the second day I was fine. Bob Whiteman, the Paramount manager, said, "Now do you think you can close the show?" "Yes," I said, "no problem." It had all been so sudden. But I was already starting to feel what it was like to be a real performer, a professional singer.

It was a good thing, too, because in that business you had to grow up fast. Strange things tended to happen, and you had to be ready for them. After my Paramount show I began working all over. In Washington, D.C., I was doing a show at the Capitol Theater. Here, as in most places, the spotlights pretty much blinded you if you were looking directly at the audience, but the wall lights illuminated the side aisles, and as I glanced over to the left I saw a man walking down toward the front. I was wrapped up in my song and didn't think anything of him except that maybe he was just going back to his seat from the men's room or something. But he kept coming down, passing one light after another, until he was right at the front. And then he came up onto the stage. As I finished the song he walked up to me and just stood there, looking at me.

"Hi," I said, trying to stay casual, but wondering if something was about to happen here. "How are you?"

"I'm good," he said. "How are you?" As if this was the most normal thing in the world.

"I'm good," I said. "Thanks." I stuck my hand out. "What's your name?"

"Name's Jim," he said, shaking my hand.

The audience was watching this, no doubt thinking it was part of the show.

"So, Jim, you here to see my show?"

"Yah," he said. "I'm a big fan. I love your music."

"Gee, that's wonderful."

The orchestra was right behind me, wondering what I was going to do, which I didn't know myself. The guy was obviously a nut job. The questions was, was he a dangerous nut job?

"Jim, listen. I've got a great song I'm going to do now. I'd like you to really pay attention to it. It's got a great lyric."

"Hey, I'd like to hear it."

I walked over to the wings and told the stagehands to get me a chair. They got one and I put it on the stage, a ways off from the middle. I didn't know what this guy might have in mind. He seemed perfectly sober and rational, just a fan who wanted to get up close. But who knew?

"Sit there," I said. "You're gonna love this song."

He sat down, crossed his legs, and relaxed. I did the song, and as soon as I finished he began clapping enthusiastically. The audience was applauding, he was applauding. He was really enjoying himself there. When the applause died down I went over to him and shook his hand again. But instead of letting go I kept my grip and put my other hand on his back. "I really appreciate your coming to see my show," I said. "I'll see you later." And I guided him off into the wings, where the stagehands grabbed him.

Back at the microphone I said to the audience, "I don't know who that gentleman was. I guess just a fan. He came up, so I thought I'd talk to him a bit." The audience was laughing, I was laughing. But it easily could have turned into something else. Mel Tormé used to tell the story of one especially disruptive person in a club where he was singing, who waited for him afterward to beat him up. Mel pulled a gun on him. He thanked God he didn't have to pull the trigger, but it was a close call.

I never had anything like that happen, but for some reason I did attract nut jobs on occasion. Some time later I was playing the Paramount again, with Tex Beneke and the Glenn Miller Orchestra. I had had several other hit songs by this time, the biggest of which was "You're Breaking My Heart," which had gotten up to number one. I was closing the show with this song, and in the middle there's a passage that's very pianissimo, very pretty. I'm singing softly, keeping as sweet a tone as I could, when I heard a *click, click, click* sound coming toward me, as if someone was walking in high heels on a bare floor. When I looked over to my right, I saw a woman, who had come up from the audience just as that fan had in Washington. Wearing high heels, of course. And halfway toward me she stopped, pulled a half slip down from under her skirt, and started swinging it over her head, saying to me—the audience couldn't hear her, but Tex and the band could—"This is my bridal slip. We're engaged."

I was still in the middle of "You're Breaking My Heart," but I was staring at her. Tex and the musicians were staring at her, too, though they were still playing. The entire packed house was staring at her as she walked right up to me, waving the slip.

I stopped singing. "Hello," I said. "What did you say?" Giving Tex the "cut" sign so he'd stop the music.

"I said, 'This is my bridal slip and we're engaged.'" Close enough to the mike so that everyone could hear.

"I'm sorry, I don't even know who you are. What's your name?"

"Lillian."

"Hi, Lillian," I said. "I'm Vic Damone." We shook hands. I'm thinking, Christ, am I some kind of magnet for these people?

"But Lillian, I can't talk to you now, I'm in the middle of a show. Why don't we talk later. This is not a good time."

"Oh," she said, as if she hadn't quite realized where she was. "Oh, okay."

I turned to Tex. "Tex, why don't you walk Lillian here over to the exit curtain."

"Sure," he said, and he took her hand and walked her off.

The audience was staring at me, absolutely hushed. I didn't know where to go with this. "I'm sorry," I said to them. "We were trying to do 'You're Breaking My Heart,' but why don't we finish up with 'Sorrento' instead. Jack"—this to my piano player, Jack Kelly—"Jack, let's do that wonderful Italian song 'Sorrento.'"

I sang "Sorrento" with just piano, and as I did Tex Beneke walked back from the wings, alone, thank God. As I was singing I looked at him and gave him the sign that this was the last song, so he knew that, as soon as I finished, he would play my bow music. I hit the high note at the end, and that was it. I took my bows and headed offstage, looking for the girl. But she was nowhere. When I asked the stage manager, he said, "What girl? We didn't see any girl." Then one of the guys said, "Oh yeah, some girl walked right through here and out the exit."

"That's it?" I said. "Didn't you guys see what happened out there?"

"Nah," he said. "We're just waiting for them to cue the lights back here."

At the time this incident happened I was working on radio as well as in clubs and theaters. I had gotten a call from the *Pet Milk Saturday Night Serenade,* a popular music show on the CBS radio network. *Saturday Night Serenade* featured a major male and female singer, a big orchestra led by Gus Haenschen, and a chorus, the Emil Cote Serenaders. The female singer was Vera Holly. Would I consider coming on as the lead? they asked. The billing would be the *Pet Milk Saturday Night Serenade with Vic Damone.* There were a couple of other big radio music shows at the time: *Your Hit Parade,* with Frank Sinatra, *The Chesterfield Supper Club,* with Perry Como. *Saturday Night Serenade* was going to put me into as rarefied company as you could possibly get.

6

Frank's Stand-In

In 1949 I was appearing at the Paramount again, along with doing my weekly *Saturday Night Serenade* radio broadcast. The Paramount was a heavy schedule, five shows a day, starting at eleven A.M. and finishing in the evening, which made things very tight, since I also had to rehearse for and perform the hourlong radio show, which went on at ten P.M.

One day in the middle of the Paramount run I got a call from Frank Sinatra. It was a Friday afternoon.

"Hello, Dago. How are you?"

"Good, Frank. How are you?"

"I'm okay. Listen, I know you're busy, you're doing a lot of shows there, right?"

"Yeah, five a day."

"I know, I've done it, even six or seven shows."

"Well, I'm lucky. I'm only doing five. What's up?"

"Listen, I want you to do me a favor."

"Sure, Frank. What can I do for you?"

"I've got a problem. My throat isn't up to what it should be. I want you to go on for me tomorrow night, on the *Hit Parade*."

"Frank, I'd love to, but I'm doing five shows here, then I've got my *Saturday Night Serenade* show. I don't know how I could possibly do it."

"But would you if I can work it out?"

"Sure. But how're you going to do that?"

"Well, I'm going to arrange it, okay?

"Okay, but hold on a minute. What songs am I supposed to sing? This is Friday. We're talking about tomorrow night."

"Don't worry about it, Vic. You know them already: 'Night and Day,' 'Maam'selle.' Easy."

"Okay. If you can arrange it. It'll be an honor."

"Trust me," he said. "I'll arrange it."

I don't know what to say about what happened next. It showed what a consummate operator Sinatra was, and how utterly meticulous. First, he found out all my show times at the Paramount. Then he found out my rehearsal time at CBS. And he worked out a kind of choreography, changing all the rehearsal times so they would fit together. That Saturday I did two early shows at the Paramount, then went off to rehearse *Saturday Night Serenade,* then went back to the Paramount for my third show. Then I ran from there over to NBC to rehearse Frank's show with Axel Stordahl, his arranger and the leader of the Lucky Strike Hit Parade Orchestra. Axel had been Tommy Dorsey's arranger, and was already famous for arranging many of Frank's hits. Axel was a big talent, with a special gift for tailoring orchestra music to a singer's voice.

At NBC I rehearsed "Night and Day," "Maam'selle," and the rest of the *Hit Parade* song list. Then Axel said, "Okay, let's do 'Civilization.'" "Civilization" may not have been the number-one song in the country at the time, but it was close. Everybody knew it, and everybody was singing it: "Bongo, bongo, bongo, I don't want to leave the Congo, oh no no no no no." It was a very catchy number. Easy, a snap. "Okay, Axel," I said. "Bongo, bongo, bongo, right?"

"Right," said Axel. "But that's the chorus. You have to sing the verse."

"The verse? What verse?"

"The verse to 'Civilization.'"

"I don't know the verse to 'Civilization.'"

"Well, you'll learn it."

"No I won't. How can I learn it? There's no time. We're almost out of time here."

"Don't worry about it, Vic. You'll learn it."

Axel pulled one of the kids out of the chorus to stand next to me and sing it to me. And it was one of the hardest verses I ever heard in my life. It started off: "Each morning, the missionary advertises ba ba ba ba bi bi." Sixteen bars. And only then, "Oh, bongo bongo bongo, I don't wanna," and so on. And the melody for those sixteen bars was not obvious, it wasn't intuitive, it went up and down and did strange things.

"Axel, Jesus, I can't learn that. By tonight? You've got to be kidding."

"Please. Don't worry about it," said Axel. "I'm sending my piano player back to the Paramount with you."

So I hustled back to the Paramount with Axel's piano player in tow. And when we got there, somehow they had moved a piano into my dressing room. So while I got dressed for my next show, the piano player was playing the music for the verse: "Each morning, the missionary advertises . . ." He played it, stopped, played it over, stopped, played it over, and over, and over, and over, and I'm thinking, Jesus Christ, give me a break already. The thing's coming out of my ears, and I have to do a show. Actually, I had to do three shows, and then *Your Hit Parade,* and then *Saturday Night Serenade.* But he's playing and I'm singing. I put my pants on, I'm singing, "Each morning, the missionary . . ." I put my shirt on. "Each morning, the missionary . . ." I'm knotting my tie. "Each morning, the missionary . . ."

I get down to the Paramount stage, and the damn thing won't leave my head. But somehow I got through the show. Then I'm up in my dressing room between that show and the next, and it's the same thing all over again, with that damned piano player.

When I finally finished at the Paramount I took a car over to *Your Hit Parade* at CBS, and I got there at about twenty minutes to nine. Sinatra had not only reserved the car, he had also arranged a police escort so we wouldn't get caught in the Saturday night traffic. Axel and the orchestra were onstage waiting for me. The audience was in their seats. "Ladies and gentlemen," Axel said. "Please ignore us. We have to work on a song here. Mr. Damone is taking Mr. Sinatra's place tonight, and he's not familiar with this particular number. We're just going to work with him a bit before we go on the air. Thank you."

Then we did the song, once, twice, three times. And suddenly the red "On Air" light went on, and the announcer's voice boomed, "Ladies and gentlemen, this is *Your Lucky Strike Hit Parade,* starring Frank Sinatra. Filling in for Mr. Sinatra tonight is Vic Damone. And now, here's Vic Damone, singing 'Civilization'! Bam! I had just heard the thing a moment ago, and it was right there on my lips. "Each morning, the missionary . . . Oh, bongo bongo bongo . . ." And it worked perfectly. I glanced at Axel and he winked at me, as if to say, "I told you you'd get it, you son of a gun." I was never so happy in my life that a show was finally over. I think a lot of people of a certain age still have that song in their heads, but not like I do, nothing at all like I do.

That show went so well that Frank made an arrangement with Lucky Strike to have me there for the rest of the season, just to be available in case his voice wasn't up to it. Those periods when Frank took care of himself, when he concentrated on his singing, his voice was pure. It had an unusual richness to it. It was fluid and had depth. And that was aside from the fact that he was the greatest interpreter of lyrics popular music has ever had. But he often didn't take care of himself. He loved to party. He smoked and drank, and that had consequences. One time, when he was performing at Radio City Music Hall, he could hardly talk. He still went out—the man was fearless. But the first three or four songs, before his voice warmed up, he could barely sing a note. At one point he told someone, "I have a great voice. It just happens to be in Vic Damone's throat." That was flattering, but it was only true when his voice was breaking down from all the stresses he put on it.

At any event, for thirteen weeks I backed him up on *Your Hit Parade.* I'd rehearse my radio show, rehearse his show, go sit in the control booth at NBC in case he needed me, then do my show on CBS. In actual fact, even though I was ready, I never did have to go on for him after that one appearance. I sometimes wondered not only why he was keeping me there but also why he was doing the *Your Hit Parade* at all. He was the country's leading popular singer, with hit records and albums, and he was under contract with MGM, starring in movies like *Anchors Aweigh* with Gene Kelly. He hardly needed it. The thought struck me more than once while I was watching from the control booth that maybe he was doing it partly for me, to help me learn by hanging out and rehearsing with him and Axel Stordahl. Maybe that was a little too self-centered on my part, but maybe not. I was still at the beginning of my career, and ever since that night at Madison Square Garden, it had been obvious that Frank had a protective feeling about me, and was doing whatever he could to help bring me along.

By the time I started in radio my relationship with Lou Capone was on a steep downward track. I was still working under the terms of our contract, which meant he was paying me $150 a week, while all the other income I was generating went to him. At first I had been so thankful for that $150. As hard as my father worked, he didn't make nearly that much, and we had a lot of mouths to feed. When I signed that contract it had seemed as if God was smiling on me. But then I had the hit record, I started working full time at clubs and theaters, and CBS gave me the radio show. A lot of money was coming in, of which I was seeing only that same $150. But besides that, as I came to understand the business better, it became clearer and clearer that Lou was not really a manager. He made elementary mistakes. He let things slip. He was just not professional at it, and it became obvious to me that he never would be.

One incident between us was so blatant that it set all my negative thoughts about him in stone. At the time, I was working at the Adams Theater in Newark, New Jersey. On Saturdays, I'd finish my first show there, jump into the limo CBS provided for me, drive back to Manhattan to rehearse *Saturday Night Serenade,* get back in the limo for the next shows in Newark, then race back to Manhattan again to do the radio show before a live studio audience.

One Saturday—it was the day before Easter—I was supposed to sing "Avé Maria" on the radio. Anyway, in the middle of all this rushing around, I finished my last show at the Adams and went outside to jump into the limo for my ride to the city, only to find that there was no limo. I'm thinking, Goddamnit! Where the hell is it? Then I remembered that Capone had said something about taking it to go see his girlfriend. He was going to take it, then have the driver bring it back to the theater.

My anxiety level was skyrocketing. I was supposed to go on at CBS in half an hour. I looked around the corner, across the street. The limo was nowhere! He hadn't sent it back.

By now the musicians were leaving the theater, and one of them saw I was in some kind of trouble.

"Hey, Vic," he said. "What's the matter? Can I help with something?"

"I don't know. I've got to get to New York for my radio show, and my limo isn't here. I don't know what happened to it."

"Here," he said, tossing me his keys. "My car's the Buick over there. Take it. You can bring it back here tomorrow."

I stood there with his keys in my hand as he walked off with some of the others. I couldn't tell him that I wasn't that good a driver. I had learned how to drive and passed the test, but I hadn't done it that much. To say I was shaky would have been putting it mildly. And driving to Manhattan? On a Saturday evening? I didn't know how to do this. I wasn't even sure I could find the way.

I still don't know how I got to the Lincoln Tunnel. It had to have been dumb luck. What I do remember is that I was scared to death the whole way, especially inside the tunnel. I finally got into the city, though, and now I had to find my way to Fifty-fourth near Broadway, where the theater was. I got up to Fifty-second, which went east, the direction I needed. I wasn't sure which direction Fifty-third or Fifty-fourth went. I was confused. Time was ticking down. How was I going to get to Fifty-fourth? The traffic was maddening, all those cars, all of them honking—at me, I thought. People yelling. I turned right on Fifty-second, figuring that might be the safest. But after a couple of blocks I realized my mistake. I turned back on Fifty-third, thinking, What now? What should I do? I'll never make it! And right then I saw a cop on a horse, right next to my car. I knew that cop. He had seen me coming and going into the theater for my show for a long time. We often said hello to each other. "Vic," he said, "what are you doing? Where's your limo? You're on the air in a couple of minutes. What the hell are you doing out here?"

"I don't know. I've got to park this car. I don't know what to do with it."

"Stop right here," he said. "Give me the keys. I'll take care of it. Go through that alley. The stage door's right on the other side."

"Oh, man," I said. "Thank you, thank you. You're the greatest."

I sprinted through the alley, and there, standing outside the stage door with his arms folded, was Lou Capone. "Oh," he said, "there you are. I knew you'd get here."

"Get the fuck out of my way," I said, pushing past him. I ran into the theater. My conductor, Gus Haenschen, was telling the orchestra, "Okay, you do eight bars, you do eight bars." Giving them the melody lines, so at least they could play the songs, even if I wasn't there to sing them. It was two minutes to airtime. I came running in and Gus said, "Oh, he's here, he's here. Forget it. Just do it as usual."

I was out of breath from running when they gave me the keynote for "I Have But One Heart"—my theme song. But I sucked in a breath and let out: "I have but one heart, this heart I bring you." With that the orchestra came in and we rolled through the show.

When it was over I got hold of Capone backstage. "You can't do that to me!" I told him. I was shaking with rage. "I'm doing shows, I've got to come back here for the radio show, and you take the car? To see your girlfriend? You stay out of my way! How could you do that to me?"

"Ah," he said. "I knew you'd find a way to get here."

That was the straw that broke my back. Sinatra knew about my contract, and he couldn't stand Capone because of it. He thought Capone was taking advantage of me, and Frank had had his own bad experience with the same kind of situation.

One time, while I was backing Frank up on *Your Hit Parade,* I was sitting in the glassed-in control booth with Capone watching Frank do his opening number. He finished his song, with the kids screaming, as usual. Then he looked toward us, and when he saw Capone in the booth he walked away from the microphone, came over to us, and pointed. Frank had those steely blue eyes; he looked really pissed.

"You," he said, pointing up toward us. "Get out of there. Get out of that booth!"

We couldn't hear him, but we could read his lips.

"Who, me?" I said, pointing at myself.

"Not you. Him!" Pointing at Capone.

"Me?" said Capone

"Yeah, you. Get outta there. Get out of the booth."

"You're okay," he said to me. "You"—staring at Capone . . . "You! Out!"

Frank's own problem had been with Tommy Dorsey. That situation was why Capone's relationship with me aggravated him so much. Sinatra's original contract with Dorsey was similar to mine: Dorsey was paying him a small salary for the life of their agreement. Then, as Frank became popular and wanted to go out on his own, Dorsey had demanded a punitive settlement, in which he took a hefty percentage of Sinatra's future earnings for an extended period. When Sinatra tried to break that, Dorsey sued him. But then Dorsey suddenly and unexpectedly agreed to settle the suit. Rumors flew around that a couple of mob guys had visited Dorsey and persuaded him. Much later Dorsey himself said that Willie Moretti, a big-time underboss, had threatened to kill him if he didn't settle. Of course, Frank did know the mob guys well, and a lot has been written about what happened between him and Dorsey. But Frank never talked to me about that, so I don't know personally. That was what Francis Ford Coppola's *Godfather* scene was based on, though, the one where Al Pacino tells his fiancée, Diane Keaton, that the Godfather got Johnny Fontane (the Sinatra character) out of his contract by making the bandleader "an offer he couldn't refuse."

To digress a bit, the Johnny Fontane/Frank Sinatra character in the movie was a role I was offered but had to turn down. What I heard was that Coppola told the casting person that he wanted someone like Vic Damone for the part. At first they had a couple of people come in who were possibilities, but then someone said, "Why don't we just get Vic Damone?"

After I went in and read for the part, they told me it was mine if I wanted it. But when I saw the whole script, it turned out there were only two pages. Johnny Fontane sings at the Godfather's daughter's wedding, then there's one scene between him and the Godfather. When my agent asked how long the shooting was going to take, he was told ten weeks. I would have to stay in New York for that long, because they had to shoot the scene according to Marlon Brando's schedule, and no one was sure when he might be ready to do it. But whenever he was, I would have to be available. The fee would be eleven hundred dollars a week, out of which I'd have to pay my own expenses.

At that time—this was in 1971—I was paying large sums in alimony and child support, a lot more than they were offering. I was working as hard as I could to keep my income up, which meant I was fully booked in Vegas and at various nightclubs.

"What am I going to do?" I asked my agent. "Am I supposed to cancel my jobs? I can't afford it."

On the other hand, this was supposed to be a portrayal of part of Sinatra's life. So I called him.

"Frank, you know this part, it's like your life story."

"Yeah, yeah, I know."

"What do you want me to do?"

"I don't know," he said. "It's up to you, pal. It could be good for your career, but it's a story about the mob and all that. You've got to make up your own mind. It's your career, I can't tell you what you should do."

So that didn't settle anything. In the back of my head I was still thinking, This is definitely the Sinatra story. Who's going to do that better than me? Besides which, the song Johnny Fontane was supposed to sing at the wedding was "I Have But One Heart," my song. If I took the part I'd be singing my theme song in front of millions of people. On the other hand, the script made him out to be a kind of weakling, a whiner. Of course, Sinatra had seen the script; there was no way he wasn't going to get hold of it. But he didn't say anything about the characterization to me, only that I had to make up my own mind. I can't imagine he cared much about the way the movie presented him. He was above that. But he was never, ever a whiner. So how could I do that?

When I turned it down, my excuse was that I wasn't able cancel my bookings. Afterward I got a call from one of the networks asking to interview me about it. And they asked if Sinatra had wanted me to decline it. I said, No, it was my schedule. Of course, I would never ever discuss the fact that I had spoken to Frank at all. I said it would've been nice, and I would've been honored to work with Francis Ford Coppola—which was absolutely true—but I couldn't do it because I was booked.

One more little tidbit about *The Godfather.* Al Martino ended up playing the Johnny Fontane role. After he sings he meets with the Godfather and begs for a favor. There's a part in an upcoming blockbuster movie that would be perfect for him, that would revive his flagging career. But the studio head won't give it to him. Could the Godfather do something? Fontane is groveling and begging, and he's supposed to cry. At that point Brando, the Godfather, slaps him and tells him to "be a man." But that slap wasn't in the script.

Martino didn't expect it. It shocked him. Brando felt Al needed to put more emotion into the performance, and that slap woke him up. All of a sudden he was emoting. It made the scene. I knew about that when I saw the movie. I thought about how I might have played it myself, and whether Brando would have had to slap me or not. I'd like to believe that he wouldn't have. I actually think Al did a good job, especially after the slap. But I knew Frank so well, his life was so real to me, that I might have been able to give that scene something extra. And playing with Brando, who inhabited the Godfather character? Who *was* the Godfather? Man, would I have loved that! Who knows? It might have changed the movie a bit.

Of course, my relationship with Lou Capone had nothing to do with the mob; it was just us, my extreme unhappiness with him and his insistence that I had signed a contract, and that was that—a contract that still had four-plus years to run. I finally said to my father, "Pop, I can't handle this guy anymore. He's doing all the wrong things. I have to get rid of him. We need a lawyer." I was twenty years old at the time, still living with my family. My father was what he always was, a hardworking, honest Italian man who did not have a sophisticated understanding of certain areas of his adopted culture.

Among other things, neither of us had ever hired a lawyer. We had no idea where to turn. It was a mark of our naïveté that the only lawyer we could think of to represent us was Irving Sussman, the same lawyer who represented Lou Capone. Irving was a sweet man, very congenial and straightforward. We both liked him a lot. "Irving will be good," my father said. "He'll be fair with us, for sure."

We had to go to court, of course, and when our case was called the judge said to Irving, "Wait a minute, who are you representing?" And Irving said, "Well, I'm kind of representing both of them."

In the end, the court allowed me to buy back the contract. The judge saw that I wasn't getting much of the money I was making. "That's not good," he said. "That's not good at all." Actually, that was the first time I had seen a full accounting of the income myself. I was shocked at how much was coming in, which, of course, just made me even angrier. On the other hand, both my father and I had in fact signed the contract. The judge's decision was that, in return for canceling the agreement, I would have to pay Capone forty thousand dollars out of my future earnings. I wasn't happy about it. I felt I had been getting screwed for quite a while already, so this was an added insult. On the other hand, I was most definitely happy to be rid of Capone. I felt I could get on with my career now, without the problems and obstacles he represented.

One Sunday morning, not too long after I bought back my contract, the doorbell rang. I answered it, still in my pajamas and robe. "Hello," this person said. "Mr. Damone? My name is Pat Genaro." He shook my hand.

"Yes?" I said. "What's up?

"Mr. Damone, I have a song for you." And he handed me the lead sheet, that is, the song, with the melody and words. The title was "You're Breaking My Heart."

I looked at it. I knew the song. "This is an Italian song," I said.

"That's right," he said. "I put English lyrics to it."

I didn't just know the song, I knew it well. It was one of my father's favorites—"La Mattinata." The great Gigli had sung it. So I said, "C'mon in." I introduced him to my mom and pop. "Pop, he's showing me this Italian song. He wrote English lyrics to it."

"Which Italian-a song?" This from my father.

I started singing. "L'aurora di bianco vestita. Già l'uscio dischiude al gran sol."

"Aah, good. I like this," said my father. "That's a good song."

My mother said, "You look hungry, sit down."

Pat Genaro looked at me. It was the middle of the morning. "You better sit down," I said. My mother was already out in the kitchen fixing him a dish of pasta and sauce.

The next day I took it to Mercury Records. Mitch Miller was the A&R man there, an accomplished classical and jazz musician himself who later became famous as a record producer and television musical personality. "Mitch, this guy Pat Genaro came to my house the other day with this. I think it's pretty good."

Mitch brought in a piano player and I sang it. "Oh," he said, "that *is* nice."

"Yes, I love it," I said. "I think it's great. I'd love to do it."

We were just about to record four new songs, all of them arranged by Abe Osser. In a day or two Abe had an arrangement for the new one, and Mitch said, "Let's try to add it. We'll do it if we have time."

One of the songs we had scheduled to record was "The Four Winds and the Seven Seas," which we all thought would be a hit. We did that one and the other three, and at the end of the session we still had twenty minutes left. "Okay," Mitch said. "Let's do that new song, 'You're Breaking My Heart.'"

I did two takes on it, singing in both Italian and English. The next day, when I went to Mercury, Mitch said, "Listen, I want to play you 'You're Breaking My Heart.'"

"Okay, but what about 'Four Winds and Seven Seas'?"

"No, I want to play you 'You're Breaking My Heart.' I want you to hear what you did with it."

He played it. "Oh my God," I said, "that's awful."

"Really?" he said. "Do you think so? This is a hit record, my friend."

"Mitch. Let me do it again. I'm a little off in one spot, it's terrible. Don't release this, please."

"No," he said. "I believe it just the way you did it. Everyone who listens to this will believe what you're singing there. That's the important thing. This is a hit!"

"What about 'Four Winds and the Seven Seas'?"

"I'll put it on the B side. You'll have the two of them, two good numbers."

"You're Breaking My Heart" was on the charts for twenty-six

weeks, peaking at number one. We forgot about "Four Winds." It just wiped that right off. We sold over three million records. Later the song was covered by the Inkspots, Buddy Clark, and various others. In between "I Have But One Heart" in 1947 and "You're Breaking My Heart" in 1949 I had had a number of big sellers, but those two were major hits. And after "You're Breaking My Heart" George Wood at William Morris told me he had decided it was time for me to hit the West Coast. He booked me at Los Angeles's Mocambo Club. If you were going to play Tinseltown, the Mocambo was the place you'd most want to be. Hollywood's biggest stars liked to party there.

7

"The Bar?" Said Ava. "Sure."

The Mocambo was definitely it! There was one other big club venue for singers in Los Angeles, Ciro's, but the Mocambo had the buzz. The place was right on Sunset Boulevard, The Strip. It was decorated in a Latin American theme, colorful and intimate. I read somewhere that when it first opened it had glass cages along the walls with spectacular tropical birds in them, but if that was so, they were gone by the time I got there. When CBS started filming *I Love Lucy,* they used the Mocambo as the home for Ricky Ricardo's Latin band. I'm not sure if Desi Arnaz really ever did play there, but the Mocambo was a magnet for Hollywood celebrities who used to come to dance, drink, schmooze, and catch the big-name acts. They all came: John Wayne, Sophia Loren, Humphrey Bogart and Lauren Bacall, Clark Gable, Errol Flynn, Marilyn Monroe, Ava Gardner—on any given night at least some of Hollywood's A list would be partying there. Sinatra had made his own West Coast debut at the Mocambo six or seven years earlier.

When they booked me there I had been working at the Paramount, the Copacabana, the Riviera, and lots of other name spots around the country. I had opened for Joe E. Lewis at the Copa and Danny Thomas at the Riviera. For a young singer, I was hot. But

California? The Coast? I had never been, and now, here I was. In Hollywood! With the movie stars! I was scared to death.

I started going to the Mocambo to rehearse two or three days before I opened, so I could get acclimated to the room and the sound. My bass and drum guys and my wonderful English piano player, Ronnie Selby, came with me in the afternoons, before anybody was there. Then, the day before my opening, the Mocambo was closed, which meant I could be there at night and work with the lights as well as the sound. I had never rehearsed more thoroughly. I sang. I heard what we all sounded like. I got used to the acoustics of the room. We knew exactly what we were going to do and how we were going to do it. I wanted this show to be absolutely perfect.

The day of the opening I finished my rehearsal and drove back to my apartment with my new manager, Marvin Cain, and a friend, Ivan Mogul. Marvin had worked at the Shapiro Bernstein Music Publishing Company back in New York, where I had been doing most of my rehearsing, and Ivan had his own publishing business. Marvin was an especially dedicated music person with a great ear. I found I could always rely on him for excellent advice as I was working up songs. We had become good friends, and when I dropped Lou Capone I asked Marvin if he would take over as my manager, which he did. So there he was in Los Angeles with our other buddy from Shapiro Bernstein, Ivan Mogul, helping me prepare for my big date.

Back at the apartment I took a short nap, and when I got up I started preparing myself, getting myself into the mood. I showered and shaved, thinking about the show. To relax, I got my shoes out from the closet and started polishing them, and while I polished I went over the whole show in my mind, the lyrics to all the songs, the order, the tempos, the mood I wanted to set for each number. By the time we got into the car for the ride back to the club I felt great. I was clean, my tux looked good, my shoes were polished; I was ready to sing. I could feel myself getting into the zone.

At nine o'clock I was backstage, listening as I was introduced. Then I walked out and went right into my first song, Cole Porter's "In the Still of the Night," a great opener: "In the still of the night/ My thoughts all stray to you." Perfect lyrics for coming out and opening up. The response was terrific. Two spotlights were on me, so at first I couldn't tell who was out there in the audience. But after a bit, my eyes got accustomed. The stage and mood lights bathed the front tables, and the first person I made out, sitting right in the middle, was John Wayne. Jesus Christ, I thought. John Wayne! But it wasn't just him. The room was loaded. I felt numb for a moment. I was singing to the stars.

The whole two-week run was wall-to-wall. It was great. I couldn't have been happier. But at the same time I was lonely, out there by myself, not really knowing anyone. I had rented an apartment at the Garden of Allah, an apartment complex that appealed to up-and-coming entertainers and actors. I'd often see Jackie Gleason at the pool there. He had been in a few movies and had a nightclub act, but this was before his great television successes, *The Jackie Gleason Show* and *The Honeymooners.* We'd say hello to each other, but every time I saw him out there, he seemed to be drinking. One drink, then another. The man never seemed to eat anything, which couldn't be good, given the amount of booze he was downing. So one day I said, "Jackie, you're always drinking. You don't eat enough. How about some food?"

"Nah," he said. "I don't feel like eating."

"But you like Italian food, right?"

"Yeah, I love Italian food."

"Good. I'll go and cook something for you. If I cook it, will you eat it?"

"What are ya gonna make?"

"Pasta and sauce."

"Yeah," he said. "Okay, go ahead."

So I did, and I gave it to him. Brought it out on a plate, with the cheese, silverware, everything. And he ate it.

"Wow," he said. "Hey, this is good, man. I loved it." Then he poured himself another drink.

From the run at the Mocambo I went out to the Flamingo in Las Vegas. This was in 1949, when the Flamingo was still new and far and away the top hotel casino in Vegas. I had heard about its history with Bugsy Siegel and Meyer Lansky, how the mob had come into Las Vegas using the Flamingo, and how they had killed Siegel for siphoning off their profits. Of course, I knew some of those guys from my near fatal engagement to Franny D'Angelo, and Joe Adonis and his friends liked to come to my shows in New York. I was to have a future contact or two with them as well, which I'll come to later on. But to the wise guys I was basically a square, a Charlie Brown—in their circle of acquaintance, but not of the circle. So while I knew about the Flamingo, it wasn't the mob ties that interested me, it was the showgirls and the exposure. It was the atmosphere, the packed house, the combination of money and sex and electricity that you could practically smell, that made Las Vegas what it was even then. First Hollywood, now Vegas. I had spent my teenage years watching the great bandleaders and singers at the Paramount. But this was different, a different world, with a different feel, looser and wilder. I was barely twenty-one, and I was right in the middle of it.

I came back from the Flamingo to a second booking at the Mocambo. I had done so well there those first two weeks that Charlie Morrison, the owner, was itching to see if we couldn't keep bringing them in. And we did. The first run had built some momentum. I was a new face in town. I had hit records. People liked the shows and they kept coming; the house was always full. I was as happy as a clam. And if I was happy, Charlie was even happier. He had been having money problems, but now he was "in green" for a change. He was so happy he gave me a beautiful gold watch. And one day as we were talking on the phone he said, "Vic, tell me, what else can I do for you?"

I thought about it for a moment. "Well," I said, "how about getting me a date with Ava Gardner?"

"What?" Charlie said. "Ava Gardner? What makes you think I can get you a date with Ava Gardner?"

"Charlie, come on. I'd just like to take her to dinner. You know her, right?"

"Yeah, a little. She comes to the club."

"So? Give it a try, okay?"

Not that I expected anything would come of it. I mean, really. Ava Gardner was a goddess—so unbelievably beautiful and unbelievably sexy. She could and did have her pick of guys, anyone she wanted. So why would she go out with me? And Charlie Morrison knew her a little, but it wasn't as if they were close personal friends.

Fifteen minutes after we hung up, Charlie called me back. "You got it!" he said.

"Hello, Charlie? I got what?"

"You got a date with Ava Gardner."

"You gotta be kidding me!"

"No, you got the date. On Monday." That was my one off night. "Pick her up at her house—you can take my car. Take her to Chasens. You'll be my guest at Chasens."

"You're putting me on."

"No, here's her phone number. Pick her up at eight. Here's how you get there."

"Oh, oh, okay."

Monday night at eight I was at Ava Gardner's front door. I rang the doorbell, nervous. She opened the door. Oh my God, she was so gorgeous. You have no idea. She looked like spring. She was wearing a light dress that flowed around her like silk. She had a perfume on that smelled like heaven. I felt dizzy just looking at her. It was all I could do to say, "Hi, I'm Vic Damone."

"Hi," she said. "We're going to go to Chasens, aren't we."

"Uh, yes, to Chasens. We're going to Chasens. To have dinner. At Chasens." I hardly knew what I was saying. I was looking at her eyes. "Forgive me, I'm a little choked. Looking at you, you're just so beautiful." She tossed it off, as if she didn't even hear me.

When we walked into Chasens the maître d' said, "Mr. Damone, good evening. We're getting your table ready. Would you care to go to the bar while it's being set up."

"Ava?" I said.

"The bar?" she said. "Sure."

The bartender came over. "Good evening, folks, what can I get you?"

"Ava?"

"I'll have a double vodka on the rocks."

"And you, sir?"

"Oh, I don't drink. I'll just have a Coke"

Ava looked me right in the eye and said, "You are going to be such a fucking bore."

"In that case . . ." I turned to the bartender. "I'll have a double vodka on the rocks."

"I thought you said you don't drink," said Ava.

"Well, I'm damned if I want to be a fucking bore."

And she started laughing, an infectious, earthy laugh. I thought, This is going to be an interesting night.

Next thing I knew I was drinking the double vodka. It was strong as hell, and it didn't taste that good, either. I had literally never had an alcoholic drink before. Then she said, "I'll have another one." I thought, Jesus Christ, another one? But I said, "I'll have another one, too."

I had three double vodkas at the bar. Ava was laughing, I was laughing. I didn't even know what we were laughing about, but we were having a great time. I was having such a good time I was hardly even in awe of her gorgeousness anymore.

"Mr. Damone." It was the maître d'. "Your table's ready."

"Great, the table's ready. Ava, let's go eat," thinking to myself, I better get some food in my stomach fast.

All during dinner she was telling jokes. I was laughing, relaxed. More than relaxed. I was loose as a goose. I was ready for anything.

"Listen," she said as we finished dessert. "Can you dance?"

"Dance? Sure I can dance. I'm from Brooklyn. The Lindy, all that stuff."

"Good," she said. "Let's go to the Palladium. Woody Herman's there."

"All right! You just have to show me where it is."

I drove to the Palladium, bombed. Just terrible. Ava Gardner could make you do terrible things.

I have no idea how we got there, but we did. We got a table, and she ordered another drink. "Sure," I said, "give her anything. I'll have one, too." I think she kept drinking double vodkas, though I had long ago lost track.

We danced. I was a pretty good dancer, lucky for me. As long as I could stay on my feet I could handle it, and I was still on my feet. And who did we see on the dance floor but the swashbuckling actor Cornel Wilde and Jean Wallace, a beautiful blonde he later married. Ava introduced us. Cornel said, "Here, let me dance with Ava, you dance with Jean." We spent the rest of the night on the dance floor, switching on and off. I was having the best time of my life with two of the most gorgeous women in the universe. If there was something disappointing about Hollywood, I couldn't have named it. I had been out there maybe four weeks. I was thinking, I could get used to this.

Finally, the place was closing down and it was time to call it a night. With Ava directing we drove back to her house, which was on one of the hills. I drove around the hillside there and stopped in front of the property. The house was behind a stand of hedges. And as my headlights hit the hedges I saw somebody in there—half hidden in the bushes.

"Look," I said, slurring my words, "there's a guy in there. See? In the bushes."

"Oh, God," Ava said, "that's Howard." But in a tone that was more annoyed than surprised. Like, "Oh, for God's sakes, it's that Howard again."

"Howard?" I said. "What Howard?" I thought it was Howard Hughes, who I remembered used to date her. Was he still? Had they been married at some point? I couldn't recall. Howard Hughes hiding in her bushes. Jesus.

"Howard?" I said. "Howard who? Howard Hughes?"

"No, silly. Howard Duff."

"Howard Duff?"

"Yeah, he thinks he loves me. It's a long story."

"Howard Duff?" I got out of the car

And here he came, out of the bushes. Howard Duff. A big guy.

I turned to Ava. "What should I do?"

"Look at him, will you?" she said. "He's obviously drunk." (*He's* obviously drunk? I'm thinking. *I'm* obviously drunk.) "But don't worry about it, Vic. I'll handle him. When he's drunk he's . . ." Her voice trailed off, so I didn't catch what he was when he was drunk. I'm thinking, When he's drunk, what? Now he was out of the bushes and he started giving it to me: "You took my girl! She's my girl, and you took her!"

"Hey, whoa, fella. I just took her to dinner. What is it with you?"

"Yeah? You . . . you . . . you . . ."

Ava looked at me. "You better go," she said. "It's better if you just go."

"Okay," I said. "Thank you for a wonderful evening. And my first drink." My first drink? Christ, my first six or eight drinks. I had no idea. I got back in the car and drove off.

That was my date with Ava Gardner. We didn't go out again after that, but I got to know her well. She used to come to visit her sister on Havenhurst Drive, in the apartment building where I was living after the Garden of Allah. Mickey Rooney also lived there, in the unit to the right of mine, and Ava's sister, Bea, lived just above him. Mickey had met Ava at MGM when she was nineteen, and married her. His first marriage, and hers too. That was seven or eight years back, and they were only together a short time; I think one day Ava just decided to divorce him, no reason given. But they were friends. Mickey got along with everybody, former wives and everybody else. Later, when I got to know her, I told her how nervous I had been on our date. She laughed. I told her I'd never had a drink before. She laughed even more at that. "You certainly did that night," she said. "Yeah, well, I didn't want to be a fucking bore, you know. Jesus, did we have fun."

Charlie Barnet and his wife lived in the Havenhurst Drive building, too, in the apartment above mine—the great Charlie Barnet who played saxophone, and had had one of the best of the big bands. Lena Horne had sung for him, Doc Severinson played trumpet, Roy Eldridge played with him, Oscar Pettiford. Sometimes I'd cook dinner for Mickey, and he'd invite the Barnets and Bea and Ava, too, if she was visiting.

Mickey enjoyed cooking himself, and he asked me to teach him my sauce, which was really my mom's sauce with a few little variations. So I did. Here's the recipe, which I still make on occasion:

For the Sauce

Cut some pancetta up into small pieces.
Heat one-third cup of extra virgin olive oil in a large pan over low heat.
Sauté the pancetta for eight to ten minutes.
Add a third of a medium or large onion, chopped.
Sauté until just translucent.
Add two cloves of garlic, minced.
Sauté for a couple of minutes.
Add a large can of San Marzano brand tomatoes—crushed by hand.
Add kosher salt to taste.
Bring to a boil.
Lower heat and simmer for about forty minutes.
About ten minutes before finish, tear three or four leaves of fresh basil by hand and add.
Add a touch of oregano.

For the Pasta

To make sure pasta is tasty, taste the water while the pasta is cooking. If the water is flat, add more salt. If the water is flat, the pasta will be flat.
My mother gave it a pinch of sugar, but I don't do that myself.

After I taught Mickey I'd sometimes come home and there would be a wonderful aroma in the hallway. Oh, oh, I'd think. Mickey's cooking the sauce again.

I had met Mickey a little earlier, while he was making a movie called *The Strip* for MGM. Joe Pasternak, the MGM executive who was about to start me off in movies, was producing *The Strip,* which was about a drummer—Rooney—in the Los Angeles nightclub world. Pasternak wrote in an extra scene that gave me a cameo singing "Don't Blame Me" at the Mocambo. Though I only found out about it later, Pasternak was the person who was really responsible for bringing me out to Hollywood in the first place.

What had happened was that Pasternak had seen me in New York when I was working at the Riviera with Danny Thomas, who had acted in several of his movies. He had gone to hear Danny, who was such a great comedian and storyteller, and I was opening, so he saw me, too. Afterward he told William Morris and Charlie Morrison to book me at the Mocambo, which was how I got there.

I hadn't known anything about that, though. Pasternak had never introduced himself at the Riviera, not that I would have recognized his name, anyway. And I hadn't been thinking about Hollywood at all. I was having a great time as it was in New York, still learning my trade, picking up more and more performance understanding from the stars I worked with, including right then from Danny Thomas.

I was opening for him, doing thirty-five or forty minutes worth of songs, and when I was finished I'd go out to sit with the audience and watch. Danny was a mesmerizing storyteller, using all sorts of material, some of it from his own Lebanese background, some Italian, some Jewish. He had a great sense of irony, too, which he'd use to give a surprising and funny edge to his stories. I loved how comfortable he was onstage, and how comfortable he made the audience feel, how easily he communicated with them. Among the things he taught me was how to take a bow. I watched him carefully. He was a comedian, but the opposite of a baggy-pants guy. He was very regal up there. And when he'd take a bow—it was just the greatest bow I had ever seen. There was something indefinable about it. He'd finish, go offstage, come back to the applause, and take this incredible bow.

After about two or three nights of this I went to him backstage after his act.

"Danny, I've been watching you. You're magnificent."

"Thank you, my boy. Thank you, my boy."

"But Danny, there's something about you when you take a bow. I've never seen anybody take a bow like that. I worked at the Paramount for years. I saw all the great stars there taking bows. But you . . . there's something different. How come your bow is so powerful?"

"Oh, so you noticed?"

"Yes, I did. What is it about that bow?"

"Let me teach you," he said. "When you bow your head, you do everything you can, you let it come through your face, your eyes, your body. You let them know."

"What? What do I let them know?"

"You let them know, your whole attitude, your whole thinking is: I am your humble servant. I am here only for you. That's on your way down. But on your way up . . ."

"On your way up, yes?"

"On your way up, you have your whole body say, 'But don't screw with me!'"

Danny Thomas, the most elegant of performers. The friendliest and most genial. To hear him say "screw" . . . that was a shock. But I never forgot what he said about how to take a bow. And after that I always did it that way myself: "I'm here to serve you, to make you happy." For Danny, that meant to make people laugh. For me, it was to make people feel romantic with their girls, with their wives and husbands. I'm here to sing for you, only for you. To entertain you. But understand, I'm someone to respect, too. Don't ever mistake that. Don't screw with me!

So, Joe Pasternak had seen me at the Riviera. And when I opened at the Mocambo he came out to see me there. He was already thinking of what I might do in the movies, and after I came back from Las Vegas, he asked me to come to MGM for a screen test.

That was an experience. "Well," I asked when I got to the studio, "what do I do?" And someone said, "Just stand there. The director will come in and ask you questions. All you have to do is answer them. They want to see what you look like on camera."

They put makeup on me—I had never had anything like that done. I stood there. A director came in and said, "Okay, Vic, you walk out, you sit on the stool, I'll ask you questions. Okay, action!"

I walked out. "Hi," I said.

"What's your name?" said the director.

"Vic Damone."

"Where were you born?"

"Brooklyn, New York."

He started asking me questions about Brooklyn. Where did I go to school? Was I a good student? What subjects did I like? Then I heard a loud voice behind him, saying, "No, no, no, you're not doing it right! Get out of that chair!" And this woman practically pushed him out of the chair and sat down herself. It was Judy Garland. "Hi, Vic!" she said. "It's me. It's Judy!"

I thought, Oh my God, it's Judy Garland, whom I'd never met in my life. "Hi, Vic," she said. "It's Judy!"

"Vic, hi. I love your songs. I've got your records."

Judy Garland!

"Vic, what's your favorite song?"

I hardly heard her. Judy Garland, who had done *The Wizard of Oz* when she was sixteen. "I love your singing," I said. "You're fantastic."

And all of a sudden the screen test turned into something else. Before I had been answering in a monotone. "Yes, I'm from Brooklyn." "Yes, Lafayette High School." "What did I like? Uh, I don't know. Geometry?" Now it was, "Yeah! That's great! Wow, Judy Garland!" I lit up. And they signed me that day. At twenty-five hundred dollars a week. In 1950. My God, that was a lot of money. Suddenly I was a rich man.

My first movie for MGM was going to be *Golden Boy,* which was why I hired Al Silvani to teach me how to box. But Joe Pasternak decided to hold off on that and make another one first, *Rich, Young and Pretty. Rich, Young and Pretty* was about a girl who goes to Paris and, of course, unexpectedly falls in love. Janie Powell was the girl. She was actually pregnant while we were shooting, though not far enough along that you could tell. I was the lucky guy in Paris. Fernando Lamas was in it, and Danielle Darrieux. Sidney Sheldon wrote the screenplay, and Sammy Cahn and Nicholas Brodszky wrote some of the songs. Norman Taurog was our director, an awfully nice guy, a very patient man.

Which was what I needed. I, of course, had never had an acting lesson or appeared before a camera in my life. My innocence was breathtaking. I thought you had to face the camera. Singing, you face the audience. Acting, you face the camera, no? "No," said Fernando Lamas. "No, no, no. You're acting with the person you're having the scene with. If it's you and me, you're talking to me, not to the camera. They'll still get you. So, talk to me. Look me in the eye. It's a conversation."

Fernando was wonderful. "Watch that nobody upstages you," he said. "Janie's great. She's wonderful to work with. But you'll find people who aren't."

"Okay, I'll watch. But what do you mean, 'upstaging'? What's upstaging?"

"Upstaging is, let's say you're having a scene with someone. What they'll do is turn around so they're full face to the camera, and the only thing of you is the back of your head. Or you're talking, and while you're talking, the guy you're talking to starts doing something, moving, doing something with his hands, something that's going to catch attention on the screen, when it should be on you. Watch out for those guys. If someone pulls that kind of stuff, just say, 'Hey, I'm talkin' to you.' Then they have to come right back to you, so you're controlling the scene."

The first scene I worked on with Jane Powell, we were supposed to be walking down the street together. We come to the corner. We stop. We talk. So the camera rolled, and we walked to the corner. We stopped, and the camera moved around us to get a better shot of us both. But as we talked I turned away a little, which I wasn't even aware of, and Janie took my arm, very naturally, and turned me back, so I was as much in the camera as she was. I never forgot that. I did other movies with her later on: *Hit the Deck* and *Athena.* But I never forgot that first scene.

Rich, Young and Pretty did well, though by the time it was released I was in the army, so I didn't get to follow much of what was happening with it. But one of the songs I sang, Sammy Cahn's "Wonder Why," was nominated for an Oscar. My mom came out during the shooting, which gave her a lot of pride. Unfortunately, my father had to work, and somebody had to stay home anyway, to look after the family. I know that he and my mom were a little overwhelmed by what had happened with my career. Singing was one thing. I had been singing by my mother's side since I was three. But Hollywood?

I was a little overwhelmed myself. There I was, acting with Mickey Rooney and Jane Powell. Going out with Ava Gardner. Okay, only once, but still. And then I started dating Elizabeth Taylor.

I don't think Elizabeth Taylor was even eighteen when we first went out. Of course, I was only a few years older. I had met her at MGM, but she was still living at home with her parents. When I arrived to pick her up for one of our early dates, she was still up in her room, so her father took the occasion to look at me sternly and say, "I want you to make sure you have her home by eleven."

"That's fine, sir," I said. "We're just seeing a movie. We'll be back right after."

"And I want to make sure that you'll always be a gentleman with my daughter."

"Yes, sir."

And he put out his hand, so we shook on it. I didn't think that much about it. We were just going to see a movie.

We got into the car and were on Wilshire on our way to the movie when Elizabeth said, "Keep driving."

"Why?"

"Just keep driving."

We went all the way down to the end of Wilshire, to the coastline, and then turned up toward Malibu. She was directing me. "Make a right here, now go straight, now make a left." We finally pulled up in front of a house, and she said, "This is where we spend our summers."

"Okay," I said.

"Let's go and sit on the porch."

"Okay."

So we were sitting there and talking, and the next thing you know, we were hugging and kissing and necking, and it was getting nice and heated.

I was thinking, Damn, I shook hands with her father. Damn. I promised. Why did he make me do that? Am I a man of my word? Or am I going to . . . ? And after a bit I said, "Don't you think it's probably time for us to get back?"

I don't know what she thought. I could only imagine. Maybe I wasn't completely straight? Maybe I thought there was something wrong with her?

We got home fifteen minutes late. Her father was waiting for us outside when we drove up. "You know," he said, "you're fifteen minutes late." And I was thinking, If you only knew what I've been through just to keep my word to you. But all I said was, "Yes, sir, I know. I'm very sorry."

I never did tell Liz about my promise to her father even though we kept going out for a while, and stayed friends afterward, and even talked seriously about life on one or two occasions. But I never mentioned what I had told her father. I hope she didn't think it had something to do with her. If she's reading this, now she'll know.

I went out with Elizabeth for five or six months. We were seeing each other a lot, not heavy heavy, but seeing each other. Until one evening when I cooked dinner for her and her parents at her house. In the middle of dinner a phone call came for her and she left the table to answer it—and she didn't come back. I was sitting there with her mother and father, and she was off someplace on the phone with Glenn Davis, a football star for the Los Angeles Rams. We must have been sitting there for a half hour.

Finally, I left. I told her parents to tell her to call me when she grew up. I got into my car and backed out of the driveway, fuming. And as I was turning to drive away she came running out of the house and stood in front of the car. She came to my window and said, "Vic, where are you going?"

"I cooked for you? I'm there with you? And you're on the phone with this guy for half an hour? It's ridiculous. Who needs it? When you grow up, call me. I'll see you." And I drove off.

The next day I was hanging out with Mickey Rooney in my apartment, telling him about what had happened and talking generally about music and other things. Mickey was a hugely talented guy. He was a great athlete. A wonderful actor. He had been a singer and dancer. He said, "You know, I write songs."

"C'mon, you're kidding."

"No," he said. "I write great songs."

And he did. Mickey Rooney could play the piano and sing, and compose, too. I liked one of his songs so much I later recorded it: "Where I Belong." "Where I belong isn't far away/Where I belong is near. Close as the sun on a summer's day/Close as a cheek with a tear."

But that day, as we were talking, the phone rang. It was Anne Strauss, a PR person from MGM. "We have a problem," she said. "Elizabeth is upset. She says she won't work unless you say you're going to have dinner with her tonight. We're in the middle of shooting, and she won't come out of her dressing room."

I told Mickey in a whisper, my hand over the phone. He said, "Tell her to go to hell."

"Ann," I said, "you know what she did to me? Tell her I'm not going. Tell her to grow up."

Ten minutes later Ann called back.

"Look, Vic, Mr. Mayer himself is telling me to tell you to have dinner with her tonight. Louis B. Mayer. I suggest you tell her you'll have dinner."

"Okay," I said. "Tell her I'll have dinner."

At which Mickey said, "You know, you're a schmuck."

"I'm a schmuck? You think I'm a schmuck? That was a message from Louis B. Mayer."

"Oh," he said, "Louis Mayer. I take it back, you're not a schmuck."

I did have dinner with her, and we did talk. But that's as far as it went. And not long after that she got married, not to Glenn Davis but to Conrad "Nicky" Hilton, son of the Conrad Hilton who founded the hotel chain.

We did stay friends, as I said. And since I had dinner with her I got to stay employed by MGM. But my next movie would have to wait, because on April 9, 1951, I found myself drafted into the United States Army.

8

The Beautiful Pier Angeli

I had actually been in the National Guard for two years already, based out of New York. I trained once a month and went on maneuvers for two weeks during the summer, but there was enough flexibility so that it didn't disrupt my career. But in 1951, with the Korean War raging, the draft was expanded, and I was called up.

I knew it was coming. I actually had received notice from the army a couple of months earlier, so George Wood, my agent, had filled my schedule with as many bookings as I could squeeze in. My last appearance, the night before I was supposed to report, was at New York's Copacabana. I had opened there various times, but now I was headlining. Buddy Hackett, already a big name, went on first, then came the showgirls, then I sang, accompanied by the truly great Copacabana band conducted by Dick Stabile, who later conducted and arranged for Dean Martin and Jerry Lewis. So there I was, starring at the number-one nightclub venue in the country, in a tuxedo, with showgirls, with Dick Stabile's musicians—that was at night. The next morning early I was lined up at Fort Dix, New Jersey, with a couple of hundred other disheveled, sleep-deprived, mostly hungover draftees.

We were all standing there, in alphabetical order. Since I had never formally changed my name, I was with the Fs, for Farinola. And as we were waiting, some tough guy recognized me, and I heard: "Hey, get a load of who's here. Vic Damone—and he doesn't have his bodyguards with him. Hey, get a load of this! Hey, the big star! Who's gonna protect you now? Huh? Hey, hey, the big singer, big star. Yeah, yeah, yeah. Now you're in the army." The guy started a singsong: "Now you're in the army/And you got nobody here to protect ya." He started it up, and three or four other guys chimed in.

Right behind me was a guy named Gazzo. F, G: Farinola, Gazzo. Lou Gazzo, from Trenton, New Jersey. And he said in this gruff voice to the main guy giving me the raspberry, "No. We're still here!" I turned around, and he winked at me. "Don't worry about it," he said. "Isn't that right, Otulo?" he boomed out to another guy back with the Os, another Italian. "Hey Otulo, isn't that right?" And Otulo boomed back, "Yeah, that's right."

"Hey," I said. "I can handle it."

"Nah," said Gazzo. "Don't worry about it."

After we got sworn in, we went to get our gear, our sheets and blankets and so on, which we carried over to the barracks. "Here," said Lou Gazzo. "I'll take the top, you take the bottom."

"Okay, sure."

"And don't worry about a friggin' thing, okay?"

Lou was a tough guy, a real street guy. After basic training they put him right where he belonged, in the military police. But meanwhile we did our basic together, and we hung out. We even managed to get away from Fort Dix a couple of times on short passes. One time we did that Gazzo took me to a little club in Trenton. "There's a guy here you've got to see," he said. "Funny as hell. A comedian name of Joey Bishop."

So we went out to see this Joey Bishop, and Gazzo was right. The guy was funny. More than funny. I thought he was brilliant. I sent a note to him with a waiter. "It's Vic Damone. I'd like to meet you."

"Vic Damone the singer?" Joey said to the waiter, as he told me later.

"I guess," said the waiter. "But he's in an army uniform."

After the show I went backstage and introduced myself.

"Hey, Vic," he said, kind of mumbling, his voice low.

"Joey," I said. "I just saw the show. You're really funny. I'd like you to come and work with me."

"Yeah, right," came the mumble.

"Look, I'm in the army here, as you can see. But when I get out I want you to come and work with me, be my opening act."

"Yeah, yeah, yeah." Very dour. He obviously didn't think I was serious.

"I said, I'd like to work with you, in clubs." A little louder.

"Yeah, yeah. I heard you. But I know you'll never call me."

"What? You don't even know me."

"Yeah, but I've heard it before."

Joey Bishop sounded like a man who had experienced some disappointment in his life.

"All right. But let me tell you something. I'm in basic training, so I've got two years in the army. But when I get out, I promise you that on my first job you're going to be with me. Give me your number, your agent, if you have one. I'm with William Morris. They'll contact you. Let me tell you, that's what's going to happen. You'll be there with me."

"Yeah, yeah, yeah." Mumble, mumble, mumble.

"You'll see."

And that's what happened. My first show after I got out was at the Riviera nightclub, just across the George Washington Bridge from Manhattan, and Joey Bishop opened for me, billed as "The Unhappy Humorist." The lineup was Joey, Marge and Gower Champion, and me. Marge and Gower Champion were by then the hottest dance act in the country, taking up where Fred Astaire and Ginger

Rogers had left off a few years earlier. I had managed to stay somewhat in the public eye even while I was away, so there was a lot of interest in my comeback performance. Barry Gray, a famous talk show personality at New York's WMAC, had promised me he'd keep playing my records, which he did. My publicists had also done a good job promoting my return. So the Riviera was packed. It was one of those great nights.

Joey, meanwhile, for all his brilliance, was still struggling to get out of third-rate clubs. Nobody knew him. "Hello, folks," he said when he walked out onstage. "My name is Joey Bishop. Let me tell you why it is they put me on first. This is Vic Damone's show. He didn't know what to do with us, so he decided to go alphabetically. That's the only reason I'm on first. B, C, D. Bishop, Champions, Damone. If we had had an 'A,' he would have been on first."

Joey was terrific that night. So was Burt Bacharach, who had also just gotten out of the army. I needed a piano player and arranger now that I was restarting my career, and Ivan Mogul had told me that this young guy Bacharach was pretty good, that I should audition him, which I did, and I hired him immediately. Burt worked for me for the next three years, until we had a falling out, and John Williams of *Star Wars* fame took his place.

But I don't want to get ahead of myself. After the Riviera I took Bishop along with me to the Paramount. Later, when he joined up with Sinatra, Dean Martin, Sammy Davis, and Peter Lawford in the Rat Pack, he began telling people that Frank had discovered him. But we both knew what really had happened, and I still claim credit.

When Bishop had his TV talk show later, Regis Philbin was his announcer and sidekick. He had me on a number of times (after all, I had discovered him). One big night for the show—the night Joey was going head-to-head against Johnny Carson, who had just moved out to L.A.—I was the first guest. I watched from the wings as Regis introduced him and as Joey did his monologue. Then Regis went out again, but instead of the usual patter between them, Regis started talking about how maybe his presence was hurting the show's ratings. He didn't want to drag things down, so he wanted to tell Joey and everybody that he had decided to quit.

Joey seemed shocked. He made some lame joke about how he didn't want Regis to quit, that if he did the network might find out he himself was the one pulling down the show's ratings. Then Regis just walked out, right by me. And I was the first guest! I had to follow, in front of an audience that had lost the mood, to say the least. Later I found out that the whole thing had been manufactured by Joey and Regis as a ploy to boost interest and help counter Carson. A week or so later, after fan letters had poured in demanding Regis's return, he rejoined the show, and things went back to normal. Regis and Joey were both friends of mine, so I forgave them. But that had to have been one of my most uncomfortable moments as a performer.

Now, the truly strange thing was, a year or so after this I was booked on the show again. Again I was standing in the wings waiting to go on. Regis had introduced Joey, as usual, and he was now standing there with me, both of us looking at the monitor watching as Joey began his opening monologue. "Folks," Joey said, "I wanted to come out and thank all of you. You've been a wonderful audience. But my agent has been talking with ABC, and it looks like we just can't come to any kind of agreement on a new contract. So I've come out here to say good night. And good-bye."

I look at Regis. "What did he say?"

"I think he said he's saying good-bye."

"He's saying good-bye? What?"

"It looks like he's going to walk off the show."

"Listen," I said, "if he does, don't worry about it. You can do it. I'll do whatever you need to help. I've got my trio here; we know a thousand songs. Don't worry about it."

As we watched, Joey said something about going home to have dinner with his wife, and then he walked offstage, right by where we were standing, without even glancing at us. He didn't say a word. He just walked right on by and out the exit. There was dead air. The camera was on the exit door he had just left through.

Then Regis went out onstage. "Vic Damone and I are standing back there at the exit where Joey walked off, and we heard him say good-bye. He really said good-bye. He left. And folks, listen to me, he is gone. He's out the door. So now, let me bring out Vic Damone."

For the next hour Regis and I did the show. We talked, we sang, we did the whole thing. And that's how Regis started. Regis has a pretty nice singing voice, actually a good voice. He still tells the story when he does his club show. If you ever want to leave a show, he says, just invite Vic Damone on as your guest. But that was how Regis got his first break. He handled Joey Bishop's walk-off beautifully. After that ABC looked to him and gave him his own show, which kicked off his career.

When we finished basic training at Fort Dix, Lou Gazzo was assigned to the military police and sent to Germany. I asked to go to Korea with special services, so I could help entertain the troops who were fighting there. At that time I was probably the number three or four male singer in the country, along with Frank Sinatra, Perry Como, and Dick Haymes, so it seemed pretty much a no-brainer that the army would send me out with an entertainment troupe, and Korea was where the real hardships were, so that would have been the right place. But no. This was the army. They did put me in a special services company, but in Germany, not Korea, and not singing with a performance troupe, but working in a costume shop. Various army entertainment troupes in Germany put on shows and plays, and the army's big costume warehouse and shop was located in Nuremburg, in the former Palace of Justice. Which is where I found myself sitting behind a desk handing out costumes.

That's what I did, day after day. I sat there at my desk, logging costumes in and out and listening to American Forces Radio play records, quite a few of them my records. So since the American Forces Network was based in Nuremburg, one day I decided to go over and introduce myself to the disc jockeys.

The first DJ I met there was a fellow named Al Evans.

"Jesus Christ," he said. "You're here? Where are you stationed?"

"I'm at the Palace of Justice."

"You're kidding! Doing what?"

"They've got me working in the costume shop."

"The costume shop? For chrissakes! Don't they know?"

"No, it's the army. Forget about it."

Over the next couple of weeks I got to know Al and the other jocks, and one evening after work they said, "Listen, there's a big network party. C'mon with us."

This party turned out to be a pretty big deal. All the top brass from the American Forces Network was there, majors, colonels, generals, and I'm, of course, a one-stripe private first class. At one point a general walked by and looked at me. "Hey, soldier," he said. "Where do I know you from?"

"Sir, maybe from show business."

"Really? What?"

"My name's Vic Damone, sir."

"Vic Damone! Of course! I've got your records. They've brought you over to sing for the troops, huh? That's just great!"

"Sir, no."

"What do you mean, no? You're here, aren't you?"

"Yes, sir, I am. But I'm not singing. I'm in special services, but they have me working in the costume shop."

"Costume shop?! Jesus Christ, what the hell's wrong with this damned army?" And he collared a full-bird colonel who was standing nearby.

"Colonel, come here! You know who this is?"

"No, sir."

"This is Vic Damone. He's one of the top singers in the world. They've got him working in a costume shop! For chrissakes! I want him singing for the troops! You understand me, Colonel?"

Then he turned to me. "Vic," he said. Not "soldier," not "private"—"Vic." "Vic, I want you to be singing. I want you to put a show together for me. Colonel, you get this man whatever he needs! Am I clear?" Then he walked off, shaking his head.

Now, the colonel, Colonel Rodriguez, I still remember his name, said, "Well, what do you want to do?"

"I don't know. This just happened. I haven't even thought about it."

"Well, why don't you come up with a concept for a show and let me know. We'll do whatever's necessary."

"Yes, sir, I will."

Now, Al Evans and the other disc jockeys were listening to all this. They couldn't believe it. They take me to a party, and I meet a general? So we were all talking about it, and about the fact that I had to come up with some kind of show. And we finally put together a concept: an amateur show. We could go to all the camps. The talent in that camp would audition. I could sing maybe twenty minutes, a half hour, then we'd have a talent show.

Everyone thought that was a great idea. So now I had to put a traveling band together. I auditioned for a drummer, a piano player, a bass player, a guitarist. And I found four really good guys, one of whom, Johnny Janis, the guitarist, was really a special talent as a musician, arranger, and singer himself. So now we had our band. Then the colonel got me a public relations guy, who informed all the camps that we'd be coming through, looking for talent.

Before we started our tour I said to the colonel, "By the way, there's a man I worked with in the States. He's a real expert with light and sound and everything we need for staging. There's no one better. I need him to be part of this. His name is Lou Gazzo. He's in Bremerhaven, in the military police there. I'd like him to be with me; he'll do a great job for us."

Two days later Lou Gazzo showed up.

"What's up, Vic?" he said. "What the fuck am I doing here?"

"Hello, Lou. You're with me. We're going to do shows. I told them you knew all about sound and lights."

"I don't know a fuckin' thing about sound and lights."

"Well, you're going to learn."

I told him what to requisition. I taught him—the spotlights do this and that, they've got different gels. Then we've got these other lights on the side for a little atmosphere, blues and reds. You got it? We need instruments, we need music stands, we need chairs. Lou picked it up fast, and from that point on he was right on top of it. He took care of everything for me. He was that kind of guy.

Once the colonel got us a bus, we started going from city to city, from camp to camp to camp. In the camps beforehand they put out a call for talent, and when I arrived I'd audition everyone who had put his or her name in. We kept lists indicating what they did, whether they were male or female, and rating them. Then when we got back to Nuremberg we decided among all those we had rated "exceptional," and before long we had put the show together.

The first time we made the circuit around Germany we were finding the talent, then the next time the best people toured with me. We had a couple of WACS who were funny and good singers;

we had a guy who played harmonica; there was a comedian. It was great. Like a traveling circus. That was my show. And that was the main thing I did in the army.

The one other memorable thing that came out of my military service, for me at least, was seeing Anna Maria Pierangeli, whom I married a few years later. Anna Maria was an exceptionally beautiful Italian movie star who was under contract at MGM, as I was. She had first appeared in the prize-winning Italian movie *Domani e troppo tardi* (*Tomorrow Is Too Late*) with Vittorio de Sica, then had moved to Hollywood with her mother and equally beautiful fraternal twin sister, Marisa, who was also an actress. Anna Maria and I had run into each other a few times at MGM, and the last time we talked I had told her I was about to go into the army. She asked how long I was going to be away, and had given me her phone number. "Why don't you call me when you get back," she said. I'm pretty sure I kept that number.

Anyway, at one point I was in Berlin with my traveling talent show and there was a big USO performance scheduled to go up right afterward. Danny Kaye was touring for the troops, and he had other performers with him, including Anna Maria, who was going by her stage name, Pier Angeli. When he found out I was there, Danny asked me to do a song as part of his show, and when I did, there was Anna Maria, with her mother. We talked a bit. I can't say we flirted. Her mother was as watchful as a hawk, and not an easy person, as I was to learn a lot more about later. But our brief encounter did remind me to get in touch once I was back in the States.

When my tour in Germany was up, the army sent me to Fort Sam Houston to finish out my two years. I sang with the Fort Sam Houston Army band there, but also managed to get free for a recording session in New York. By the time I completed my service I was dying to get back to work. I felt ready to take on the world, singing, acting, or anything else that might come along. MGM was waiting for me; my agents were lining up gigs. I couldn't wait to throw myself into all of it.

Back in Los Angeles, I rented a place at the Havenhurst Apartments, where I had lived before I left. At MGM I started working on *Athena,* a Joe Pasternak movie in which I played a crooner roped into a love affair by Debbie Reynolds. My old friend Janie Powell was in it, too, the second of "two nubile maidens," as one reviewer put it, carrying on her own affair with Edmund Purdom. Steve Reeves, the famous pre–Arnold Schwarzenegger muscle man, had a small role, too—this was before his epic star turn as Hercules.

Acting with Debbie Reynolds was an experience. She was so spontaneous, so vivacious—and that was her actual personality, as well as her personality in *Athena.* She was as lively as a kid in school; she lit the set up. At one point she was supposed to give me a kiss. But when she did, it was no movie kiss. Whoa, I thought, what's going on here?—just as I heard the director say, "Cut, cut, cut! Debbie, what is that? You look like you're swallowing him."

"What do you mean?" she said. "It was just a kiss." Which was all it was. She was an uninhibited, free spirit of an actress if ever there was one. Still is, too.

MGM had been the dominant production company in the studio contract days of the thirties and forties, and in the early fifties it was still a powerhouse. Fred Astaire was there, among other giant names, and we got to know each other pretty well. I would see him at the studio, and also from time to time at the Hollywood or Santa Anita race tracks. Actually, more than from time to time; Fred was at the track a lot. In fact, he eventually married Robyn Smith, a former actress turned jockey who rode for Alfred Vanderbilt.

One friend I used to go to the track with was Nick Castle, an MGM dancer and choreographer. Nick had worked quite a bit with and for Fred. We'd see Fred at the track and chat a bit, then catch him between races on our way to or from the ticket window. Fred would walk by and say, "Hey, Nick. Hey, Vic," or just "Niiick? Viiiic?" And he'd saunter on by. We'd turn to watch. Fred Astaire carried himself so elegantly you just couldn't help watching him. Nick, the choreogapher, would look on and say, "Walk it, Fred, walk it." And every time he'd have a different walk. Whatever mood he was in, that's the walk he had. If he won, he'd bounce a little. If he lost, he'd slow down or maybe shuffle slightly. But a graceful shuffle. "Walk it," Nick would say. "Walk it, Fred."

Fred's dancing, needless to say, was above and beyond. Both George Balanchine and Rudolph Nureyev called him the greatest dancer of the century. He was a good singer, too, and his interpretation of lyrics was impeccable.

Fred was also a friendly guy, with an exuberant side to him. One day I was leaving the Bel Air Country Club, where I had just played a round of golf, and as I was walking toward the parking lot I saw someone doing strange things around my car. That was my special model Dual-Ghia, the one Frank Sinatra's bodyguard, Pooch, later threatened to pick up and throw.

When I got closer I saw the man was Fred Astaire, dancing around the car. By himself, in the Bel Air parking lot. No one was around, no one was watching; he was just dancing, popping and sliding and twirling, throwing his arms out, as if he were onstage, going oooh, aaah. All around the car.

"Fred!" I said. "Fred, look at you. What are you doing?"

"I love this car!" he said, without stopping. "Vic, I love this car. Is it yours?"

"Well, yeah, it is."

He was dancing on his toes, tapping with his heels. The man was unbelievably graceful. "Vic, this is the most beautiful car I've ever seen in my life. Look at that grille. Look at those little fins. What's it called?"

"It's a Dual-Ghia, Fred."

I loved that car myself. If it came out today, it would look like next year's top sports model. And that was fifty years ago. But I had never quite been inspired to dance around it. Or sing to it. But Fred Astaire was not as shy as most. When something made him feel like dancing, the man danced!

Fred's dancing partner most people remember, of course, was Ginger Rogers. One of my greatest thrills was getting to dance with her myself. I was having dinner at Danny's Hideaway in New York once with some friends when I saw her come in with her agent, who left after they had talked for a while. Since she was sitting alone, I invited her to come and have dessert with us. While we were talking, I had a sudden thought.

"Ginger, why don't we go dancing?" I was kidding, really. Me dancing with Ginger Rogers, Fred Astaire's partner? I loved to dance, but give me a break.

"Oh, I don't know," she said. "I'm really tired. But . . . maybe just one dance. Where did you have in mind?"

I could hardly believe this. "What about the El Morocco?" I said. "They've got a great Latin band there."

At the El Morocco we had that one dance, then another, then another, nonstop. All Latin numbers. By then I was thinking that she had claimed she was tired so she could have an excuse to get out of there if I turned out to have two left feet. Three hours later we finally called it a night. I dropped her off at the Waldorf Astoria, thinking, Oh my God, I've been dancing with Ginger Rogers. I might not have been Fred Astaire, but hey, she had stayed on the floor with me till quitting time. I felt positively high. I had watched her dancing with Fred in the movies when I was a kid usher in Brooklyn. I still felt like I was a kid in Brooklyn. The whole thing was surreal.

I danced with another of Fred's partners, too: Rita Hayworth. I met her in London, where she was with Bert Lancaster and her husband, the producer James Hill. They invited me to dinner and asked me to sing the theme song for *Separate Tables,* the movie they were working on. I agreed to that; "Separate Tables" was a beautiful Harry Warren song. I also got to dance with Rita that evening. She was an extraordinary dancer. Her father was a famous flamenco dancer, and Rita had been dancing professionally since she was a child. Fred Astaire said her ability to pick up steps and routines was uncanny. She was so powerful on the floor that, even though I was in the lead position, there was no question who was doing the leading. She was. In her movie dance routines you see her grace and energy, but it's her power that really sets her apart.

Another friend of mine from MGM was Mario Lanza. Mario's parents were from Abruzzi, and he was born in South Philadelphia's Italian neighborhood as Alfredo Cocozza. He took his stage name from his mother's maiden name, as I did, since Cocozza just would not have worked in those days. He had been a truck driver back in Philly, but was also classically trained. He had played the part of Enrico Caruso in *The Great Caruso,* which was a huge success; critics actually compared him to Caruso himself. When I met him he was just about to start *The Student Prince.* Mario's voice was phenomenal; it was an unbelievably powerful instrument. He was a big, good-looking guy, too, so the studio saw him as one of their prime upcoming stars.

One night I was fast asleep in my apartment when I had a dream that someone was calling my name: "Vittorio, Vittorio, Vittorio." The voice kept getting louder and louder until I woke up. "Vittorio, Vittorio. Where are you, Vittorio?" Now the voice was louder, much louder. There was no mistaking it. Nobody else had a voice like that. I had met Lanza not too long before and he had never visited me, but I had told him I lived at the Havenhurst Apartments, right up the street from Sunset Boulevard. I looked at the clock. It was 2:15. He was outside somewhere in the dark, calling for me. "Vittorio, Vittorio! Where are you, Vittorio?"

I got up and opened my door. And there he was, disheveled, like he had just been in a fight. He had blood on his shirt and only one shoe on. He was bombed.

"Mario, Jesus. What's the matter? What happened to you?"

"Vittorio, Vittorio, I really did it. Oh, Vittorio."

"Did it? Did what? What did you do?"

"I was having a drink at the bar."

I knew the bar he must have meant, on Sunset, just across from where Havenhurst came to a T.

"I was just relaxing, Vittorio. I was ready to go home, because it was two o'clock. You can't drink anymore after two o'clock. Do you know that, Vittorio? These two guys were there, cops, plainclothes cops. And they tried to take my drink away from me. I told them, 'Let me finish it.' And they said no. Vittorio, they took my drink. My drink! I told them, 'It's my drink. I paid for it. Let me finish my drink.' Then they got rough with me, Vittorio."

Now, Mario and I had several things in common, one of which was boxing. He used to work with an ex-fighter named Terry Robinson. Terry trained him; they worked out all the time. Mario was a bull of a man to begin with, and he was in great shape. Mario hit one cop in the jaw. "I broke his jaw, Vittorio. I know I broke his jaw." He gave the other cop one to the body and another to the jaw, and knocked him out, too.

"They called an ambulance, Vittorio. And I ran away to look for you."

After I got Mario cleaned up a little, I made him a cup of coffee. "I'm okay, now," he said. "I'm okay. I'm leaving you now, Vittorio. I just wanted to stop by to say hello." And he got up to go, one shoe on and one shoe off. His car was still parked down on Sunset, and we had given the ambulance plenty of time to load up and leave. "Goodbye, Vittorio," he said, as he closed the door behind him and walked off into the night.

It was a great loss that Mario died so young. What we heard was that he had received an injection for something, but it wasn't administered properly, and a bubble in the syringe went to his heart and killed him. This was in Italy some years later, where he had gone to live with his wife and children. Such a physically powerful guy, too. Serge Koussevitzky apparently had told him when he was young that he had the kind of voice that only appears once in a hundred years.

When *Athena* was finished I started on another film, *Hit the Deck,* also a big Joe Pasternak musical production. Janie Powell starred in this one, too, along with Debbie Reynolds, Tony Martin, Ann Miller, Walter Pidgeon, and Russ Tanblyn. I was one of three sailors on leave who just happen to bump into three girls looking for romance. Hijinks ensued, as the MGM ad put it, along with quite a bit of singing and dancing. It's a little hard to remember which other sailor was stuck on which girl, except I know I was head over heels for Janie Powell. That was in the movie. But sometime while we were making it I really began to fall head over heels for another MGM actress, the beautiful Anna Maria Pierangeli.

Hollywood is not a place where you have to be lonely. I had a lot of dates, but nothing serious. It wasn't that I had anything against the idea, but I was always so busy I didn't even know how I'd fit such a thing in. The movies were coming one after another, and when I wasn't in the studio I was singing. And if I wasn't working somewhere I was on the golf course.

Golf was my therapy, physical and psychological. I had been playing golf for years already, ever since my uncle Mike had introduced me to the game back in Brooklyn. The game absorbed my attention. Playing golf, my mind was a million miles from work. It left me refreshed; it set me up to get back to the movie sets or the nightclubs full of energy. So I played whenever I could. I practiced and practiced and practiced. At night I'd be out at the open-till-midnight range on Wilshire, along with Dean Martin and other movie people or entertainers who were busy working off their own tensions or finding their own balance. But I can't say my mind wasn't on the girls, too, one of whom initially was not Anna Maria, but her sister, Marisa.

Back in Hollywood from the army I had it in mind to call Anna. But when I telephoned her house, she was out, and I got to talking with Marisa instead. Marisa was at Paramount, not MGM, but I had met her one or two times before, which meant that I knew her almost as well as I knew Anna. So I asked her out instead.

Marisa Pierangeli was every bit as beautiful as her fraternal twin, but she was a very different kind of person. She had started acting after Anna, so when she did go into the movies she had to change her name to avoid confusion. That was how she became Marisa Pavan, taking the last name of an old family friend. Where Anna was lighthearted and spontaneous, Marisa was thoughtful and introspective. That came through in her acting as well, which tended to be quieter and more underplayed, though still moving. Both sisters lived with their mother and their baby sister, Patrizia, in Brentwood. Their father had not come to America with them, and had died in

Italy. So this was a house full of women. A house full of Italian women, which meant that there were a lot of emotions flying around, wonderful Italian cooking aromas in the air, and the constant sound of Italian being spoken. There was a lot about that household for me to like.

Marisa and I went out a few times, but it didn't take long for me to find that I was more attracted to Anna. I can't explain why. Maybe it was Anna's vivaciousness or happy laugh. Maybe it was just a chemical attraction. Whatever it was, I was soon dating her rather than her sister, which caused more than a little friction, and a little friction went a long way in that household. A few years later, though, I introduced Marisa to Jean Pierre Aumont, whom she married. Jean Pierre was an important stage and screen actor who had originally gained fame in France before coming to Hollywood and MGM. During World War II he joined the Free French forces and fought in Africa and across Europe. We were friends from the studio, and one evening we saw each other at a party, where I was with Anna.

"Too bad she doesn't have a sister," Jean Pierre said, looking at Anna, who was hard not to look at.

"She *does* have a sister," I told him. "A twin sister. You ought to meet her."

Marisa was a serious person. She and Jean Pierre were married for more than forty years, until his death. But I was in love with Anna. We went to the movies together, to shows at the Coconut Grove. She was like an angel, a breath of fresh air. Sweet and innocent, almost girlish in her natural friendliness and enjoyment of people. She had a completely charming Italian accent when she spoke English, and, of course, her Italian was beautiful to listen to. She was delightful in a hundred ways. And we seemed so comfortable together, so compatible. I was completely smitten. We had been

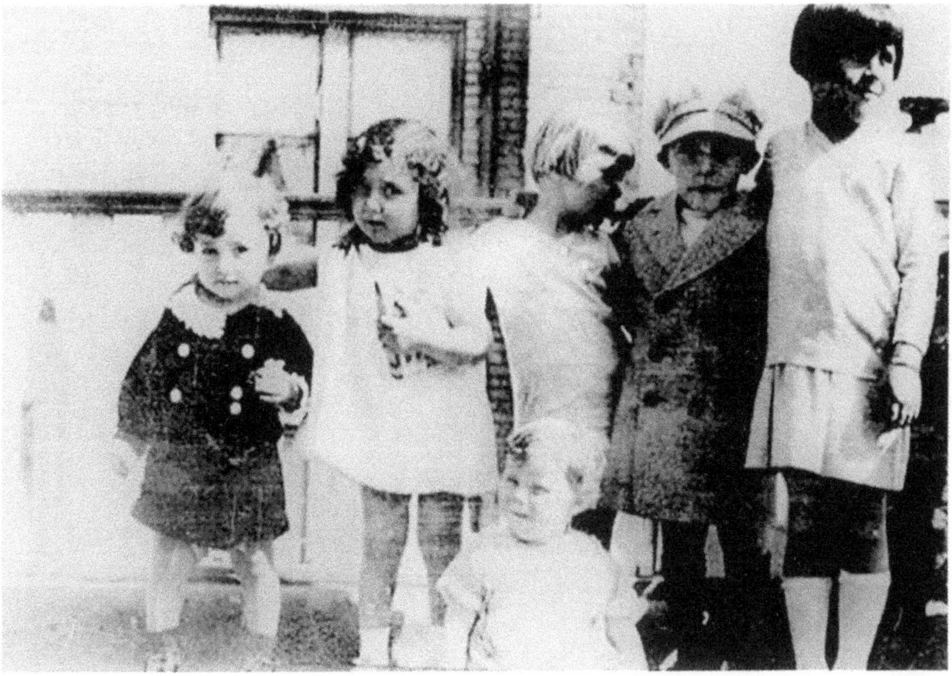

I'm the cute one on the left, with my sister Pearl and our uncle Mike and aunt Carmela's kids.

The family that sings together... Mom on the piano, Dad on the guitar, and sisters Terry, Pearl, Elaine, and Sandy.

Recording for Muzak at age seventeen. I did eighty songs. Everyone in New York who rode an elevator must have heard me sing.

My father and mother. A harsh word never passed between them.

Mom and me with Joe Pasternack, the great producer. I was twenty-two years old and acting in my first movie, *Rich Young & Pretty.*

With Dad and Perry.

Perry Como, me, Eddie Fisher, and Merv Griffith in 1953. Merv played piano and sang with the Freddy Martin Band.

Backstage at the Mocambo with Jack Benny and George Burns. George is teaching me to sing.

Best man at Jay Sebring's wedding. Jay was later murdered by the Charles Manson family with Sharon Tate and others.

My partner Sol Branker. Our ranch was in Exeter, California—six hundred acres, fifteen hundred head.

With Arnold Palmer. I'm receiving the JFK Award for Entertainer of the Year in Golf.

On Red Skelton's show. I'm the mob guy (just kidding).

With Connie Stevens and Shirley Jones honoring the great songwriter Jimmy McHugh.

With Andy Williams and Anthony Newley on Andy's show. I loved singing with Andy. What a voice!

Catching a bite with my good pal Nat King Cole at Luigi's, next door to the Las Vegas Sands.

With Tony Bennett.

Steve Lawrence and me at a Frank Sinatra birthday bash singing a medley of Frank's hits "from A to Z," arranged by Nelson Riddle, who's on the podium.

With Jack Leonard. A funny, sweet man.

Carroll Shelby asked what my favorite car color was, then gave me this silver Cobra, courtesy of Lee Iacocca. I was starring in Lee's Ford-sponsored TV show, *The Lively Ones.*

Perry at age thirteen visiting me from military school.

With my second wife, Judy Rawlins.

My wonderful daughters: Daniella, Andrea, and Victoria.

Singing a Richard Rodgers medley with Peggy Lee and Lena Horne. What a thrill to perform with such legends of song.

The great Jake LaMotta (left), after one of my shows!

With Marvin Hamlish, Liza Minnelli, and Bobby Short after performing for President and Nancy Reagan at the White House.

My old pal Larry King presenting me with the Songwriter's Hall of Fame Lifetime Achievement Award.

With my mom in her later years.

With the love of my life, Rena Rowan Damone, after performing at a benefit for her homeless charities.

seeing each other for only a couple of months before I proposed, and she accepted.

One of the things I did not know about Anna before our wedding was her relationship with Kirk Douglas. This had been before my time—actually, very shortly before my time—but she had never mentioned it. I found out only many years later, after Kirk wrote his autobiography, *The Ragman's Son.* I had great respect for Kirk as an actor. He also had a strong, fearless personality, which I admired in him. Kirk and I were friends, and I was reading along in his book, innocently enjoying the story of his life, when all of a sudden I turned a page, and the next chapter was entitled "In Pursuit of Pier." Then there was "In Pursuit of Pier Part Two," then "In Pursuit of Pier Part Three."

I thought, What? Why in the world is he writing about Pier—Anna? And what's with this pursuit business? It turned out that Kirk had been madly in love with Anna, whom he had met when they costarred as trapeze artists in *The Story of Three Loves.* Apparently, at least according to Kirk, Anna was equally enamored of him, so much so that they were engaged to be married, with a ring and mutual promises and talk of the future—a full-blown engagement. Reading on, though, it seemed that she had only been playing with him. They would plan to meet in Rome, but when he got there she was in Venice. He shot a movie in Israel and came back to Rome to meet her; she was in Sardinia. He tried to see her later, but she was in Capri, or London—with Dean Martin. With Dean Martin!? Dean had been one of my ushers at our wedding! What had she been doing in London with Dean Martin?

Whatever it was, I don't think they had been sleeping together. She was, I am sure of it, an innocent girl. Kirk had never managed to sleep with her, and Kirk slept with more or less everybody. But Anna's mother never let her out of her sight, except with a trusted chaperone. She was like a medieval guardian of Anna's chastity. Kirk at first blamed all those missed rendezvous with Anna on her. Later he realized that Anna's friendly, flirtatious personality had misled him into thinking that her love was real. She was, he finally saw, emotionally still a child.

At the same time, it was true that Anna's mother, Enrica, guarded her fiercely from all dangers, and a Jewish actor sixteen years older than Anna must have been pretty high on the danger list. So was James Dean, with whom Anna also had a relationship, this one still going on when she and I became involved. That, too, was more or less a surprise to me. She never mentioned him while we were dating. She never gave any indication she might have had an emotional attachment elsewhere. And Jimmy Dean was a bad boy—moody, troubled, unstable—absolutely terrible husband material. Not Catholic, either. He must have driven Enrica up a wall. On top of which, of course, Dean was what Italians call *un finocchio.* He wasn't quite sure if he was a girl or a boy.

My own feeling, thinking about it afterward, was that Anna was probably playing with Jimmy, a little like she had been playing with Kirk. I think he was most likely playing with her as well. Shortly after we were married she told me that she would like us to have dinner with him, since he was an old friend. I was happy to invite him. We went to the Villa Capri together, except that Dean brought a male friend with him. Just a year or two ago (I'm writing this in 2008) William Blast, a film and television writer, wrote of his five-year lovers' relationship with Dean in *Surviving James Dean.* I cannot remember the name of Dean's friend at the Villa Capri that night, but it was likely Blast. I wonder if Anna knew what was going on there. I certainly didn't.

In any event, when the dust settled with Kirk and Jimmy, I was the one Anna married, at St. Timothy's Church on Pico Boulevard, on November 24, 1954. It was one of those grand Hollywood weddings. Joe Pasternak and Bob Sterling were my ushers, along with Dean Martin. Boo Roos Jr., a close golfing friend whose father managed John Wayne, was my best man. Marisa was Anna's maid of honor. Marisa was beautiful beyond words, but Anna was simply resplendent. The MGM publicity machine cranked up the volume as loud as it would go. "People lucky enough to observe Pier Angeli and Vic Damone in unguarded moments," one magazine read, "are treated to an intimate, undisguised, delightful look at the enthralling heights to which love can carry a boy and girl."

When we came down the church steps, a Harley Davidson parked across the street revved its engines high, then roared off down Pico. Everyone said it was Jimmy Dean, but I was too busy staring at Anna to notice.

9

Divorce Italian Style

Almost nine months to the day after the wedding, Anna gave birth to our son. I named him Perry, after Perry Como, who had agreed to be his godfather. I thought that would be auspicious. I had gotten to know Perry over the years, since he had first treated me with such kindness when I was an usher at the Paramount. And Perry Como, I thought, was the finest human being I knew, a great performer, yes, but also a wonderful husband and father—the kind of person my Jewish friends would call a mensch. As my son grew up I used to tell him that he should not be like me, with my various failings; he should try to be like his godfather.

Perry's birth was a joy. But Anna's pregnancy had brought trouble. It wasn't the pregnancy itself. Anna was healthy; she took care of herself well, and we both loved the idea of having a child. The trouble was her mother, Enrica. And the trouble there was money.

Anna had started acting at the age of sixteen, and ever since then Enrica had hovered over her like a mother hen. She had protected her and chaperoned her, carefully watching over both her personal life and her acting career. She was Anna's full-time life manager, including her business manager. And as her business manager, Enrica was paid by the studio when Anna was working, but not when she wasn't. And since Anna got pregnant practically on our wedding night, that meant she wasn't working. No pregnant star ever worked then; few or none do even now. Which meant that Enrica was not getting paid. And that was the trouble, for me especially, since I was the culprit.

"Why weren't you more careful?" Enrica asked angrily as soon as we found out there was a baby on the way.

"Be careful about what?" I said. I was so happy about the news, Enrica's attitude really got under my skin. "About what, Enrica? I want children. Anna wants children. What's the matter? What are you talking about?"

To make matters worse, when Anna discovered she was pregnant, she insisted that we move in with her mother so Enrica could cook for her and help take care of her. I understood that; she wanted her mother near while she was expecting. But living in the extra bedroom of Enrica's house wasn't exactly ideal. Enrica was upset, and she was not a person who kept her feelings to herself. She did lavish attention on Anna, which was fine, but she also lavished it on me, which wasn't. "How could you do this to me?" I heard this refrain from her time and again.

"Do it to you? What do you mean, do it to you? What do you have to do with this?"

"She doesn't work, I don't get paid. I'm her manager! You know what that means!"

"This is my wife! What are you talking about? She wants to have children. So do I. Jesus!"

"Yes, but she doesn't work if she's pregnant."

"Well, that's your problem!"

Sometimes a man doesn't understand a woman's dilemma. I know I didn't at the time. But looking back on it all, I can undestand Enrica's anger a little better. Enrica's husband was dead. Marisa's acting career was just getting started—she was playing Anna Magnani's daughter in *The Rose Tattoo,* her first role. And fickle as Hollywood was, who knew if her first role might not have turned out to be her last. Anna was out of commission. Then there was Patrizia to raise, the youngest daughter. And here was Enrica, a widow without an income. I understand now, but I didn't then. Enrica Pierangeli was a person who took things to extremes. If a woman ever had a temper like a four-day tropical storm, it was her. Her emotions were right out there. And she wasn't the person to back off, either.

When Anna went into Cedars of Lebanon to give birth, we all were in the waiting room—Enrica, Marisa, Patrizia, and me—all of us as nervous as could be. After many hours the doctor came out to tell us that he might have to do a caesarian. Anna was small boned and delicate; she was having trouble getting the baby out.

"No!" Enrica yelled at him. "Absolutely not! You are not going to scar my daughter!" She was shouting at him, out of control. But this was Dr. Red Krohn, the head of obstetrics there, one of the first to do horizontal C-sections rather than vertical, which enabled him to hide a C-section scar. When he described his procedure, Enrica calmed down. But it was quite an outburst.

An hour or so later the doctor came back with the news that we had a beautiful baby boy, which was a great relief to us all. And, not too long after Perry's birth, Anna and I moved into our own place, which was a big improvement. But Enrica's attitude toward me didn't change. I might have saved Anna from Kirk Douglas and Jimmy Dean, but that did nothing to keep me off her black list—not a good list to be on.

After I married Anna my performing and recording career moved into high gear. I was busy on the movie front, too, but my next film after *Hit the Deck* became a problem. This was *Kismet,* a film version of the hit Broadway musical. Howard Keel starred in it with Dolores Gray, Anne Blythe, and myself. Vincent Minnelli was our director.

Kismet was a big production, but Vincent Minnelli was putting together another picture at the same time that meant a lot more to him. That was *Lust for Life,* with Kirk Douglas playing Vincent Van Gogh. *Lust For Life* was going to be shot largely on location in France, with all the complications that involved. And whether it was for that or some other reason, Minnelli didn't seem to have good focus in directing us, and extremely little patience. For some reason that I was never able to figure out, a lot of his impatience was directed at me.

I knew I was far from a great actor. My only real advantage other than my singing was that at least I was natural. I tended to play myself. When that worked, I did well. In *Kismet* I was the caliph, and maybe my style wasn't exactly right for that part, though I thought I was doing fine. Minnelli didn't, though.

It started when I was doing a scene with Ann Blyth. I was singing "Stranger in Paradise" to her as we walked through a lush garden down to an ornate gazebo, where I was supposed to finish the song. As we walked, the camera moved backward in front of us, taking in the garden, which was meant to enhance the romantic imagery—the "paradise" of the song. And as I was nearing the end, Vincent suddenly yelled, "Cut, cut, cut, cut!"—so angrily that I was a little startled. I said to Ann, "Did I miss a lip-sync?" We recorded all the songs in studio, with an orchestra, then we lip-synced them on camera. "Did I miss a lip-sync? Or what did I do here?"

"No," she said. "It was perfect. The mood was right, everything was right. It couldn't have been better. We had great contact, everything."

It turned out that what had happened was that there was a peacock in the garden we were walking through, with its tail displayed.

And when the camera moved back the peacock's tail was supposed to be in the scene, for the decorative effect. But apparently the peacock's tail had gone down during the song, actually at about the song's climax. And Minnelli wasn't looking at me or Ann, he was looking at that tail.

By now he was yelling at the peacock trainer—"Get that tail up! I want that tail up! Get that thing up!" When the trainer couldn't coax it up, Minnelli had him get down in the bushes with the poor bird and shove his little finger up the peacock's ass. Damned if those feathers didn't stand right up. Why the peacock didn't run off, I'll never know. I sure would have. But the poor bird must have been tied down to the spot, and he never moved. And that's what was really going on while I was singing "Stranger in Paradise" to Ann Blythe. Now, I'm sure it wasn't a pleasant experience for either the trainer or the peacock. And let me tell you, it didn't do much for the love scene, either. You try singing a beautiful love song to a girl while there's a guy practically under your feet with his finger up a peacock's ass. Believe me, that kind of thing does absolutely nothing for the mood. It took us two full days to get that scene finished—and we had it on the first take, too.

After that, something happened with Minnelli, at least regarding me. He just let me have it from start to finish. For one scene I walked into my throne room—I was the caliph. I was supposed to walk in, sit down on the throne, and sweep my cape around me so that it would end up right where it was meant to be visually.

I rehearsed it a couple of times, then played the scene. On the first take, Howard Keel forgot a line. Back again. "Roll 'em. Action." I walked in again, up on the dais, swept the cape around me and started the scene—and somebody else forgot a line. Back again. We did it again and again. Thirteen times. And each time something went wrong, though not with me. I can tell you that by then I was a past master at that cape sweep.

The fourteenth time, I was the one who forgot a line. And Minnelli yelled, "What's the matter with you? Why don't you know your lines? We're working here—why don't you know your lines!" He hadn't yelled at anybody else after the previous thirteen takes, when I had been fine. But now I had goofed up, and all of a sudden there was this explosion. Howard looked at me and said, "Why don't you just slap him?"

Howard was as tired of this as the rest of us were. But that's the movies. Sometimes you need a lot of takes to get a scene right. But I think everyone was especially frazzled by Minnelli's impatience and demands, and no one could understand why he had come down on me.

One of the other actors was Mike Mazurki, who had a bit part. Mike was a former professional wrestler, a huge guy with a craggy face you'd never forget, which got him a lot of tough-guy parts in movies. Mike said, "If you don't hit him, I will. Why would he do that to you?"

But Minnelli did those kinds of things to me all through the filming of this movie, from that damned peacock scene on, as if maybe I had been responsible for the peacock losing its display. I just took it on the chin from him. Ann Blyth said, even long afterward, "I felt so bad for you, what he did to you on that movie. You were his whipping boy. If you did something wrong, he always embarrassed you with it. He wouldn't do that to Howard or me." "You've got to talk to him about it," said Howard, during the filming. "It's not right." Mike Mazurki said the same. "Tell him you're going to smack him one," he said. "Or maybe I should do it."

I do have a temper, which I've lost on occasion in my life. But I didn't say anything, or really even think about hitting Minnelli. I loved Metro. I didn't want to cause any trouble there. He was relentless, though. Kirk Douglas had exactly the opposite experience shooting *Lust for Life*. "I always seemed to do the right thing," he wrote. "I felt like the teacher's pet." It was interesting to me to read what a lift Minnelli's approval had given even such an accomplished actor as Kirk. His disapproval did the exact opposite for me. At least, as far as acting went, it did something to my spirit.

Some years later I saw Minelli at Pipp's restaurant in Hollywood, where I was having dinner one night with John Raitt. Minnelli walked in, went by our table and into one of the private rooms. I excused myself and went in after him. I told him how I felt about what had happened. How none of us could understand it, how embarrassed I had been, and how under other circumstances I might have just whacked him one.

"Vic," he said. "I didn't mean to do that. Please forgive me."

"Okay," I said. "It's over." We shook hands. I was happy, I told him. What happened on that set had bothered me for years.

Fortunately, even though I became shy about doing movies, my life as a singer was busier than ever. I was headlining regularly in Las Vegas, and performing in the premier clubs around the country. So many of my songs were charting I could hardly keep track of them.

Ever since I had gotten out of the army, Burt Bacharach had been playing piano and conducting for me. But Burt was clearly bound to go out on his own. He was an exceptionally talented, classically trained pianist, with very clear ideas on the musicality of songs, how they should be played, and what they should sound like. I appreciated his gifts, and for several years our sensibilities about the standards I was mostly singing more or less coincided.

But over time, as he became more and more decided in his tastes, we began to have differences. Finally, I decided it was time for us to part company. The breaking point was a disagreement over some musical issue I can't even remember. But he wanted to do something his way, and I was just as sure it should be done mine. When I told him that this just wasn't working anymore he said, "Are you firing me?"

"No," I said. "I'm not firing you. I'm letting you go. You're so adamant about what you believe in musically—to me that means you're ready to be on your own, and you should be on your own. You have such a strong belief in what you want to do. I respect that, so go ahead and do it. And good luck."

And, of course, he did do it. Burt's subsequent career was dazzling. First he got a job conducting for Marlene Dietrich, then he began collaborating with Hal David, writing songs in the legendary Brill Building. Burt's songbook is like a tour through the greatest hits of the last forty years: "Raindrops Keep Falling on My Head," "What's New Pussycat," "Say a Little Prayer," "I'll Never Fall in Love Again." One after another. I still hear his classic songs being played all the time.

After Burt left, George Wood and Milt Ebbins, my manager at the time, arranged for some piano players to audition for me in George's office. The first one came in and started playing as if he were in a concert hall, showing off all the pyrotechnics he had. The second one was so tentative I could hardly make out what song he was playing. As the third candidate came in and sat down, I went off to the side to talk to George and Milt. "Who are these guys?" I said. "I need somebody who can accompany and conduct and maybe do some arranging. Those two didn't have a clue."

While we were talking, the third one started doodling around on the piano, just to keep himself occupied until I was ready for him. But the chords he was playing were so beautiful, I stopped talking. "Wait a minute," I said to George and Milt. "Wait a minute. Listen to that. This might be the right guy." I went over to the piano.

"God, those are beautiful chords you're playing. What's your name?"

"Thank you," he said. "I'm John Williams. Would you like to sing a song?"

"Yes. How about 'Embraceable You'?"

It's Gershwin. Everybody knows it. He hit a note. "The key all right?" he said.

"Yes, fine." I started: "Embrace me/ You sweet embraceable you." I'm listening to what he's playing against what I'm singing. He waits for me. "Just one look at you." I stopped, waiting to see what he would do. He played something to round out the phrase, and ended with the chord. I could have come in right then or an hour from then. I had the chord. The man was completely attuned to what I was doing. He was breathing with me.

"Oh," I said, "that's beautiful. Just right. Do you arrange?"

"Yes."

"Can you conduct?"

"Yes."

"Well, you've got the job, Mr. Williams."

Fifty years later when John and I talk he still calls me "boss." This after a career in conducting and composing that outshines that of any other popular master. That "boss" always makes me smile.

Burt Bacharach played and conducted, but John became my arranger as well. His taste was unerring. In 1956, the first year he was with me, Mitch Miller, at Columbia Records now, where I was, too, called me up to say a new Lerner and Loewe musical was testing in Philadelphia. The show was titled *My Fair Lady.* Columbia owned a piece of it and had first rights to the music; Mitch wanted me to listen to the score and pick one of the songs to record.

I was doing shows at the Copacabana just then, and John and I were staying at the St. Moritz in New York in a two-bedroom suite with a piano, so we could rehearse. When Mitch sent over the score, we went through the whole thing. I especially liked the song "I've Grown Accustomed to Her Face." But John said, "No, that's a nice song, but *this* is the song for you: 'On the Street Where You Live.'" He played it for me and I sang it. I thought, Yes, this is interesting. John had already pictured what I might be able to do with it.

After we rehearsed it, I called Mitch Miller.

"Mitch, John and I agree that the song to record is 'On the Street Where You Live.'"

"Well," he said, "unfortunately, they're taking that song out of the show. Why don't you come down to the office and we can talk about it."

So John and I went down to Columbia, where the three of us, Mitch, John, and I, went in to see Percy Faith, who was Columbia's chief arranger. Percy was sitting at his desk when we came in, writing an arrangement. I'd never seen anything like it. Arrangers don't arrange at their desks; they arrange at a piano. They play chords, they play harmonies, they hear what it sounds like, they find something better, they play around with that, then they put down the notes. "Jesus Christ," John Williams whispered to me. "He's writing a score at his desk." Percy Faith heard things in his head. He didn't need a piano.

We told Percy that we liked "On the Street Where You Live," and he said, "Too bad. They're going to take that out of the show."

"We know, Percy," we said, "we know."

"Well," he said, "let's hear it."

So we got to a piano, and John and I did it for him. "You're right," he said. "That's too good not to do."

"We've got to record this quickly," Mitch said. "If it's a hit, they'll have to keep it in the show."

Two days later John and I and Milt Ebbins went down to the Columbia studio, which was in an old church on Thirtieth Street that had wonderful acoustics.

Percy was already there with the orchestra. I stepped into the three-sided glass-walled booth that gives the engineer what they call "separation," which enables him to keep the singer's voice separate from the sound of the orchestra. I was ready to go, but there was no microphone. When I asked Mitch, he pointed up to a foot-long, black pencil microphone hanging three or four feet above my head, aimed downward.

I had never seen that kind of setup. "What's that?" I asked him.

"That's your microphone."

"Come on, Mitch, give me my regular mike."

"Okay," he said, and he had the engineer bring in a stand-up microphone.

Percy had the orchestra run through it for me, to hear the arrangement. He had opened the song with "Oh, that towering feeling," which then led into the first line: "I have often walked down this street before." The power of that opener, contrasting with conversational tone of the first line, was just wonderful. The whole arrangement was wonderful.

"Gee, Percy," I said, "that's just great."

"Thanks, Vic. I thought you'd like it."

We did two takes. Then we did a B side. I had to get to the Copa for my next show, but I was eager to hear what we had sounded like, so we went into the control booth and the engineer played it. I was absolutely thrilled by the way it had come out.

"You see, Mitch," I said. "Don't give me that stuff about those hanging microphones. This is how it's supposed to sound. Forget that newfangled jazz."

"Come here," he said. "I want to show you something."

We went out to the booth, John, Milt Ebbins, and I. Mitch picked up the cord to the mike I had used. It wasn't plugged in.

"That recording was done with that mike"—he pointed up at the hanging mike.

I was so embarrassed I made John and Milt walk with me the thirty blocks uptown, at a fast clip. But "On the Street Where You

Live" was a huge hit. It reached number four on the charts and stayed there week after week. They did have to keep the song in the show, and it was the record that did it.

A little more than a year later, I was at home one Sunday with Anna and Perry when the phone rang. "Vic?" I heard. "It's Alan Lerner. Frederick and I are out here. There's something we'd like to talk to you about."

Lerner and Loewe—I knew they were at MGM filming *Gigi*, their follow-up to *My Fair Lady*.

"Yes, hi, Alan. I know, you're doing *Gigi*."

"Right. Listen, we'd like you to record something from *Gigi*. We'd like you to hear the score."

All I could think of was that they must have decided, based on what had happened with "On the Street Where You Live," that I was good luck.

"Sure, I'd love to. When would be good?"

"Could we do it today?"

"Yes. Where do you have in mind?"

"Well, we can come to your house. You have a piano?"

"Sure."

"Good, we'll come to your house."

"You mean you and Frederick?"

"Yes. What's the address?"

An hour later Anna and I were sitting on our sofa listening to Frederick Loewe playing the piano and Alan J. Lerner singing the entire score for us. Everything from "Thank Heavens for Little Girls" to "Yes, I Remember It Well" to the title song. Songwriters have a special way of singing; they're selling the song as they're performing it. Sammy Cahn used to say he "leaned into it." Alan Lerner was leaning into it in our living room.

After he went through the score, Lerner said, "You pick a song. We'd like you to do it the way you did for *My Fair Lady*."

"'Gigi,'" I said. "I'd like to sing 'Gigi.'" "Gigi, am I a fool without a mind/or have I merely been to blind to realize?" "This is gorgeous," I told them. "It's beautiful. I want to record this one."

"You've got it," Lerner said, and they packed up and left. Anna and I just sat there for a while. I knew we had just experienced something we'd remember forever. I did record "Gigi," which made the charts and did well. The song also won the Oscar that year, one of the nine Academy Awards for the film.

Anna and I were close in so many ways. I thought we had a fundamental compatibility with each other. And, of course, we had Perry, whom we both loved dearly. But our marriage wasn't completely smooth. Anna had her career, I was away a lot on singing engagements, in Europe as well as around the United States. We didn't have much of a shared life with friends. Anna was lonely, and I wasn't as aware of that as I should have been. And then there was always and forever that aggravating factor—her mother.

My original sin was getting Anna pregnant. Enrica's anger over that never seemed to go away; it just simmered and was redirected. Another part of it was that she and Anna had been so close for so many years, and now I had separated Anna from her, which just ate her up. When we bought a house on Moraga Drive, Enrica bought one nearby, with good sight lines, so she could watch us with her binoculars. She'd see when I left, and then go over to spend time with Anna. I knew I wasn't wrong in my conviction that she just out and out hated me. But I wasn't ready for Enrica's accusation that I was stealing Anna's money.

The way we worked our finances was that Anna had her bank account, I had mine, then we had a third account that I paid the household expenses out of. And one day Anna said to me, "My mother is telling me that you are taking money out of my account for your gambling."

My gambling was a bit of a sore point between us. I didn't gamble that much, but I often worked in Vegas, and there wasn't much to do there other than gamble or screw around. So I did spend time gambling, sometimes winning, sometimes losing. But never enough to make much of a difference in our finances. "Would you rather that I screwed around with broads, Anna?" I asked. "I've got to do something when I'm not singing. I'm not going to sit there and stare at a wall."

Of course, it wasn't just me. We all gambled, all the entertainers. The casino managers and owners encouraged it. Customers would see that Dean Martin or Jerry Lewis or Robert Goulet was gambling next to them, and it gave them a thrill, something to talk about when they got home. It was part of the game the owners played, part of the Vegas scene.

But I wasn't going to excesses, and I for sure would never take anything out of Anna's account. So when Enrica accused me of this I scheduled a meeting immediately with our accountants—for that day. "I want you to have your mother there," I told her. "I want her to accuse me of this in front of the accountant."

So we sat down with the accountant, and when he was finished going over the accounts and statements, it turned out that there actually was money missing from Anna's account. But I hadn't taken it; her mother had.

When this came out, Enrica was embarrassed. She was left speechless for a change. But I knew that our marriage was in trouble when Anna didn't apologize to me. She didn't say, Vic, I'm sorry, I was wrong. It was my mother. I apologize for having accused you. When she found out it was her mother, she just said, "Okay."

It was still a tremendous shock, though, when I came back from a European tour to hear Anna say that she wanted a divorce. And when I found out that she had been having an affair with Al Hart, it drove me wild. Only Frank Sinatra could have stopped me from killing him, which, thank God, he did.

The great mystery was why. Why Al Hart, who was a lot older than Anna, and who looked even older than he was? Anna was one of the most beautiful women in Hollywood. If she had wanted to have an affair, she could have chosen anyone, someone she'd have things in common with, or at least feel a physical attraction to. Hart didn't have any of that.

The reason came out in the divorce proceedings, and when it did it came as another body blow. "I had to do it," Anna told the lawyers. "I had to do what I did because I had to support my sisters and my mother. He promised me I'd have a million dollars in an account. No matter how much I spent, he promised me I'd always have a million dollars."

After that, the divorce was unavoidable. But even then we still had feelings for each other. She was the mother of my son. I was Perry's father. Perry loved us both, and of course he had no idea why we weren't going to be a family anymore. I lost my respect for Anna over what had happened. What she had done was unforgivable. But after my emotions cooled I could understand it, at least somewhat. Anna was looking out for her mother, who was in trouble. That was a feeling I knew about. I always took care of my parents. And when my father died I continued taking care of my mother until the day she died. She always had a nice place to live; there was always a check in her mailbox.

So while I couldn't accept what Anna had done, I could understand why she did it. And very quickly it turned out that she couldn't even keep her side of the bargain with Hart. She couldn't stand the old son of a bitch, and she couldn't go through with what they had agreed. Instead, she took Perry and went off to England to make a movie.

I felt this failure badly. I loved women, and there were plenty of them around. But I loved the idea of a home and family more. I missed Perry terribly, and as time went by I missed Anna, too. But whatever I was feeling inside, I still had a career to carry on, which included a big industry show coming up in Florida. All the radio program directors, producers, and big name DJs would be there, and each of the major labels was showcasing its talent. Columbia had asked me to represent them, so I arranged to get myself and my musicians down to Miami.

We were booked on a night flight. But that day I got a call from my drummer.

He was in bed, sick as a dog. He wasn't going to be able to make it. The only person I knew to turn to was to my previous drummer, Sidney Bulkin. Sidney Bulkin was a great guy, but a little wild. It's probably enough to say that he was a drummer. He liked to drink; he was a real party animal. Like I said, a drummer. Wonderful, but nuts. Sidney had been with me for many years. He knew all my music. I called him.

"Sidney, hello. It's Vic. How are you?"

Now, usually if I called Sidney, it would be, "Hey Vic, man, what's goin' on, man? Everything cool, baby? Yeah."

This time he picked up the phone and said, "Hello."

"Sidney? Sidney, it's Vic, Vic Damone."

"Vic. Oh, hello, Vic. Gee, it's nice to talk to you. How are you, Vic?"

"Sidney, what the hell's happened to you?"

"I'm sorry, what do you mean?"

"You don't sound like Sidney."

"Oh, I'll tell you about it someday. Anyway, what's up?"

"Listen, I have to leave for Miami tonight to do a show for Columbia Records, and my drummer can't make it. I need you to come and play for me. You know my book. Can you do it?"

"Sure. What time are we leaving?"

"TWA to Miami, the red-eye."

"You got it. I'll be there."

Sidney sounded straight. He sounded sober. I had John Williams with me, my bass player, and now Sidney. That was it. I got to the airport, met everyone, and we boarded the plane.

TWA's cross-country flights at that time had first-class seats that faced each other, with a table in between. Sid and I found seats opposite each other, and when the stewardess came by and asked if we wanted a drink, Sidney said, "Yes, I'll have a Coke, thanks."

I almost fell over. Sidney had played with me for years, and I never once saw him have a Coke, or refuse a drink.

I, on the other hand, almost never had a drink. But I was feeling extremely low about what had happened with Anna. So low I felt I could use one. "I'll have a scotch on the rocks," I said.

"What?" Sidney was sitting there, looking at me with his arms folded. He'd never seen me have a drink, just like I'd never seen him not have one.

"Vic, you're drinking?"

"Oh, I don't know. I miss my kid, my son. My wife and I are separated. I don't know what to do about it. It's very hard, Sid. Very hard."

A bit later the stewardess came by again and I ordered another scotch. Now Sidney knew something was really wrong. "What?" he said. "Another one?"

"What about you?" I said. "Look at you, for God's sakes. Are you really Sid Bulkin?"

"Yes, it's me, all right."

"What is it with you?"

"Vic, I've found God."

"Found God? What do you mean, you've found God?"

"Vic, I have. And it's a wonderful feeling. Listen, you're going through a very tough time, aren't you?"

"Yes. Yes, I am."

"Why don't you do what I do, what Baha'is do?"

"What?" Baha'is? I'd never heard of Baha'is.

"Why don't you pray?" said Sidney.

"Pray? What do you mean, pray?"

"Well, every day at noon Baha'is pray. We acknowledge God. We say our prayers."

I didn't know what he was talking about. Baha'is? But I looked at him. He was certainly an example of something. Sid was a good Jewish kid, but a total party animal for all the years I had known him. Now I looked at him, and he was different. He was a changed man.

"I don't mean to say 'Our Father Who Art in Heaven,'" said Sid. "I mean, talk to Him. Tell Him what's on your mind."

"Just talk?"

"Yes, just talk. Tell Him what you're thinking. Tell Him how you're feeling."

"Sure, Sid. Okay. Right."

Next morning we landed in Miami and had a few hours' sleep. When I got up I was thinking about the rehearsal, which was at one o'clock with the Count Basie Band. Count Basie was also with Columbia, and I was going to integrate my group with his guys for the performance. They were going to play our music.

I ate breakfast in my room and checked the time. It was noon; the second hand was just coming up on twelve. All I was thinking about was getting to rehearsal and how things were going to work with Count Basie. But the fact that it was approaching exactly noon suddenly reminded me of what Sid had said on the plane—he prayed every day at noon.

It was twelve. I had nothing to do until one. Why not? I thought. What is there to lose? So, sitting at the table in my suite, I started off, "God. Please listen. I have to talk to you." Out loud. But then I pulled up. I felt self-conscious. What if room service walked in to get the dishes, or if a maid walked in. What in the world would they think? They'd think I was nuts.

So I got up, walked into the bedroom, closed the door behind me, and went into the bathroom. I locked the door and started over.

"Now, listen to me, please. I'm so unhappy, I cannot tell you. I miss my wife, I miss my son. Please, listen. I feel like I'm going crazy with all this. I have never felt so bad. I'm lonely. I like being married. I can't stand this being alone. I love Perry. I love my boy. Please. I just want another chance with Anna to make it right. I'll give her another chance, she'll give me another chance. We could work it out, I'm sure we could. Please."

I was going on and on, pouring my heart out about this, about my feelings, my love, my loneliness, my desperation, my hopes. All of it. And finally I felt like I had said it all, all the things I had never said to anybody that had been welling up inside me. I looked at my watch and it was one o'clock. I had been in the bathroom for an hour, getting it all out of my system. I thought, Oh my God, the rehearsal. And I ran out.

That night at the show my voice seemed unusually full. I surprised myself, it felt so good. I finished with "Maria" from *West Side Story,* a big song, full of longing and hope and desire. Afterward I told the guys that we would meet the next day at the pool. I had rented a cabana. We weren't going to leave until the following day, so we had a day to just take it easy and relax.

The next day I got up late and began getting calls from Columbia. They were hugely pleased with the way it went. It had been a really important performance, they said. The jocks and radio execs had loved it. According to them, it was my best performance ever.

I had my breakfast, glanced at my watch, and strangely, again it was coming up to exactly noon. It was weird, as if I were in some kind of Alfred Hitchcock movie. And I thought, Damn, I have to go pray.

So I went to the bathroom and locked myself in again. "God, listen to me. In case you didn't hear everything from yesterday. But first . . . thank you for the show. You helped me there. It really went well. I know it was with Your help. But listen, I'm truly dying inside . . ." And again I went on and on and on. Just like the day before. It all came out. Everything. And when I looked at my watch again, it was one o'clock. I had told the guys I would meet them at twelve.

I went down to the pool and the attendants pointed out my cabana. "Right over there, Mr. Damone." I went over and there they were, John, Sidney, and my bass player, luxuriating in the sun. Musicians love relaxing like that between shows and after shows. We sat around in the warmth and talked about the performance, how great it had gone, how well things had worked out with Count Basie's guys, how happy we were about the audience's response.

At some point Sidney went into the cabana to get out of the sun and while he was in there the phone rang.

"You want me to answer it?" he called.

"Yeah. Please. Answer it."

"Hello," I heard. "Yes. Yes, this is Vic Damone's cabana. Yep. Who's calling, please? Who? *Who?* Calling long distance, from where? His wife? Just a minute, please. Vic, Vic. It's from England. It's your wife."

"Get out of here."

"No, it is. It's from England."

The first thing that jumped to my mind was that something had happened to Perry. Something terrible. Why else would she be calling me? And how did she find me?

I took the phone. "Hello, hello?"

"Veek!" Anna could never say "Vic." "Veek, Veek."

"Anna, Anna. What's wrong? How's Perry? What's happened?"

"Nothing happened. Perry's fine."

"Let me talk to him."

Perry got on the phone. He wasn't even four yet. "Daddy, Daddy," he said. "I love you, Daddy."

"I love you, too, Perry. I love you, too. Okay, Perry, put Mama back on the phone."

"Anna, what's up? What's the matter?"

"I don't know. I just know I had to talk to you."

"How did you find me? How did you know where I am?"

"I've been trying to get you for the last two hours. I finally got in touch with George Wood. He told me where you are and what hotel, so I called."

"Okay, okay. Anna? Anna, I'm so happy to hear from you."

"Veek," she said. "I had to call. I had to talk. I wanted to say, Veek . . . Do you think? Do you think we could try again? Could we try again? Could you come here?"

"Anna, where are you?"

"I'm in London. I'm doing a movie here."

I got off the phone. I couldn't believe it. I'd been praying, like Sidney said. It made me feel better, just getting everything off my chest. Friday and Saturday I had prayed. Or anyway, talked, talked to God. But this?

The next day, Sunday, I flew to New York. George Wood got a jeweler friend of his to open up his store so I could buy a piece of jewelry as a gift. And Sunday night I flew to London. I got in Monday morning and an hour later I was with my family. Which was exactly what I had prayed for.

That's when I began to think seriously about Baha'i.

10

Let Me Put You on with Sam Giancana

Anna and I tried to make it work. But we couldn't quite get over the things that had happened between us. Anna had changed, at least it seemed so to me. Part of it was the awful circumstances that had caused our separation. They had had an effect. But that wasn't all, or even most of it.

Anna had been on her own now for a while, for the first time in her life. Her mother wasn't hovering over her, as she had been before we were married—and while we were married, too. She hadn't had me to take care of her, as I had been for the previous four years. She had been managing her own life and making her own friends, among whom was Richard Attenborough—"Dickie" Attenborough—a British war hero and actor who was not a lover, but a strong influence. She had grown more worldly; she seemed to have lost a lot of the freshness and innocent charm I had always found so winning.

After our reunion in London, Anna and Perry came back to the States so we could be together, but work separated us again. I was singing in Vegas and all around the country. She was making movies in England. It was all too much for us, and after six or seven months of trying we decided it wasn't working, and the only thing to do was get a divorce. Actually, Anna was the one who decided, but I didn't argue. It was sad for both of us, and especially for Perry, who was so attached to me as well as to her. But at least we felt we had tried. At least we had given ourselves another chance.

One positive fallout from our breakup was that Sid Bulkin had introduced me to Baha'i. He had gotten me thinking about spiritual things in a way I had never thought about them before. But I didn't really get serious about it until the divorce estranged me from the Catholic Church I had grown up in.

I want to say in advance that I still love Catholicism. I feel that in some ways I am a better Catholic now than I was before my troubles with the Church. But at a very tough time in my life, I did find something spiritual to hold onto that was different. Some might say very different. But I'd say that at heart it wasn't that different, after all. Here's what happened.

As the divorce was being finalized, I went back to the church where Anna and I had gotten married to talk to the monsignor about the possibility of an annulment. I knew the Church wouldn't recognize a civil divorce, but I was still a practicing Catholic. I went to Mass, I confessed, I took communion. I might not have been the most faithful Catholic in the world, but I wanted to find a way to continue in the only religion I had ever known. I knew that sometimes the Church granted annulments, that if you looked hard enough, maybe you could find some kind of irregularity in the marriage that would allow it. That's what I wanted them to do.

At the church I sat down with the same monsignor who had married us. I told him that our marriage was not working out, I wanted to see about getting an annulment.

"Why is that so important to you?" the monsignor asked.

"Because my wife and I are getting a divorce, but I still want to practice my religion."

"Well," he said, "if you are divorced, you won't be able to receive Holy Communion anymore."

"Wait," I said. "I'm not the one who wants the divorce. She does. I want to continue in the Church; I want to receive Holy Communion."

"No, I'm sorry, not if you are divorced."

"Isn't there some way we can just have the marriage annulled?"

There was silence for a moment. The monsignor looked thoughtful. "I can do that," he said finally. "But you'll have to write a substantial check."

"No, that's not what I mean. I don't want to *buy* an annulment. Why don't you just excommunicate her—she's the one who wants the divorce. Don't excommunicate me."

"Sorry," he said. "That's the way it is."

I walked out.

Well, the fact was, even though I was born and raised Catholic, I had always had a lot of unanswered questions about my faith. I had a strong belief in God. I also believed that everyone received some kind of blessing, and the blessing I had received was my voice. I really did feel, especially as I got older, that using my voice, singing, was my way of worshipping.

I had had a regular Catholic upbringing. I had gone to Sunday school. I had learned the prayers and the catechism. I was an altar boy. But there was a lot I simply did not understand. I'd say things in Latin, but what did they mean? I used to ask the priest, "Father, why am I pouring the wine?"

"It's the blood of Christ, my son."

Okay, I thought, but how is that supposed to work?

"What's the Holy Trinity, Father?"

"The Holy Trinity, my son? It's the Father, the Son, and the Holy Ghost."

"But what's the Holy Ghost, Father? What does it mean?"

"You don't have to know that at this point, my son. Just have faith."

And so it went.

At Mass, in the back of my head I was saying, I don't know what I'm doing here. Standing up, kneeling, standing up, kneeling. My mom did it, my dad did it, my sisters did it. I followed along with them. Okay, but why?

It wasn't like I was driven to find the answers. I wasn't obsessed to know. But the questions stayed in the back of my head. Why was I standing and kneeling? Why was everything in Latin, which I couldn't understand? And what exactly was the Holy Trinity, anyway?

After that experience with the monsignor, I went to talk to Sid. "Tell me more about the Baha'i religion," I said. "I do believe in God, but I'm not sure if I'm a Catholic anymore. I want to hear about it."

Sid and his wife, Elaine, gave what they called "firesides" at his house, and he invited me to come. Firesides are discussions in which Baha'is and others who are interested come to hear the lessons of the faith and to ask and discuss questions they may have.

At one of the first fireside meetings I went to I asked what Baha'ullah—the Baha'i founder—had to say about the Trinity. The question still bothered me. I don't know what I expected; maybe I was just testing them. What would Baha'is know about the Father, Son, and Holy Ghost? But one of the people at the fireside, Sid, I think, said, "Okay, we'll explain it."

"Good!" I said. "I want to hear this!"

"Picture a perfect mirror," said Sid, "a perfect reflection. Then take it out into the sunshine. Let the rays of the sun hit the mirror, and angle the mirror so that the reflected rays are aimed directly at your chest. Those rays will burn you to the heart. Now, the sun, from which the rays emanate, is analogous to God the Father. God gives us everything, our soul, our intellect, all we have, our spiritual direction, all of life's true gifts. But how are these conveyed to us? They are not conveyed directly. They are conveyed by the mirror. The mirror, or mirrors, here on Earth are our teachers and prophets: Abraham, Moses, Zoroaster, Buddha, Krishna, Jesus, Mohammed. They are our mirrors. They teach us. They are the sons. And the reflected rays that hit us? Those rays are the Holy Ghost, the reflection of God's power.

"When people argue about their religion being better than someone else's, they are really just arguing about these mirrors. My mirror is better than yours, they are saying; it reflects better. But all these differences are only over mirrors—whichever mirror you are using, there's still only one God."

From then on I started going regularly to firesides at the Bulkins'. I learned there that religions are just labels. Baha'i, Christian, Jewish, Muslim. Names. Different names, but only one God. And Baha'is believe that since there is only one God, we should all pray together. Though we think we are many, we are actually one. I loved that. That said something to me.

I started reading Baha'i books. I traveled all the time, going to gigs in Europe, Asia, across America. On those flights I used to have a little traveling chess set with me. I'd play against myself. Then I'd read. It was a great opportunity for me to learn about God, and to learn about the things I'm supposed to be doing. The things I'm supposed to be doing as a person in this world, as a child of God.

The more I read and listened, the more I found other things I liked—no clergy, for instance. Baha'is have no priests. All Baha'is are themselves teachers. I liked the idea of reconfirming your spiritual connection every day, the noonday prayers Sid had originally told me about. I liked the acknowledgment of our powerlessness and God's omnipotence. You might think that's a simple truth for anyone who believes in God at all. But I can tell you that it's a rare thing to acknowledge in the show business world, where people's egos can get unbelievably inflated.

And man, did I like the fact that no one ever passed the basket around. You were free to contribute anything you wanted, of course, at any time. But there was no pressure, nothing in public. For Baha'is, religion was a spiritual matter, not a material one. I heard the story about the Ford Foundation check to the Baha'i central office: a quarter of a million dollars to help with the construction of the Baha'i Temple outside of Chicago, which was being built with the nickels and dimes of Baha'is from around the world.

The Baha'i administrators asked whether any member of the Ford family was Baha'i, and when they found that none were, they sent the check back. The Ford people were incredulous. "You're going to give us back $250,000?" Yes, they were told, because you don't believe in what we believe in. We believe in the oneness of mankind, the oneness of God, the oneness of religions. That told me the Baha'is were serious about themselves. They had integrity.

Another teaching that hit me right where I lived was that God gives each of us talent. And one of our reasons for living is to find what our particular talent is. And when we find that out, then it's our duty to follow it, to bring it to its full potential. That's our job, our obligation, that's one of the things we are put here to do.

Over time I found so many elements of Baha'ism that made sense to me personally that I became Baha'i. At the same time, I did not feel as if I had given up my Catholicism. If anything, I felt I understood some of the Catholic tenets a lot better than I ever had. And, as I began to understand Baha'i beliefs more deeply, I came to feel, as all Baha'is do, that, in fact, I was Catholic—and that I was Jewish, too, and Muslim, and Buddhist; that all of God's great prophets spoke the truths that their times and their cultures could understand. As a Baha'i I could grasp the truths they taught as my truths and my beliefs as well. The idea that though our faiths are many, they all spring from one God meant that at heart our faiths are one as well. And that we partake of all of them, that I myself partake of all of them.

While all this was happening, of course, I was working hard. I had an agent, Fred Apollo; a manager, Milt Ebbins; and a part-time secretary, Judy Rawlins, who came to my home office a couple of times a week to take care of the fan mail and other business and who sometimes traveled with me. Judy was very good, very smart, and very beautiful. She had had some small parts in movies—she was Elvis's first kiss in *G.I. Blues.* She was also a talented animator and worked for Walt Disney on *Lady Is a Tramp.* Before too long we were going out, and soon it developed into a real relationship. Then we started living together. This was a number of years after Anna and I were divorced.

When we were in Chicago at one point I took Judy out to the Baha'i Temple, a beautiful, nine-sided architectural marvel in nearby Wilmette I wanted her to see. While we were there, we met the head of the National Assembly. When I introduced him to Judy, he took me aside and said, "Are you going to get married?"

"Oh, I don't know," I said. "I got over a divorce not that long ago. I don't know if I'm quite ready. But yes, eventually I think we'd like to get married."

"I'll tell you what you should do," he said. "While you're thinking about it, marry her."

"Really?"

"Yes."

And I did. On October 25, 1963, Judy and I were married in a Baha'i ceremony at our home in Los Angeles. Afterward we flew to Las Vegas for a civil service and a brief honeymoon.

Meanwhile, interesting things were happening with my career. I had had regular television shows since the mid 1950s. Almost every summer for eight or nine years I was on CBS, with variety shows featuring singers, instrumentalists, and comedians. CBS got Jack Philbin to produce these *Vic Damone Show*s for me. Jack was also producing Jackie Gleason's *The Honeymooners,* and he brought his whole crew over, so I felt well taken care of in that regard. And when I asked them to get Tutti Camarata as my music director and conductor, they did that, too, which meant more than I can say.

Tutti Camarata was simply one of the greats. He was a Juilliard-trained classical trumpeter who had played with Bing Crosby and Paul Whiteman before Jimmy Dorsey stole him away to be his first trumpet and arranger. Tutti had gone on to arrange for the likes of Billie Holiday, Louis Armstrong, and Ella Fitzgerald. Then Disney brought him on to establish and run Disneyland Records. This was a man who had made former Mouseketeer Annette Funicello a singing star, and who also conducted the legendary Jascha Heifetz on one of his recordings. He played solo trumpet with classical orchestras. He knew popular music, big bands, classical, rock—he did it all. Tutti was a phenomenon.

But it wasn't just his talent that made me so happy to have him. I had known Tutti since I was seventeen. He had been a huge influence on me. Somehow, I still don't know how, Lou Capone had gotten him to work with me—this was before I ever recorded anything. Tutti taught me how to take a line apart, how to break down a phrase. I was copying Sinatra, but Tutti said, "Listen, that's Sinatra, that's *his* life. You have to do it the way *you* feel it." Tutti made the lyrics come alive; he showed me how to make songs move.

Tutti wasn't just a gifted musician, he was a magnanimous, forgiving man, which I also experienced because of an incident I still feel badly about, something that happened while I was married to Anna. I was having lunch with him one day when he said, "Vic, I have something incredible to show you." He took a letter out of an envelope. "It's a letter of Puccini, Puccini's writing."

I looked at it with him. Puccini! Unbelievable. Tutti had conducted some albums of Puccini's music. He loved Puccini. "Tutti, what does it say?"

"I don't know. I can't read Italian. Can you?"

"No. I can speak some, but I never learned to read it."

We were staring at the letter. "But listen, my wife reads Italian. Let me have it. I'll get her to translate for us."

"No, Vic. I don't want to let it out of my hands."

"Tutti, really. I'll just show it to my wife. She'll translate it. I swear to God, I'll get it right back to you."

When I got home with the letter, I was so excited I showed it to Anna immediately, even though her friend Anna Kashfi was with her. Kashfi was married to Marlon Brando at the time—a short-lived marriage, as it turned out.

"Anna, it's an original Puccini letter. It's Tutti Camarata's. We need you to translate it for us."

Anna took the letter, but before she had a chance to say anything Kashfi piped up, "Puccini! Marlon adores Puccini! Puccini's his favorite! I have to show this to him. He needs to see it. He'll just die."

"No, please. I told Tutti I wouldn't let it out of my sight. I'm sorry"

"But Vic, this is *Marlon*. *Marlon* needs to see this letter. You know he won't let anything happen to it."

And Kashfi took the letter out of Anna's hands and left. I couldn't believe it. I thought about grabbing her, but then what? Besides, Marlon. I didn't know Marlon was a Puccini fan. I would have shown it to him myself.

Needless to say, I never saw that letter again, despite all the calls to Kashfi from me and Anna. She just would not give it up. It couldn't have been too much after that that she and Brando divorced. I told him about it later and asked if I could get it from him.

"A Puccini letter?" he said. "I love Puccini. That woman never showed me any Puccini letter."

I can't describe to you how I felt having to tell Tutti what had happened. But as I said, he was a forgiving man. I know he was terribly hurt by the loss of that letter, but he never let it come between us, not for a moment.

Anyway, Tutti had showed me how to make a song move when I was just starting out. Now he was making the *Vic Damone Show* move on CBS. We had incredible guests: Benny Goodman (Tutti had arranged for him), Duke Ellington (Tutti had arranged for him, too), Gene Autry and his Riders of the Purple Sage (no arranging there, as far as I knew, but he could have if Gene had ever asked him). Errol Garner, the legendary African American jazz pianist, was on once. Errol had one of the finest ears anybody has ever had, which is how he learned piano as a kid and how he played later as one of the all-time greats. But he couldn't read a note, which a lot of people knew. During our rehearsal I put a score down in front of him. "Errol, we're changing things around a little. We're going to add a medley. You come in here and here and here." Pointing. "Okay?" I thought Errol was going to change color. Until he looked up and saw I was laughing, at which point he started to laugh, too.

At one point my director thought it would be a good idea for me to sing "Soliloquy," a Rodgers and Hammerstein song from *Carousel*.

A truly great piece of music, full of emotion and mood changes, eight minutes long, an aria really. I rehearsed the song once, twice, again. It was beautiful; I began to feel almost as if it had been written for me. But it wasn't until the big Monday rehearsal that I felt comfortable enough that I decided to include it.

My opening number that night was "The Trolley Song" from *Meet Me in St. Louis.* I'm singing, "clang clang clang," but I'm thinking "Soliloquy." Then I introduced the comedian Alan King, and while he was on I went over to where Tutti was standing on the conductor's podium, laughing at Alan's routine. "Tutti," I whispered, "I'm doing 'Soliloquy.' "

"I know," he said. "It'll be great."

When it came time, I got my Billy Bigelow outfit on for the song and launched into it. But sixteen bars or so into the song, some CBS guy came out with a camera and plunked himself down to take pictures near the number-one TV camera—right directly in front of the lyric cards. I couldn't see the words. Of course, I knew the words, but on live television you have to make doubly sure. You can't take the chance of making mistakes. I began signaling the guy to move, pointing at him, jerking my thumb for him to get out of there. But he was oblivious; he just kept snapping away. This in front of the studio audience, which couldn't see the guy with the camera but could see me gesturing angrily. Finally, the stage manager grabbed the guy and practically threw him out of there bodily. All in all, I thought the song went off pretty well. So did the audience, though I'm sure my presentation left at least some of them wondering. Afterward, a number of people told me they thought all the emotion I had put into that song had made for a really interesting interpretation.

The *Vic Damone Show* started back in the fifties. Then, in 1962, not long before Judy and I got married, NBC developed a show for me called *The Lively Ones*. This project owed its creation to Lee Iacocca, Ford's vice president at the time. Ford was introducing it's new lineup of cars, which their advertising was calling "The Lively Ones." So Iacocca, always a great salesman, thought that a TV show with the same name, sponsored by Ford, could have a powerful marketing effect. The idea was to combine sketches with appearances by the country's top musical talents—the lively ones, the best, just as the automobiles were liveliest and best.

I would host together with two beautiful sidekicks, Shirley Yelm and Joan Staley, and we'd incorporate the guest stars into the action. I'd sing, then Shirley, Joan, and I would "travel" around the country and drop in to places where great stars were performing. The roster of guests we had on that show was like a who's who of the musical world: Peggy Lee, Dave Brubeck, Mel Tormé, Charlie Byrd, Count Basie, Julie London, Woody Herman, Joe Williams—the list went on and on. On one show Ella Fitzgerald tried to teach me to scat. I'm just glad tapes of that episode haven't appeared on YouTube. In the two years it ran, *The Lively Ones* was nominated for two Emmys. But even with all the great stars who appeared, the most memorable moment came during one of the commercials—memorable and almost catastrophic.

We shot that particular commercial in Dodgers Stadium. The idea was to portray how exceptionally roomy one of the Ford models was, roomy enough for a big African lion. Dodgers Stadium was chosen for the filming just in case the lion they were going to use got away. Inside the stadium he'd have nowhere to escape to. Thinking back, I'd say that though the concept was attention grabbing, it was kind of a stretch, not to mention a little on the dangerous side. But that's what it was. We put a lion in the backseat to demonstrate the car's spaciousness, and we had one of my "girls," Shirley Yelm, in the front seat to suggest the car's glamour and ability to attract beautiful women.

We rehearsed the commercial a number of times without the lion. Then the trainer brought him out and coaxed him into the backseat. The lion was on a chain that the trainer kept hold of while he squatted on the car's far side, so the audience couldn't see either him or the chain. All they could see was beautiful Shirley Yelm in the front seat, a giant lion in the back, and me, standing next to the car, smiling and saying, "Look how much room there is in this beautiful Ford automobile, even in the backseat. Just look at how comfortable this big African lion is back there."

At this point in the commercial I was supposed to close the car's rear door, which had been open so the television audience could get a good look at the lion enjoying the outstanding comfort of the spacious backseat. When I did this the lion was supposed to be facing the camera, and I had to be careful not to close the door on anything belonging to him—his nose, his paws, whatever. I said my lines, looking at the camera, then turned to close the door on the lion, but his face wasn't where it was supposed to be. Instead the lion was hunched over the front seat with its paws on Shirley's shoulders, its opened jaws about to chomp down on her neck.

"My God!" I yelled. "The lion's got Shirley!"

Shirley herself must have been in shock for a moment, paralyzed with fear, but now she started screaming. The trainer jerked the chain, which pulled the lion's head back just as he was about to bite down. As the lion was pulled back, the trainer shoved his arm in its mouth so it couldn't bite and dragged it out of the car. By now Shirley was hysterical. Not hurt, thank God, but beside herself.

We had to call an ambulance, though by the time it got there Shirley had calmed down. She handled it amazingly well, considering she was an instant away from having her neck snapped by a four-hundred-pound lion. When the trainer had gotten the lion into its cage, he came back and asked Shirley if she was having her period. She was.

"God, Shirley," he said, "you should have told us. That can set lions off."

The TV audience did get to see a couple of those lion commercials, but not that one. I wonder if it's preserved somewhere in NBC's archives of unused footage.

One unexpected benefit from *The Lively Ones* was that I got to know Lee Iacocca. The show was his creation, and he stayed close to the production to make sure things went exactly as he wanted them. Along the way we went out to dinner a few times, then he invited me to do commercials for the cars and make presentations at industry shows. In effect, I became part of the Ford team. "Will you please call me Lee," he said, but as long as I was working for him I thought it was more respectful to keep on a "Mr. Iacocca" basis. I eventually relented, though, after I got to know his wife and children and his parents, Nicola and Antoinette. His parents were from the Naples region in the old country. His mother was a lovely Italian lady, and Lee's father, Nick, was one of the finest people I had ever met, always a smile on his face, always a kind word for everyone. He reminded me a great deal of my own father.

When Nick died, his funeral was scheduled for the day I was supposed to open at the Riviera in Las Vegas. I called Eddie Torre, the Riviera's top executive, to tell him I couldn't make it.

"What do you mean, you can't make it?"

"Eddie, I can't. I have to go to Allentown, Pennsylvania, for a funeral."

"But the contract!"

"Eddie, I don't care. This is my close friend's father, and my close friend, he was like a father to me. I just have to go."

"Well . . . Okay," said Eddie, and he managed not to hold it against me, either.

One other vignette with Lee. At one point I was in New York and he asked me to meet him for dinner. He was going to be in a meeting at a particular address, but his limo would be waiting outside. Could I meet him at his limo in the late afternoon?

I was on time at the address, and there was the limo and the driver, but Lee wasn't there yet. I waited, chatting with the driver, and eventually Lee came out and got in the car.

"How'd things go?" I asked.

"Well," he said, "I just agreed to take over Chrysler."

I was in the stock market some at that time. I knew that Chrysler was four dollars; they were plunging fast and looked like they might go belly-up. "God," I said, "that stock is so low, I should buy some." As extraordinary a salesman as Lee was, I thought, if anybody could turn the company around, he could.

Iacocca never said a word; he just looked at me and changed the subject.

I ended up not buying a share. I was the first to have the information about his switch to Chrysler, and I was afraid that if I had bought in, it might have led to some kind of trouble for him. I could have used the money, though (of course, Iacocca did turn Chrylser around, and the stock went right up), especially some years later, when I found myself in pretty desperate circumstances.

The Lively Ones was a good time. It got me lots of exposure. My singing career was also going great guns. I was headlining in all the top venues. But as time went on I didn't feel completely fulfilled. I loved singing, but singing was something I had been doing since I was a kid. I fell into it because of my voice, and I followed through with it, basically going wherever it led me. But I used to think, Is this it? Is this the sum of your life? When interviewers would ask me about my future, I'd say, "I don't know. I haven't decided what I'm going to be when I grow up." It was a favorite line of mine.

I did have another vocation, or at least an avocation: golf. I had always loved sports, and golf was perfect for me. For one thing, it was something I could do by myself, on my own schedule. It got me out into the fresh air, away from the smoky clubs and theaters, so it was good for me physically; it made me feel good, and it helped save my lungs. I thought I might have a chance at becoming a top-notch golfer. I played obsessively, and I did have a talent for it, but, as it turned out, not quite at the required level.

There was something else that attracted me, too. I often found myself playing around with ideas for inventions, having thoughts about new things and figuring ways of building them. I wasn't obsessive about this, as I was about golf, but I seemed to be drawn to it naturally. I wouldn't try to think things up, but every so often an idea would come along on its own.

Exactly this happened one night two or three years before Judy and I were married, while I was waiting in the lobby of a hotel for a starlet I was dating to come down from her room. I was sitting across from a cigarette vending machine, and as I waited I was watching people put their coins in for a pack of cigarettes. I noticed that everybody who used the machine had a certain pattern. They'd put their money in, they'd look for the brand they wanted. Then they'd pull a lever and get their pack. And I thought, Wouldn't it be funny if there was a voice inside the machine that would say, "Buy Lucky Strikes." A whimsical, passing thought as I waited there with nothing to do. But then I thought, Wait a minute, that's not a bad idea. Why can't I get some kind of machine that would say "Buy Lucky Strikes," or maybe play the music from a commercial.

So I worked on it. This was before compact recorders appeared on the market. The only recording machines generally available were big reel-to-reels. So I had a little tape player custom built, a small one that would be triggered by the coin going into the machine. Then I managed to get a tape of an L&M cigarette commercial music with the L&M message. I had looked for Lucky Strike music, since I knew people at the American Tobacco Company (which made Luckies) from the Lucky Strike–sponsored *Hit Parade* radio show, when I had backed up Frank Sinatra for a year. But L&M was the only tape I could get, so the L&M commercial went onto the recorder, which I placed in a vending machine in a restaurant one of my friends owned. Then I sat myself down nearby to see how it would work.

I'm not sure if I ever had more fun in my life. People would come by, put the coins in, then be startled when music started playing. Nobody had ever heard of music coming out of a cigarette machine before. Sometimes they'd jump back. They'd stare at the machine. They'd look around; they'd check the sides of the machine; they'd get down and look underneath. They couldn't figure out where it was coming from: the L&M music, and a voice saying, "Buy L&M. Buy L&M," which looped until they made a selection. Given all that, it wasn't so strange that most people were pulling the L&M lever.

Since I knew the American Tobacco people, I had my agent put in a call, and eventually I found myself talking to one of their top executives. He wasn't unreceptive. In fact, he sounded intrigued. But he made it clear that he would need to see an actual prototype; he wasn't going to be satisfied with a description of the idea. I told him I could have a prototype in three weeks and made an appointment to see him. When I thought about how the meeting might go, though, it seemed pretty clear that he was going to ask me how many machines I could put these devices into. I knew the tobacco companies didn't own machines themselves, leasing companies did. If I didn't have access to any vending machines, I had nothing. And, of course, I didn't have access to any machines. So, what to do?

The only person I could think of who might be able to help was Frank Sinatra. Frank had contacts everywhere and was building his own business empire. Maybe Frank could hook me up with someone who leased machines, or maybe he'd have some ideas of his own; Frank was a creative guy.

So I called him, told him what I was thinking about, and about how my restaurant experiment had gone.

"Hey," said Frank, "that sounds like a helluva good idea."

"Yeah, Frank, but I need machines.. What good is it otherwise? You have any suggestions? I've got to get machines."

"Well, I just happen to have a guy sitting right here who might be able to help you with that. Here, let me put you on with Sam Giancana. He's my house guest."

Sam Giancana was his house guest? Holy Christ. Not that I said anything. Everyone knew Frank was friendly with mob guys. I didn't follow these things closely, but I understood who was who, and I knew Giancana was head of the Chicago outfit, Al Capone's old gang. So now I had to go through the whole spiel again with him.

When I was finished, Giancana said, in his gruff voice, "Can you come down here to Palm Springs?"

"Yes. When?"

"How about now?"

"Okay."

So I drove down to Palm Springs, to Sinatra's house. And there was Sam Giancana: skinny, sharp features, an extremely serious-looking guy.

"Okay," he said, "lemee hear this whole idea again." So I went through it while Giancana and Frank sat and listened.

When I was finished, Giancana said, "The music's on a *what*?"

"On a tape."

"How do you shut the fuckin' thing off?"

"You make a selection. That turns it off."

"Hey," he said. "That's a pretty good idea."

"But here's the problem, Sam. I have an appointment with the president of American Tobacco. What I'd like to do is go into his office with a vending machine. Boom. Just wheel it right in. Put it on a dolly and roll it in. Plug it in and let him put the money in the machine. Then let him listen to the music coming out."

"Yeah, good idea."

"But he's going to ask me how many machines I have. I don't have any."

"Well, now you do."

"What do you mean?"

"When you go there, you tell 'em you got three hundred thousand machines."

"Three hundred thousand?"

"Yeah. You just tell 'em. Three hundred thousand. And if they say, How do we know that? You say, I passed by Chicago and visited some of my uncles there, and I'm telling you, I got three hundred thousand machines."

"Okay. Three hundred thousand. What kind of deal can I make with them?"

"Tell them you want three dollars a month per machine."

"Okay. What's the three dollars?"

"You get a dollar, I get a dollar, and the vendor gets a dollar."

"Okay," I said. "I like it." I was already counting the first three hundred thousand.

"Of course you like it," he said.

"But I need a machine, Sam. I need a machine to bring into the office. I've got this little tape player with a speaker on it. They have to hook it up to the coin mechanism, so that when the coins go in it triggers the tape."

"Okay."

Sam made a few calls and told me who I should call in Brooklyn a couple of days before my meeting.

"You call him and he'll set it all up for you, and he'll send a guy with you to take care of the machine."

"Okay, Sam, that's great. But I can't go in there by myself. I need to make a deal with the guy. I think I need to have a lawyer with me."

"There's a guy from Cleveland who represents a lot of us. He'll take good care of you. I'll talk to him. Adrian Fink. You call him after I talk to him."

Three weeks later Adrian Fink and I walked into the meeting with the president of American Tobacco. Behind us a guy rolled in a cigarette vending machine on a dolly. The machine had been rigged with my tape player. It worked beautifully. All we needed was an electric socket.

"Thank you for seeing us, sir," I said. "This is Mr. Fink, my attorney."

"Okay," he said. "Show me what you have here?"

We plugged the machine into a wall outlet.

"Sir, here's thirty-five cents. Please put the coins in the machine."

"No, you do it."

"Sir, you have to do it. I want you to see what it's like for a customer, how the customer is going to feel."

The president got up, put the money in, and all of a sudden Ligget & Myers music started playing and a voice said, "Want to try a great cigarette? L&Ms, L&Ms."

"Godamnit!" said the president. "L&Ms?"

"Sir, it was the only tape I could get."

He was looking for where the music was coming from, in front, in back, underneath. Meanwhile, the tape was looping over and over: "A great cigarette? L&Ms, L&Ms."

"Jesus Christ, how do you shut the goddamned thing off?"

"You have to make a selection."

"Okay." And he pulled a knob—the L&M knob.

A moment later he was back at his desk, pushing buttons and telling people to come into his office. In a few minutes the place was crowded with lawyers and PR guys; there must have been ten people in there in addition to us.

The president told them to put money in the machine. Someone did, and the usual scene started up. They were all looking around for where the music was coming from. Then somebody made a selection. I was interested to see that he made sure he selected Lucky Strikes.

The president said, "You know, I like this, Vic. Please explain how it works." I did, and he said, "Yes, I like the idea." Then one of the lawyers said, "Okay, but how many machines do you have? That you can put these in?"

"I have them."

"What do you mean? How many do you have?"

"Three hundred thousand."

"What?"

"Yes," said Adrian Fink. "We have three hundred thousand machines."

They were incredulous. Some of them actually laughed. "Where do you have three hundred thousand machines?" the lawyer smirked.

"We have them in every large city," said Adrian Fink.

"There are only seven hundred thousand of these in the country," said the lawyer. "How in the world do we know you have three hundred thousand of them?"

"Well, sir," I said. "I'm sure we can document that for you. Before I came here I visited with one of my uncles in Chicago. I told him we needed machines, and I asked him how many we could use. He said, 'Tell them you have three hundred thousand.'"

The president said, "Chicago, huh? Really? Well, you might actually have them. What kind of arrangement are you looking for?"

Adrian Fink said, "We think three dollars a month per machine would be fair to everyone. Nine hundred thousand a month for all our machines."

But then one of the company lawyers said, "Sir, it may actually cost considerably more than that. The Robinson Patman Act on pricing will most likely affect any arrangement we might make. Without knowing exact figures, I believe it could possibly cost us in the neighborhood of another four or five million dollars."

I looked at Adrian. "I'm sorry," he said. "I'm not sufficiently familiar with Robinson Patman. I'll have to examine it."

"Look," said the president, "I love this idea. It's like hypnosis. But you have to figure out a way we can use it so that we're not in violation of Robinson Patman or anything else."

So we went home, me back to Hollywood, Adrian back to Cleveland. And we never did find a way to get around the Robinson Patman Act.

So, my cigarette vending machine idea turned out to be a nonstarter. I had another business idea years later that I wish I could say the same about.

In 1970 I was working on plans to start an entertainment company that would produce records, TV shows, and movies. I had been thinking along those lines for quite a while. Sinatra had developed his own music and film company, Reprise, in the late 1950s and had subsequently sold it to Warner Brothers. I thought I might be able to do something similar. With all my friends and contacts in the entertainment world, I would have access to recording artists, show writers, producers, and others. There were a lot of talented people out there who were not happy with the exploitative arrangements they often had with their studios and recording companies. I thought I could do a lot better.

My big, immediate problem, of course, was backing. I didn't have anywhere near the resources myself to fund this project, so I was starting to look for money people who might be responsive. Rudy Duran had been a friend of mine for some years, and early on in my search he introduced me to the Shaheen family from Washington, D.C., wealthy investors who he thought might be interested in backing me.

After some positive initial discussions, Duran and I flew to Washington to meet with Tom Shaheen, the head of the family. Shaheen sent a limo to pick us up at the airport and drive us to his home, a large mansion with well-tended grounds and a household staff, as well as various business employees who worked in his offices there. I had spoken with Shaheen by phone a number of times and had met with one of his representatives. What I was hoping to do here was come to an agreement about the structure and financing for what would be called Damone Productions. Shaheen seemed ready to move ahead, and we discussed at length not just how to establish the company, but what some of our first projects would be and how we might best handle them. But Shaheen wasn't all business. He had his ten-year-old son with him, a boy who had been blind from birth. He was a really sweet kid, friendly and happy, despite his terrible disability. I liked him tremendously.

That meeting laid the groundwork for the company, and over the next period of time we ironed out the details and developed a business plan. Tom would come in as chairman of the board, and I would be president and actually run the company. When everything was ready I went with Tom's brother, the family's lawyer, to a bank in Denver that had agreed to be our lender. They were going to provide a $250,000 loan, which would constitute my share of our initial capitalization.

We went over the details of our plans for movies, records, and TV shows with the bank officer, and by the end of our meeting we had our loan. The only hitch was the bank's requirement that I had to keep a minimum balance of $50,000 in the account, which meant that I would only have use of $200,000, instead of the full two fifty. But I agreed to that stipulation, and the account was set up. We were ready to move.

Once the loan was approved, we had a meeting to formally establish the company: John Shaheen was present, as was our lawyer, Rudy Duran, to whom we were assigning a small percentage of the equity in lieu of a finder's fee. I told John Shaheen that I hadn't had a chance to read all the documents through, and that I wanted to do that. "Vic," he said, "it isn't necessary. I've gone over them carefully and they're in order. All you need to do is sign."

So I did.

When we were done, John gave me four blank checks to sign. One was to pay off back taxes I owed the government; the three others were for start-up costs. I was leery, though, of simply signing blank checks, and I put in a call to Tom in Washington.

When we got him on the phone, I said, "Tom, your brother's given me blank checks to sign. I'm not happy about doing that."

"No," he said. "They're in order, Vic. We'll use them serially, as needed. I'll keep you closely informed of the progress. We should start hiring people in two weeks or so."

I signed them.

Two weeks later I got a call from the bank president.

"Vic, I want you to know that there is no money in your account, and as you know, you agreed to keep a balance of fifty thousand."

"What do you mean, no money?"

"The two-hundred-fifty-thousand-dollar loan account has no money left; you've withdrawn it all, and our agreement was that you would leave fifty thousand in there."

"What do you mean, I've withdrawn it all?" I was already feeling a deep anxiety. I had not heard from Shaheen about any activity. "What are you talking about?

"There's nothing left in your account."

"Give me your number, please. I'll call you right back."

I called Tom Shaheen at his office and heard: "This number is no longer in service."

I called him at his house. Again: "This number is no longer in service."

By now I was feeling heart palpitations. I called the police department in Washington and explained that I had friends at the address and was not getting any response. Could they please check the house.

They called back. "Mr. Damone, that property is vacant."

"I can't believe it," I said. "I was just there a couple of weeks ago."

My heart was in my stomach when I called Rudy in. He seemed as shocked as I was. "I don't know anything about it. If they scammed you, they scammed me, too."

I hired a private detective to track Shaheen down. He came back with a report that the entire family had fled to Lebanon. I thought about trying to go after them there. I had black thoughts about making some contacts and finding somebody who would do something for me there. Even if I couldn't get the money back, at least I'd get some satisfaction. But in my heart I knew I wasn't really serious about that.

I truly did not know what to do. The only thing clear was that I was facing ruin. I owed back taxes. I was on the line personally with the bank. I had been doing well, but also spending a lot. I was paying Anna alimony and child support. I had all my family expenses—Judy and I had three children by now and a big house in Hollywood. When I went over the situation with my lawyer, he said, "Vic, there's really only one option here. I'm going to have to recommend that you declare bankruptcy. That will at least buy you some protection. There's simply no alternative."

I dreaded telling Judy. This could absolutely not have come at a worse time. Judy was not well. She hadn't been for a long time, and her situation was not getting any better. This was going to be like a death blow to her. I had no idea how she might take it.

Judy and I had started off well. We had known each other for a good while before we started going out, and even then we hadn't been in any rush to get married. We had grown a strong affection for each other. When we were married in a Baha'i ceremony in 1964, we were sure our prospects were bright for happiness, children, and a loving marriage. And when, a month or two after the wedding, we found out that Judy was pregnant, we couldn't have been happier. But the whole thing almost ended shortly after it began.

Five months after our brief Las Vegas honeymoon, I was working at Harrah's in Lake Tahoe, Nevada. Judy was with me there, enjoying the place while I was singing. She was already three months pregnant. Harrah's owner, Bill Harrah, had other interests in addition to the casino, including a business in high-end automobiles. While I was working, he told me to pick a car to drive for the duration of my show. I chose a beautiful silver two-liter Ferrari. I drove it during the gig, and liked it so much that I told Bill I wanted to buy it. He gave me a good deal, and so now I had my second great sports car, after the Dual-Ghia, which I had sold years earlier.

When the gig was over, Judy and I picked the car up at the dealer for the drive to Los Angeles. This was 1964, before people were using seat belts much. But Bill's dealer stressed that with a high-performance car like this, seat belts were essential, so Judy and I strapped ourselves in and off we went, heading down Route 395 for our trip over the mountains.

It was late afternoon when we started, and the weather in the Sierras was cold. A light snow was falling, covering the road. I was going slowly, maybe fifteen miles an hour. I turned the lights on. I wasn't used to driving in the snow and the road felt slippery, so I was being extra careful. We had brought some sandwich ingredients and Cokes along, and Judy was making sandwiches while I was navigating us around a curve in the mountain road. Next thing I knew, the car was sliding. I hadn't seen any ice, but it was obviously there, under the snow. The Ferrari slid up toward the face of the mountain and hung there for a moment. I was thinking, Uh-oh, black ice. I'll bet we hit black ice. Then we slid down and right off the mountainside.

As we went off the side, the car began to tumble. Our heads were banging into each other's as we crashed down the steep drop, rolling over and over. There was no time to think. I grabbed for Judy to try and protect her. I somehow managed to get hold of her arms. I was holding her arms as tight as I could as we slammed into one thing after another, jolting the car again and again and knocking us around, until everything just went black.

Next thing I was aware of, a voice was talking to me, saying, "You'll be all right, you'll be all right. The ambulance is coming."

I could barely hear it. Next to me someone was murmuring, "My arms are broken, my arms are broken."

I heard the voices, but I didn't know who I was or where I was. Or who these people were who were talking to me.

But I was coming around. Judy was next to me, still mostly out, but groaning about her arms. I looked up at the man who was speaking.

"How did you find us?"

"Your tracks in the snow. I was salting the road. I saw the tracks going off the side, so I stopped and looked over. I saw your headlights and called the ambulance from Bishop."

We had rolled down the mountain until the car got wedged between two trees. Somehow it hadn't crushed in. The Ferrari was like a tank, and we were buckled in, which is probably what saved us. It was dark out. I had no idea how long we had been sitting there.

After a while the ambulance arrived. I don't remember how they got us up to the road or anything about the ride to the hospital. But by the time we got there we were both coherent. They treated us for cuts and abrasions and concussions. Judy's arms, it turned out, were not broken, just bruised where I had been gripping them. Everyone said it was a miracle we weren't hurt more seriously. It was amazing we hadn't been killed. But we lost the baby.

It was another two years before we finally had our first, Victoria. Then, in short order, Andrea came along, and then Daniella. We were so happy with these three beautiful little girls, but unfortunately, each pregnancy took a progressively worse toll on Judy's health. The problem was that she had scoliosis, a curvature of the spine. With each pregnancy the scoliosis worsened. And as it worsened, her back gave her more and more pain. Judy was taking increasing amounts of painkillers and tranquilizers to manage this, and other drugs to help her sleep. She was seeing various doctors, and getting prescriptions from each.

As Judy became increasingly preoccupied with the pain, the pressure on our marriage grew. I was worried about her; I was worried about the girls; I was worried about us. I simply did know what to do about my family, especially since my need to make a living had me on the road so much of the time. And it was just then that Sheehan and his scam artists made their appearance. I didn't want to tell Judy in the worst way. How do you tell your wife that you are ruined, and that she's ruined along with you? Especially in a situation like that. But declaring bankruptcy isn't something you can hide, either.

In the end I just faced up to it and told her: "I'm going to have to declare bankruptcy."

"My God," she said, "you're kidding me."

"No, I'm not. I can't believe it myself."

"If that's true, Vic, we can't be married. I need a divorce. I can't be married to a bankrupt."

I knew that wasn't Judy talking, it was the pills, the Darvon and Valium and other medications she was taking. That wasn't the kind of person she was, not underneath.

But whether it was the pills talking or not, that was what happened. We separated, and she sued for divorce. "Irreconcilable differences" was what the divorce papers read. But that said nothing about the real reason. The Sheehans had ruined me in more ways than one. When it was all over, Judy had the big house and the kids. She sold the house to Wilt Chamberlain shortly afterward and moved into a small place in Brentwood. So she had money from that, and she had the alimony and support the court had awarded her. I didn't know how I would pay it, yet I knew somehow I was going to. I had a hard time figuring out how I was going to live from day to day. I was at the lowest point in my life. Lee Iacocca had told me once, after we had been talking about our lives one afternoon, "God, Vic, singing was the easy part." I didn't know then how much harder it could get. How I was going to dig myself out of this, I had no idea.

11

The Famous Sands Health Club

Eleven is exactly the right number for this chapter. When Judy and I divorced I was deep in chapter eleven. The question was, How was I going to get out? My William Morris agents and Milt Ebbins, my manager, were the best in the business; I tended to trust their judgment on how my career should be going. But now I began scrutinizing the business side of things a lot more carefully. And I saw that I could maximize my income by playing the smaller rooms in Las Vegas instead of the main showrooms.

The casinos called them lounges, but if you've been out there you know that they are actually big rooms themselves; they seat seven or eight hundred people. These gigs paid about forty thousand a week, not quite as much as the main rooms. But the advantage was that bookings were for four weeks rather than the week or two at the main rooms. Playing the smaller rooms, I could work Vegas four or even five months a year. I didn't have to spend as much time on the road, so my expenses for musicians and traveling would be a lot less. It gave me more stability, too; my life could be a little more normal. I could get to see my kids more. No, the baby showrooms were definitely the way to go.

These gigs had other advantages, too. The small shows went on at

10:15 P.M. and 2:15 A.M.; the main room entertainers were on at eight and midnight, which meant that the stars who were headlining would often stop by and see my show after they were finished: Sinatra, Dean, Sammy Davis, Steve and Eydie, Don Rickles, Elvis, Streisand. At any given time big names would come in, which always sent a buzz through the audience. Sometimes arranging things properly for them would take a little doing. Sinatra might have fifteen or twenty people with him. Elvis was so big he couldn't be seen in public; he'd drop by my shows incognito. Larry Ruvo, the night manager at the Frontier, was a master at handling the major stars, getting them in and out with the least amount of disruption—no easy trick. Larry's boss there was Steve Wynn; this was before Steve went on to become the great developer of Las Vegas, in essence the modern city's founder.

I always appreciated the headliners who would come to listen. Of course, everybody appreciated those kinds of visits. It was great to know that your friends and colleagues wanted to see you perform. But having Elvis there was something else. He couldn't show his face without causing a riot, which meant he had to make a special effort. He may have felt he owed me, though. One night when I was at Mac Davis's show at the Sands I noticed a couple of guys making advances to Elvis's wife, Priscilla. It was pretty obnoxious. They didn't know who she was; she just looked like some vulnerable, unattached woman. I went over to them and said, "Excuse me, you obviously don't know who this is, do you?"

"No, and what business is it of yours?"

"Fine. I just wanted you to know that this is the wife of one of the major mob bosses. I don't think you want to get too fresh here, if you know what I mean."

"Oh," they said. "Oh, we didn't know." And they backed off quickly.

One night Frank and the Rat Pack crew flew in from Utah, where they were making a movie, *Sergeants* 3. I got a little nervous when I was told backstage that they were all out there. They were performing together then and were pretty wild; in fact, they were opening the next night at the Sands. The whole town was going nuts over them. I thought, Oh, for chrissake, they're going to heckle me mercilessly, or come up onstage or something. But they didn't. They just sat at their table and behaved like good boys.

Dean told me later that Frank had made the arrangements for them to escape early from their movie shoot in Fuck-All, Utah (as one writer put it), where they were practically comatose with boredom. They hadn't known they were coming to my show, though. Frank had just told them they were going to go get a singing lesson. "You're kidding," I said. "No," said Dean. "That's the reason we didn't get up onstage with you." I felt like I had dodged a bullet. I had been wearing a paisley handkerchief with my tux that night. The next night the whole Rat Pack performed at the Sands wearing paisley handkerchiefs with their tuxes. I can't say if my singing had any influence on them, but I'm proud to say that at least my fashion sense did.

Another thing I loved about the smaller room shows was the band. Carl Lodico was the leader. We had all the first trumpets from all the other hotels. All the best musicians would come and play for us. Between their shows they would come and play my show. These guys were truly kick ass. My God, could they play! The first trumpet at the Sands might be playing fourth trumpet with my band. Actually, they would take turns. One show the Riviera's first trumpet would be lead. The next night it might be the Flamingo's first trumpet, next night the Sands's first, next night the Sahara's. These were the top musicians in town; they loved to get together and bounce off each other. The band energy was so high that the shows had a spirit and enthusiasm that just couldn't be matched. I used to introduce each of the musicians by name, the trumpets, the trombones, the saxes. The applause was deafening. Having a band like that was unheard-of. They got me as high as they got the audience.

Since I was in Vegas so much, it only made sense to move out there. Las Vegas became my home, instead of just a place to perform. I got into certain routines. I played golf during the day—to get fresh air, because of breathing in all that smoke at night. I'd get up at noon, have breakfast, then go play a round, often with Joey Bishop, Don Rickles, Buddy Greco, or Andy Williams. Sammy Davis was another partner, and Dean Martin.

Afterward I'd have a bite to eat, then meet Jack Entratter down in the Sands health club to relax before my first show. Entratter was a big guy—earlier in his life he had been a bouncer at the Cocacabana in New York; now he was running entertainment at the Sands. He would get ready for his night by taking a steam bath at the health club where I liked to go. There was a little gym there where I could do a light workout, then get a rubdown, shower, shave, and set myself up for my 10:15 show. From there I'd go straight over to my dressing room at the Flamingo or the Sahara or the Riviera. I'd put on my tuxedo and walk out onstage. I felt great, primed and ready to go. If Jerry Lewis was working, he'd be down there at the same time. That was how the famous Sands health club scene got started. Entratter, Jerry Lewis, and I were the charter members.

Before long a few of the guys I played golf with started to come along, Joey, Rickles, Buddy Greco, maybe one or two others. After golf we might have some dinner together, then duck down to the club. One day Sammy Davis was sitting in the lounge with us, and when we all got up at the same time, he said, "Hey, where are you going?"

"We're going to the health club, Sammy."

"The health club? Where? Why? What do you mean? What do you need to go to a health club for?"

"Well, we get a rubdown, we get a sauna, we get ready."

"Really? But what about your energy, your energy?" Sammy talked fast, in a kind of staccato. "Your energy. Doesn't it drain you? How do you do that, huh? How do you do that?"

"My energy? It's fine. It's great."

"Well, can I come? Can I come?"

"Sure. Come on, Sammy."

"Okay. Here I come. I'm comin' with you."

So Sammy started coming. Then Sinatra heard about it. "Hey," he said, "I like rubdowns, too."

After that Sinatra was there every day at six, along with Dean, who used to box himself and really liked the steam room, rubdown routine. Before long the place had turned into a regular hangout. We'd all be there, the guys who were working Vegas and who liked each other. Nat Cole would come down, Robert Goulet, even Pat Boone came in once—while I was shaving. "Vic," he said, "I'm having trouble with my voice." He had "Vegas throat," which came from sleeping in the direct line of the air conditioning. We started doing scales together standing in front of the mirror, trying to work him through it. Before long Entratter and the health club manager, Neil Leppo, put the place off-limits to anyone else. It became our own private little enclave.

Sinatra, of course, was the natural leader, and at some point he decided we should be more like a real club. Everyone was always there on time, since we all had to get ready for our shows. And one night Sinatra had a bunch of boxes brought in.

"Presents," he said. "Bishop, here's yours." He threw him a box. "Rickles, here's yours." He threw him a box. "Dean, here's yours."

We were thinking, What is this? When we opened the boxes it turned out they were robes, beautiful, thick white robes. And on the back of each robe was something Sinatra thought was appropriate. Rickle's robe had a big rhino's mouth, with the title "Big Mouth." Dean Martin was "Big Dago." I was "Little Dago." Sinatra's read "The Pope." The songwriter Sammy Cahn's said "The Nervous Jew." When we had all gotten our robes, only Sammy Davis had been left out. We were trying them on, laughing at our nicknames, and he had nothing. Sammy looked at Frank like some kind of forlorn puppy. "What about me?" he said. "What about me? I don't see anything for me."

"Just relax," Sinatra said. "I got yours." And he threw him a box. Sammy opened it, and it was a robe—a brown robe.

"What's this?" he said. "Why don't I get a white one?" Then he looked at the back and it said "Smokey."

"Oh, man," Sammy said.

"Wait a minute," said Sinatra. "There's more."

"More? I'm getting more?"

Frank threw him another box. Brown towels, to go with his robe. Then Sinatra threw him another box—brown soap. In case anyone had missed the subtlety of the previous items. Sammy was laughing and laughing. The rest of us were practically falling down.

That kind of joking probably wouldn't pass today, but it was part of the humor of our situation. Frank was an equal-opportunity jokester, and none of it was PC. This group was mostly Italian and Jewish, with Sammy the one black guy. We all gave it to each other. Rickles was so good at it he made it into a career—"The Mouth," as Frank called him. The fact was that Frank couldn't stand racism. He had zero tolerance for it. He brought Billy Eckstine into the Copacabana, breaking the color line there. He broke the segregationist rules of the musicians' unions in L.A.; he raised millions for the NAACP and Martin Luther King. Years later he took care of Sammy's expenses when he was dying. He helped out Sugar Ray Robinson, Redd Foxx, Billy Eckstine, and Joe Louis when they were older and in need. Frank was allowed any kind of joke he wanted, because Sammy and everyone else knew where his heart was.

Not that he couldn't be excessive sometimes, especially about women, that is to say, "broads." The health club was a little like a fraternity house full of adolescent boys. Every night, once we got there, the guys were always talking about broads. Broads, broads, broads. Constantly. This broad and that broad. "You should have seen the broad I saw." "The broad *you* saw? You should have seen the broad *I* saw. The tits on that broad?" "You think that broad had tits? You shoulda seen . . ." And so on. Broads, broads, broads. Nonstop broads.

I finally thought, I'm gonna get these guys. So I called a friend of mine who was the choreographer at the Tropicana. "I want to play a joke," I told him. "Sinatra and those guys are always talking about broads. So I want to get one of your girls to come in. I'll give her fifty bucks"—that was a lot of money then—"fifty bucks, if she'll come into the sauna with me. Walk in nude. That's all she has to do. Walk in, walk out."

"I've got just the girl," he said. "A redhead. Gorgeous. Her body will kill you, and she's fun. She'll enjoy it."

"Okay, have her there at ten after six. I'll set it up with the bell captain at the Sands. He'll bring her the back way to the health club."

I must say, one thing about Sinatra and the guys. Six o'clock came and they were there. Took their clothes off, boom, in the sauna. Right on time.

So, ten after six the door opened, and in walked an unbelievably gorgeous redhead. Jesus, talk about broads. The guys were in the sauna already. I was undressed, but I'm shy, so I had a towel around me. "Okay," she said, "what do I do?"

I gave her the fifty bucks. "Here's what you do. Take your clothes off and we'll walk into the sauna together. All the guys are in there. Sinatra, Sammy Davis, Jack Entratter, Dean Martin. They're all in there. As we walk in we'll talk about the weather. What a beautiful day it's been. No rain. Warm tomorrow. We don't even notice them."

When we walked into the sauna, Sinatra and Sammy Davis jumped up and scrambled out like scared rabbits, practically tripping over each other to run and get towels on. Jack Entratter just sat there. Dean was on the top bench, where it was hottest. He was sitting there looking, and he kept saying, "Beautiful, beautiful. That's so beautiful. Whoa, beautiful."

Then Frank and Sammy came back in, with towels around their waists now, laughing. "You dirty son of a bitch," said Frank.

"Hey, you're always talking about broads, so I thought I might as well bring one in so you could see what they actually look like."

I had told my friend at the Tropicana that I just wanted the girl to walk in and walk out, but now I couldn't get rid of her. She was having the time of her life, showing off for Sinatra and Dean and the others. She wouldn't leave. We went to take a shower, and she started washing Jack Entratter's back. "Hey, I thought you were leaving," I said, but it didn't seem to have any effect. Entratter didn't seem to mind, either.

We all had a great time there, me especially. All the guys would run to do their shows in the main rooms at eight, but I wasn't on till 10:15, so I'd stick around and enjoy myself. I'd break their *cugliones* as they were hustling to get out. "Where you going, guys? Hey, where you going? Why don't you hang around a little, enjoy yourselves?"

Of course, I was still working at two A.M., when they were all through. They would come in and see my show. Or, if the schedule allowed, we'd all go to see Rickles's late show at the Sahara. We'd walk in, and Rickles would say, "Oooh, the big shots are here, the big stars. Oooh, big, big. You sons of bitches, who let you in here? Frank, Frank, listen, I just heard your friend Vinnie Bombaloni got hit by a truck. I'm so sorry, Frank. Vic Damone. Hi, Vic. How's Maria? You find her yet?" I had had a big hit with the song "Maria" from *West Side Story*. Rickles would start running from one side of the stage to another. "Maria? Maria? Maria?" Looking high and low. "Vic, Jesus. Can't find her anywhere, huh?"

Rickles picked on everybody; he was a nondisciminatory ball breaker. Funny thing was that Rickles was and still is the sweetest man you'd ever meet. There never was a kinder human being. But onstage he was brutal. We worked together a number of times. Sometimes he'd open for me, sometimes I'd open for him. He got to be a huge draw, especially after Jack Benny began talking him up. Everyone who went to see him knew what to expect. When I opened for him I'd look down at the audience. If there was a heavy person near the front, I'd say, "You know, I just saw Don before coming out, and he's in a bad mood. Really bad. I'm telling you, he was walking his rat back there. He's in a *bad* mood." And the audience would go, "Ooooh." They knew what was coming. They were primed. "You are really in trouble," I'd say. "Maybe you should think about leaving before he gets out here." "Ooooohhh." Rickles would insult everyone in sight. "Sir? You look Italian. Are you Italian? Yes? Sorry, sir. No Italians in here tonight. FBI! Sir?"

At the Basin Street East in New York, where Don and I were both working at one point, we were having dinner together. His mother, Etta, was with us, whom he loved, whom we all loved. We were talking about religion, and Don started giving it to me about Baha'is—in his own inimitable fashion. Kidding, of course.

We were both staying at a hotel across the street from the club. And that morning at two A.M. there was a knock on my door. It was Rickles. Standing there with his head down.

"Don, what's the matter?"

"I'm so sorry, Vic."

"Sorry? Sorry about what?"

"My mother is angry at me. She thinks I was rude to you about your religion, and I came to apologize."

"For God's sake, you don't have to apologize. You didn't say it out of meanness. I know that. I love you, Don. You know that."

"Yes, but I was out of order, and I apologize."

Rickles and I have stayed good friends over the years, and just the other night—this is March 2008, while I'm in the middle of writing this book—Rickles called. He's still performing at age eighty. He said that he was sitting around with his wife, Barbara, talking about the entertainers we knew back then, and he wanted to call and tell me how he felt about my singing—which really touched me after all these years. And then he said, "Vic, you remember what I said about Baha'is? Vic, I apologize. I apologize! I was so wrong!"

There was a wonderful camaraderie among the performers then. When I was sick with the flu while I was working the Flamingo, Sammy Davis came over and did my shows. I did the same for Steve Lawrence. But it wasn't just us; people would do that for each other.

Sammy, of course, could stand in for anybody, no matter what their act was. Sammy Davis Jr. might have been the greatest performer who ever lived. He could sing, dance, mimic, do comedy—he was a great comedian. He could do it all. And he did it all with frenetic energy. He was a whirlwind.

I told him once, "Sammy, I see you onstage, I just cannot believe all the things you do."

"Yeah," he said. "I do about ten different things. But you know what? I'd give eight of them back if I could sing like you . . . but I'd keep two." I don't think anybody ever gave me a bigger compliment. I wondered which two he'd keep.

I'm glad Sammy liked my singing. There were a lot of singers I liked myself, and being based in Las Vegas now, I got to hear some of them more often.

Andy Williams was one. I loved Andy's voice. It was mellifluous, always so rich and full and beautiful. I couldn't imitate him. Jack Jones—I always thought Jack was a great singer, great musicality. Steve Lawrence also has great musical command and a smooth vocal quality. He always had a wonderful sense of humor, too; he's an excellent comic, loves to tell stories. He sings everything extremely well, but you'd always wait for him to hit you with something funny. Not that he doesn't do serious things, too. I've been listening to Steve and Eydie for years. Eydie Gorme is a terrific singer herself. They were back then, and still are today, two of my closest friends.

Tony Martin was another favorite of mine. I used to listen to him on the radio as a kid. If there was someone other than Frank who made a major impression on me back then, it was Tony. What a wonderful, powerful singer. Dean's voice had an interesting quality, too. Dean Martin—a characteristic earthiness and resonance. Many people think Dean modeled himself on Bing Crosby or Perry Como, but his real model was Harry Mills, the Mills Brothers' baritone. If you listen to any Mills Brothers songs where Harry solos, you'll hear the resemblance in an instant. I liked Jerry Vale, too, especially his renditions of the old Italian favorites. There was a period when I also enjoyed listening to Tony Bennett. He was fun onstage. He always acknowledged his musicians. We all did, of course, but he was especially careful about that. He'd also mention the songwriters, This is a Harold Arlen song, or a George Gershwin. It was very nice of him to always credit them.

Sometimes in Vegas we would go out and socialize with the fans on the gambling floor. We'd tell the pit bosses, "Hey, let us deal," and they'd let us stand in for blackjack dealers, Frank, Dean, Joey, myself, Nat King Cole, Jerry Lewis. Dean had been a real dealer in his younger days, so he was especially smooth out there. We loved to do it. It was a lot of fun, and it broke the Vegas monotony. I mean, how much gambling can you do yourself? And if you were married, you didn't want to fool around. Of course, the fans got a huge kick out of playing with us, even though the stakes were limited to five bucks a hand. The managers didn't want to chance someone breaking the bank on us. The main object was to let the guests have a good time. If they were playing with me, I'd try hard to make them win.

One way of doing that was that when I was dealing blackjack I'd let them see my hole card, so they'd know what I had.

One hand I remember in particular. I had a picture card up and another in the hole—two picture cards—which everyone at the table saw. One tourist lady had sixteen, and I asked her if she wanted a hit.

"No," she said.

I turned my cards over so she could see them better. Two picture cards.

"Now do you want a hit?"

"Nope."

"Lady, look. See what I got? Look, two picture cards."

"Yes? So what?"

"So you want a hit, right?"

"No."

"Why?"

"Well, I don't want to go over."

"But I've got twenty."

"I don't want the card!"

My relationship with Sinatra, of course, went back many years, but being in Vegas for such long stretches, I got to see more of him than when I was living in Los Angeles. He had been my model and my mentor when I was young, but even now there were things I learned from him.

There was a place in the health club where there were a few cots, where you could take a little nap if you wanted. When Frank wasn't working we'd sit there talking about singing, and about life in general. He always wanted to know about me, about whether I was happy. "How you doing? You okay? How's your voice, pretty good?" And we'd talk about the mechanics of it. If there were any problems, we'd talk about them and how to work through them.

I knew the stories about how Frank had learned about breath control from Tommy Dorsey. But he also worked hard to develop his lungs. He would go to an indoor pool during the day and swim underwater to see how long he could hold his breath, then let the air out little by little, which is what you're supposed to do when you sing. When he first started he could only go halfway across the pool. Later he could swim up and back before he had to take a breath. I never did that, but listening to Frank I became much more conscious of breath control, and developed my own little exercises to help sustain an even exhale that enabled me to support my notes better.

Frank talked about the importance of diction, too. He insisted that you should always finish your words. Don't slur the end. Hit those last consonants. Afterward I'd listen to some of my early recordings and hear that I was not doing that, I was not finishing the words. Then I'd listen to Sinatra records or watch him onstage, and I'd hear the clarity of his enunciation. Valuing each word like that helped give his singing its emotional depth. It magnified the feeling of the lyrics and could change an ordinary rhyme into poetry. That was part of his magic.

For me, though, Frank's greatest lessons were about emotional memory. He was the great master of the art of singing as storytelling. The way he got you, the listener, to believe his story, to invest yourself in it and in him, was the emotional authenticity he put into his singing. Frank's true genius was interpreting the mood of the song. And he did that by living the song. Nobody came close to him in that regard.

Maybe the best of so many examples, at least for me, is in the movie he did with Gene Kelley, *Anchors Aweigh.* At one point in the movie Sinatra meets the little kid, and the kid has to go to sleep. So Sinatra sings him to sleep with "Lullaby and Goodnight." Listening to him sing that song is like hearing it for the first time. Singing that, or something like "I Fall in Love Too Easily, I Fall in Love Too Fast," you know he is singing directly out of his own life.

The songs themselves, the best of them, anyway, come out of the depths of the songwriter's experience. I'm thinking of Ruth Lowe's "I'll Never Smile Again," the hauntingly beautiful song she wrote after her husband died. And if a song comes from a deeply felt event in the writer's life, it deserves to be sung with the same intensity of emotion that went into its creation. That's great singing. That's what Sinatra did. And the way he accessed his feeling was through emotional memory, by drawing on memories of deeply felt moments in his own life.

We talked about these things in the Sands health club, after all the male horsing around was over and the others had left. And I learned from him, even after having been a professional singer myself for twenty-five-plus years. Of course, by then I had been through plenty of my own ups and downs—and I was to experience more of them, too—so I had the maturity to understand what Frank was talking about. You don't just sing a song and think, Gee, this lyric is good, the melody is nice. No, you relive a moment in your life that fits that lyric. You think about your children, you think about your loves, your exhilaration, your heartbreak and loss. You use your emotional memory. Sinatra sang "It Never Entered My Mind" after his breakup with Ava Gardner. He didn't just sing that. His heart talked it. That's why it was so magnificent. His peculiar gift was not just his voice, not nearly just his voice. It was his unique emotional makeup, and his ability to translate his deepest personal feelings into song. That's what made him the best popular singer we have ever had.

12

So, I Tee'd the Ball Up and Said to Jack Benny, George Burns, and Ben Hogan . . .

"With Vic it's more than a love of golf. It's a passion. He's out on the course almost every day. He plays in the afternoon and fights the sun, trying to get in eighteen holes or even more before it gets pitch dark. As often as not he's out there by himself, practicing. But he's enjoying it as much as when he's playing with a foursome. Among entertainers who are also golfers, I'd put him in the top ten; out of a hundred, he'd be about number ten. Jim Garner, Mac Davis. R. J. Wagner, Don Cherry—Don Cherry's an extraordinary player. I'd have to put Cherry at number one."

That's Frank Chirkanian talking, a good golfing buddy of mine. Frank is golf's big daddy, the man who figured out how to make golf a television sport; he produced the Masters Tournament for CBS for almost forty years. There's nothing Frank doesn't know about the game, and no one over the last half century he hasn't been on a first-name basis with. I can't say if he's right about where I might fit among entertainers who golf, though I have had seven holes-in-one in my life, which is right up there for amateurs.

I can't understand why Frank would include Cherry, though. Don Cherry's an entertainer, that's correct—he's had some big hit songs, including "Band of Gold." The man can sing. But he's not exactly an amateur golfer; Cherry's pro level, for God's sake. He was on three Walker Cup teams, two America's Cup teams. He's played in eight Masters and almost won the U.S. Open one year—so I don't think he should be in there with the rest of us.

I've known Don Cherry for more than fifty years. We first met when I was in the army. This was 1953. I had come back from Germany and was winding up my tour of duty at Fort Sam Houston in San Antonio, Texas. I was singing with the army band there and even managed to get away for a few days to do some recording. I had been in for two years and was eager to get back onstage, so I was soaking up every bit of news I could get about bands, singers, records, everything. And somehow I heard there was a singer who was also a big-time golfer, who was going to be playing in the Texas Open. A singer who was also a top-level golfer? I loved golf. This singer/golfer's name was Don Cherry. I wanted to meet him.

Since the Texas Open was going to start in a few days, locating him wasn't difficult. All the pros were gathering and playing at the various local clubs. I found out where Cherry was and went off to introduce myself. "I'm looking for Don Cherry," I said to somebody at the club I'd been directed to. "Cherry?" the guy said. "That's him getting ready to tee off. The bald guy over there."

Cherry was playing that day with Mike Souchak, one of the great pro tour players; Doug Ford, another champion; and Al Besselink, also a top-flight tour player. I walked over and introduced myself. "Vic Damone?" Cherry said. He knew who I was, of course. He was an aspiring, up-and-coming singer, and when I went into the army I had been pretty hot. He hadn't just heard of me, Cherry told me; he had my records. Not only that, he used to listen to my *Saturday Night Serenade* radio show. He was as happy to meet me as I was to meet him. But he had to tee off. He introduced me to Souchak, Ford, and Bessalink, who were waiting to start.

"I understand," I said. "Would you mind if I follow along with you?"

"No, not at all." They were fine with that.

They teed off. They were playing for money, of course. Souchak and Cherry against Bessalink and Ford. This was high-level golf for pretty high stakes. As we walked down the first fairway—this was before golf carts—Cherry and I talked about singing, about songs, who was writing, who was singing, where they were performing. And despite all the music talk, Cherry parred the first hole.

The second hole he bogeyed. Then he bogeyed three and four. That didn't put a dent in our discussion, though; he just kept talking. But when he bogeyed the fifth hole, Souchak, his partner, came over to him. It's worth noting for the nongolfers that Mike Souchak went on to have fifteen PGA tour wins and was on the American Ryder Cup team twice.

"Hey, Don," Souchak said. "This is ridiculous. We're playing for a lot of money here, and you're talking music. Get back to golf. Come on."

"Please keep walking with us," Cherry said to me. "But I can't talk anymore. I have to pay attention now."

So Cherry paid attention. And he birdied the next five holes in a row. Then he turned to Souchak and said, "Now can I talk music with him?"

"Yes," said Souchak. "Yes. Go ahead. Please."

Before I went into the army I had been dating Joan Benny, Jack Benny and Mary Livingstone's daughter. We had kept in touch while I was in Germany, and when I got back to Fort Sam Houston I'd visit her in Hollywood any time I could get leave. Since I had no place to stay, Jack and Mary invited me to be a guest at their house whenever I came up.

One time I was there and Jack was on the road somewhere. "Instead of staying in the guest room," Mary said, "why don't you sleep in Jack's bedroom. It's more comfortable." Mary and Jack had separate bedroom suites. I was a little awed. I was going to sleep in Jack Benny's bed. "This is where you'll stay," Mary said, showing me the room. "Here's the bedroom, and here's the bathroom."

We walked into Jack's bathroom, and there was a music stand in the middle of the floor.

"Mary," I said, "that's a music stand."

"I know."

"Well, why is it in the bathroom?"

"Why is it in the bathroom? It's in the bathroom because that's the only place Jack's allowed to practice his violin."

"What?"

"Right. And the door has to be closed!"

I'm not sure how much Jack Benny may have loved the violin; enough so that he practiced in the bathroom, anyway. But what he did love, almost to distraction, was golf. In addition to his house in Hollywood, Jack had a place in Palm Springs, where he was a member of the Tamarisk Country Club.

I was a member there, too. I used to go down and play with Mervyn Leroy, a famous director I'd met at Metro—he did *30 Seconds Over Tokyo, Mr. Roberts, Quo Vadis,* and many others.

"Are you a member?" Mervyn asked.

"No."

"You have to be, no buts," he said.

"But I don't know if I can afford it."

"I said no buts. Of course you can."

So I became a member. The fee then was three hundred dollars. I don't know what it is now; probably more than half a million.

I had gotten friendly with Jack Benny initially when he and George Burns came to hear me sing a couple of times at the Mocambo. Mary and Gracie Allen, George's wife, were along with them, and Joanie came, too—my memory is that that was how she and I met and started going out.

When I'd go to Palm Springs to see Joanie and play golf with Jack, I'd stay in their house there as well. George and Gracie were constant companions of the Bennys, and every night we'd all have dinner together.

Ben Hogan was the golf pro at Tamarisk then, and he and Benny loved each other. The two men had a tremendous mutual admiration and respect, and they played golf together regularly. When I was there, I made a third, and George Burns would always come along with us, even though he wasn't a golfer. He and Benny were practically inseparable.

One day we went to play and Jack and George were hungry. I had eaten already, so I told them to go have lunch. I'd go to the driving range and wait for them there.

I started hitting balls at the range, and I saw that Hogan was also hitting balls, from his private area on the far end, a special area the club had put aside for him that was always roped off. No one else was on the range, just Hogan and I. But when Hogan was in the roped-off section, all the members knew they were not allowed to talk to him or disturb him in any way. So I knew he was there, but that was it. No hellos, no how are yous, no nods of recognition. Ben Hogan was in his zone.

But as respectful as I was being, just attending to my own drives, I still managed to bother him. More accurately, my drives bothered him. He was watching the way I was hitting, and after about fifteen minutes he just could not stand it any longer. He simply could not bear the way I was driving the ball. Apparently I wasn't making a full back turn. That is, I wasn't turning my shoulders adequately. So my drives were fading, as they will if you don't have the power of your shoulders behind them. And Ben Hogan could simply not bear to stand there and watch me hit the ball that way. It was beyond his tolerance level.

On the other hand, Ben Hogan did not teach. That was the hard and fast rule, his and Tamarisk's. He was Tamarisk's pro, but that was just a title. He had his desk there, his office. He took care of his business. He played the course with his friends. But nobody would ever think of imposing on him for pointers or, God forbid, lessons. After all, the man was a legend. Maybe the greatest golfer ever, up till then at least, and still today revered by Jack Nicklaus and Tiger Woods. He was also reserved by nature, not to mention that he and his wife had just barely survived a horrible head-on collision with a Greyhound bus several years back, and even though he still won tournament after tournament, he suffered chronic leg problems. The doctors had told him after the accident that he might never walk again, that he would for sure never play golf. But the man was so utterly determined that he worked on his body until he had brought himself back to the game, and to dominate the game. All of which meant that people gave Ben Hogan lots of space, as well as respect bordering on reverence.

But Hogan needed so badly to correct my swing that he could hardly control himself—except that he didn't teach anybody, ever. Categorically. So he stuck his club in his golf bag and walked past me, never said hello, never said anything, never made eye contact. Except that as he walked by he balled up both fists in frustration and hissed through his clenched teeth: "Turn, goddamnit. Turn."

Hanging out with Jack, I got to know Hogan well. They played together, and I played with them. One day we were out and we got to a par three, a short hole. I was twenty-three, twenty-four years old at the time, and kind of cocky. Not rude, I was never rude, but I was a young, hot singer—I was cocky. We were in our usual foursome,

Hogan, Jack Benny, myself, and George Burns. George Burns never played, but he always came along with us, walking—as I said, this was before carts—and kibbitzing. "Jesus," he'd say, "do you guys stink." Not to Hogan, of course. Hogan would tee up, and George would say to us, "You two are awful. Terrible. Why don't you pay attention to this guy for a change."

So we were on a par three. Jack Benny hit first, as always. Then it was my turn. Hogan always hit last. After Jack hit I put my ball down, but instead of placing it on a tee, I dropped it on the ground. I was moving the ball around with my club to find a nice spot to hit from, on the ground, not on a tee. A cocky thing to do. I must have I thought I was being cool.

As I was pushing the ball around, Hogan walked over to me.

"Hold it, hold it, hold it!"

He put his face right up next to mine.

"My name," he said, "is Ben Hogan. I'm a professional golfer. I'm a tour player. I've won a lot of tournaments." In a controlled voice. Quiet, but with an edge. All this with his face inches from mine.

"When I play a par three," he said quietly, "I tee the ball up." Then he screamed: *"Tee it up!"*

Jesus. He scared the crap out of me. "Okay," I said. "Okay, Ben."

Jack and George were laughing so hard they almost wet their pants.

Every night I was there we'd go to dinner, Ben and his wife, Valerie; Jack and Mary Livingstone; George and Gracie; Joanie and me. Ben just loved Jack, and he was good friends with George, too. Me he could probably have done without, but I did my best to fit in.

Whenever we went to dinner, Hogan would always come to the Bennys' house. One night the doorbell rang, and I went to get it. Something was wrong with Jack. He seemed very depressed. Not talking to anyone. Just down. Sitting there in the living room by himself, holding his head in his hands. I don't know that he even heard the doorbell. He had gotten dressed to go to dinner and was waiting for the Hogans and George and Gracie, but he was in a silent, dejected mood for some reason. I'd never seen him like that.

I opened the door. "Hi, Ben. Hi, Valerie."

"Hi, Vic. Is Jack ready?"

"Ben, something's wrong. I don't know what it is. Jack is very depressed."

"Really? Why?"

"I dunno. Maybe you could cheer him up. He's not talking. He's just sitting by himself in the living room."

So we went into the living room. Jack looked up and saw Ben. Ben said, "C'mon Jack, let's go eat."

"No," Jack said. "I don't think I can eat anything tonight."

"Why?" said Ben. "What's the matter with you?"

"Well." Pause. "I've lost it, Ben. I've lost it."

"What, Jack? You've lost what?"

"I've lost my swing."

"You lost your what?"

"I lost my golf swing. I'll never play golf again."

"Get outta here," said Ben. "You're crazy."

"No. I'll never play again. I stink. It's over for me."

"Jack," said Ben. "What are you talking about? What do you mean, you lost your swing?"

Jack was such a sweet man. He looked up at the ceiling with his big, sad eyes. Anyone who remembers Jack Benny's TV show can picture this. He just lifted his eyes to the ceiling.

"I used to have such a beautiful swing," he said. "I knew exactly what I wanted to do. I had a vision of it in my head. But I can't see the picture anymore, Ben. I've lost the picture. And I'll never play golf again. Never."

"Jack, please. You and I play almost every day. We're playing tomorrow."

"No, Ben. It's over for me. It's all over."

We were all looking at each other. I was trying to smother my laughter. But Jack was serious. He was devastated. He had lost the picture.

"Okay," said Ben. "That's it!" He took off his jacket and laid it carefully on a chair. Hogan was meticulous about his clothes. "All right," he said. "You have a golf club here? Anything. Just bring me a club."

Jack practically jumped out of his chair. "Yes. Yes I do, Ben." He left and came back a moment later with a club, a six iron.

Ben Hogan took the club and sat down on the edge of a chair, with his back straight. Slowly, gently, he began swinging the club back and forth, back and forth, back and forth. Right left, right left, right left. And as he was swinging it he started getting up, still swinging, rising slowly from the chair. And as he raised up the swing got bigger and bigger and bigger and bigger, until he was standing all the way up, and he swung the club exactly as if he were teeing off . . . and as he finished his swing, he stopped dead still. He held the club there just like that, an image frozen in time. The greatest golfer in the game, acknowledged even today as having one of the most perfectly balanced swings in golf history, frozen at the finish of his swing.

"There's the picture, Jack. You see it? That's the picture! And that's the last time I'm showing it to you! Now, let's go eat."

George Burns had a weird kind of effect on Jack Benny. George always had this twinkle in his eye and a smile on his face, as if he had just that moment heard something really funny, or maybe he was on the verge of telling you something really funny, maybe some hilarious old vaudeville joke. And, of course, the effect was enhanced by the big cigar he was never without, puffing on it or flicking the ashes. George might have actually been thinking about something else altogether, what he was going to have for dinner or something. But whatever he was thinking, his look said that something funny was about to happen. And that look never failed to break Jack Benny up. Never. If Jack was standing there and George Burns turned to look at him, Jack would start laughing. George would do nothing at all—and Jack would just crack up.

At one point we all had to go to a funeral in Palm Springs. Jack was distraught. The man who died had been a good friend of his and Mary's. The limousine was waiting for us outside of Jack's house. And Jack said, "George, George." Very somberly. "George, this is serious."

"Yes, Jack. I know."

The deceased had been a friend of George's also.

"George, please, no joking around. This is just awful, terrible. When we go in there, please, please don't do anything to make me laugh."

"Jack, of course. He was my friend, too. What do mean, laugh? There's nothing to laugh about here."

"Okay," said Jack. "Let's remember that, please. Do we understand each other?"

"Yes, Jack. Jesus. Of course. Let's just go, okay?"

So we went. I walked into the funeral hall first with Joanie and Gracie and Mary. The place was full, all of the family and friends. Jack and George walked in behind us. Everyone sat down, Joanie and me and Mary and Jack in one row, George and Gracie sitting behind us. We weren't in there two minutes when Jack turned around to say something to George. He looked at him, and suddenly he started laughing. He had to run out of the place. Literally. He just ran out of the funeral hall, trying to choke down his laughter. And

George said to Gracie, "What did I do? What did I do? I didn't do anything. I swear."

We all had to get up and leave. Jack was out on the street, laughing hysterically and beating his hand against the limo. "Gracie," George said. "Really, I didn't do anything. It's not my fault!"

I have to say, it was more than George's look that gave him that effect. The fact was that he *was* always telling jokes, or singing songs, in that low-pitched guttural voice of his: "Rararara, ba dib a di da bum." Songs I never heard of, from vaudeville, which I'm sure Jack knew—Jack's original stage act had been musical, with his violin, not comic. I think George actually thought he could sing. He'd start one of these things and Jack would be on the floor.

Jack and George probably associated those ancient jokes and songs with long-forgotten comedians and singers from the old, old days. Which was what made them so funny—to them. And what made them so funny to others was watching the two of them, and what they did to each other. You simply could not have a bad time when you were with Jack Benny and George Burns. Or with Gracie Allen and Mary Livingstone, who were both extremely funny people in their own right.

George Burns wasn't the only one who sang on the golf course. I'm still amazed when I think of all the golfers who felt they needed to sing, at least, if they were playing with me. Starting with Clark Gable.

Actually, Clark Gable didn't sing for me on the golf course. He just talked about his singing. Anna Pierangeli and I had moved to a house next to the Bel Air Country Club, and I had applied for membership. When you do that they give you a two-week guest card while they're considering your application. If they turn you down, at least you've had two weeks playing the golf course.

So I didn't miss a day. Every morning I'd be there at nine o'clock to play, usually by myself. But one morning the starter, who tells people when to begin playing, came up to me and said, "Mr. Damone, there's a member here who wants to play. Would you mind playing with him?"

"Not at all. I'd like to meet all the members."

And Clark Gable walked up. "How are you?" he said. "Nice to see you. You're at the studio, aren't you"—in his deep Clark Gable voice. "You're a helluva singer, a helluva singer. You know, I sing, too. Did a musical once."

So I played nine holes with Clark Gable. I was glancing around to see who could see me there with him. I wanted people to know that I was golfing with him. But there wasn't a soul around. Meanwhile, all Gable wanted to tell me about was his singing. He wasn't a bad golfer. Not a great golfer, but not bad. To this day I don't know what kind of singer he might have been.

Tom Watson was, and still is, a great golfer. He won eight major championships in the seventies and eighties and, I believe, was the PGA tour's top money maker for a number of years. He was ranked number one in the world for a time and was Jack Nicklaus's great rival.

I was playing with him in the Las Vegas Invitational, the Pro-Am, and he said, "You know, I sing, too."

"Really?"

"Yes. Every Christmas my wife and I go out caroling."

This was in Las Vegas. It must have been 110 degrees on the course, and we were walking down the fairway singing Christmas carols together.

Jim Demaret was another all-time golfer who just had to sing. When I lived in Houston he made me an honorary member of the Champions' Golf Club. I played with him regularly there, and he never failed to launch into some serenade. "Okay," he'd say, his eyes lighting up. We'd be a couple of holes in and he'd say. "Okay, let's sing."

"Jimmy, come on. I want to play golf."

"Sure. Of course . . . but let's sing while we're playing."

And he'd launch into one of the old standard love songs. He had a very nice voice, too.

Jimmy introduced me to Gene Sarazen, who was one of five players to win all four majors, along with Ben Hogan, Gary Player, Jack Nicklaus, and Tiger Woods. Demaret had invited me to play in a new tournament they were holding in Austin, the Mutual of Omaha's Legends Tournament. This was the very beginning of the Champions Tour—the senior tour. I played in the first and second one. And that first tournament I was playing with Gene Sarazen, who was quite a bit older by that time; he had won his tournaments back in the twenties and thirties. Sarazen had actually invented the sand iron.

He and I were introduced, but Sarazen didn't hear my name, or more probable, he hadn't heard of me, so it didn't register. He had no idea if I was a singer or a car salesman or what. When we had finished the eighteen holes, I asked him if there was anything in my swing he thought I should work on.

"Yes," he said. "If you move your right hand under just a little bit more, I would do that."

"Just that little thing?"

"Yep, that's what I would do."

"Thanks, Mr. Sarazen," I said. "Thanks very much for your help."

Now, Demaret had asked me when he invited me to play if I would mind singing a couple of songs at the big dinner for all the golfers. So that night Demaret introduced me, and I went up onstage to sing. I did the first song, and there was Gene Sarazen sitting right out there in front, and he's looking at me, his golf partner that day, as if to say, What are you doing up there? What did you say your name was?

While I was singing I caught his eye and winked. He was smiling to beat the band. He had been playing with the evening's entertainer and hadn't even known it. After I finished, while people were applauding, I looked at Sarazen and put my hands together as if I were holding a golf club, looking right at him. Then I turned my right hand a little bit and said, "How's this, Gene?"

"That's it!" he said. "That's it!"

What a privilege it was to play with guys like Tom Watson, Jimmy Demaret, and Gene Sarazen, not to mention Ben Hogan. For someone as in love with golf as I am, playing with such people is like a baseball addict getting to play ball with Mickey Mantle, Willie Mays, and Joe DiMaggio. I played with other greats too, in Pro-Am tournaments and charity fund-raisers—with Sam Snead, Lee Trevino, Jack Nicklaus, and Ken Venturi. Ken Venturi, I can tell you, is a very ballsy guy. I was at a club one night with him in Chicago. They had a pretty good trio going, and they asked if I would sing a song or two. "Thanks," I said, "I'd love to. I'm here with my buddy, Ken Venturi, and our wives." After I sang they said, "Ken Venturi. Hey, Ken, why don't *you* get up and sing?" They were kidding. But Kenny said, "Okay." And he not only sang, he got the drummer out of his seat and started playing drums. He wasn't bad, either. Who knew?

I played Sam Snead once in something called Celebrity Golf. This was a televised series in which Snead played nine holes against various celebrities, a thousand dollars going to cancer research in the name of the winner. Snead's opponents included Perry Como, Bob Hope, Jerry Lewis, Dean Martin, and others.

Sam Snead was Hogan's great contemporary, another of golf's all-time bests. Like Hogan, he was known for his perfect swing. Before we started he asked me what my handicap was. "Thirteen, Mr. Snead." My handicap tended to fluctuate all over the place, depending on how much I was able to play. Just then I was doing two shows a night at the Sands, not getting to bed before four in the morning, and not playing nearly as much as I'd like. "Fine," he said. "Do you want to play the front nine or the back?" "Can we play the back side?" I said. I knew there was an out-of-bounds on the right on the first hole—this was at the Desert Inn. I didn't want to take any chances. I mean, I was playing the great Sam Snead, and they were filming it. "Okay," he said. "The back nine. I'll give you seven shots."

Playing the back nine, we started off at the tenth hole, which I parred. "What did you say your handicap was?" Snead asked. That was all he said until we got to the seventeenth hole (our eighth), the one with water off to the right. I was doing well; with my handicap I was playing him even up. As I was thinking about my shot, Snead came up and pointed down the fairway. "Watch aht for the wohtah," he said, in his Virginia mountain twang. Needless to say, that's exactly where I put my drive, right directly into the water. With the penalty stroke to get out, I lost to him by one. As Chirkinian says, a friendly game of golf is an oxymoron.

Another actual singer I played with was Mike Douglas, which many fans of his TV talk show may not have known about him. I didn't discover Mike, but I did play a role in starting him off on his career, and that had to do with golf, too.

I was working at Lake Tahoe, at the Cal Neva—this was in 1960—golfing during the day, as usual. Hitting balls on the range one afternoon, I noticed another guy hitting balls, obviously a good player. We saw each other on the range for a couple of days and then introduced ourselves. "Want to play?" I said. "You've got a great swing." "Sure," he said. "Yours isn't bad either. Let's go play."

We played together that day, then the next. When I asked what he did, he said, "Oh, I'm a singer."

"Really? Where are you singing?"

"In a bar. Right around the corner from where you are."

"Why didn't you tell me this? I'm a singer, you're a singer."

"No need to mention it," he said. "We both love golf. We're out here doing what we like."

So we got to be buddies, and I went to see him. He was wonderful, a good singer, good-looking guy, very bright. I didn't know then that he had a strong singing background. He had been a vocalist for Kay Kyser's band—Kay Kyser, the "Ol' Professor of Swing" who had been very popular until he had just quit and left the scene about ten years earlier. Mike had done other things, too, including furnishing the voice for Prince Charming in Walt Disney's *Cinderella*. Not that he made a big deal out of any of this. In fact, I didn't even find out about it until years later.

One day on the golf course Mike said he wanted to talk to me about something. Could he see me between my shows?

So that evening, after my first show, we got together. His wife, Ginny, had come along with him. "Vic," he said, "I have to make a big decision."

"What's the decision?"

"I was offered a job, a TV talk-show host thing."

"Well, would you be able to sing?"

"Yes."

"Good. Because you're a good singer. Could you have your own musicians?"

"Yes."

"So? What's wrong with it? Why don't you want to take it?"

"It's in Cleveland, for chrissakes."

"Well, I don't give a damn where it is. I think you should take it."

And Ginny said, "I told him that. But he used to be a teacher. He wants to go back to teaching."

"Mike," I said, "give me a break."

"No," he said. "Give *me* a break. Cleveland? I don't want to go to Cleveland."

"Mike—take it!"

"You really think?"

"Yes. Take the damned thing. You'll be singing, for God's sakes. You'll be on television, you'll have your own show. You'll have your guests. You're very smart. You'll be a great host."

"You really think so?"

"I'm telling you, take it!"

He took it. After a year his show was a big hit, first locally in Cleveland, then nationally. After that the network moved it to Philadelphia and Mike became a major star, winning a number of Emmys and staying high up in the ratings year after year. He used to have guest cohosts, who would be with him for a week. He called me and asked me to be his first cohost. After that I used to be on two or three times a year. All that from playing golf. He was a first-rate player, too, a three- or four-point handicap, someone who never lost his love for the game. I remember that he had Tiger Woods on when Tiger was three years old, demonstrating what was already a freakishly mature swing. We lost Mike a few years ago, which was a real sorrow for me and his many other friends. I didn't know the circumstances, but Ginny apparently told the press that he had become seriously dehydrated out on a golf course.

Among all the people I've played with through the years, a number were especially frequent partners and especially good friends: Andy Williams, John Williams, James Garner, Mac Davis, George Scott, Bob Newhart, Don Rickles—Bob Newhart and Don have been the closest lifetime buddies, both of them wonderful guys.

Pierre Crossette, who produced the Grammys. Peter Falk, who in real life comes across just like his famous detective character. All he needs is a raincoat.

More recently I've played a good deal with Gene Hackman, whom I met on the Las Campanas course in Santa Fe. Gene has always been one of my very favorite actors, and golfing together led to a close friendship. I'll tell you what a competitor the man is. One day we were part of a foursome and we played a skin game on the last hole—that is, a separate bet on who could win that hole. This was for high stakes—five dollars, I think, or maybe ten. The first time, we both parred, so it was a tie. The second time, too. "Damn," Gene said. "Let's play it again." Three times we had to go back. The man simply likes to win. I understand that. So do I.

That was for five or ten dollars. I played a lot of golf with Perry Como, too, and with Perry the bet was always a quarter a hole. Before we teed off he'd always say, "You got your quarters?"

"Why?

"Because every hole I win, I want my quarter."

"Well, you got your quarters?"

"Yes, I've got two quarters."

"Why only two?"

"Because I don't plan to lose. But you better have a lot of them. In fact, I want to see them." Perry would not play with you until you had actually shown him your quarters.

Perry was an excellent golfer. At one point he was a five handicap. The fact was he did win a lot of quarters, and some of them from me.

Perry and I used to play at Ballen Isle in Palm Beach with a fellow who was a pro there, Harry Pazzullo. All the old pros will remember him. Pazzullo played a lot with Bing Crosby. He taught Humphrey Bogart.

One day Pazzullo asked me, "How well did you know Bogart?"

"Well," I said, "I only met him once."

"Oh, he was a hell of a guy. A hell of a guy."

"Well, he was Bogey."

"By the way," said Harry. "Bogey. You know who gave him that name, don't you?"

"Bogey, from Bogart."

"No way. They didn't call him Bogey because his name was Bogart. I played with him every day and he'd bogey every hole. So I called him Bogey. That's how he got the name."

If Perry was still around, he could attest to that.

I probably played as much with Dean Martin as with anyone—Big Dago, as Frank used to call him. Dean would have his big bets and I'd have my little bets. Once I joined his foursome, and I saw the other guys kicking the ball, moving it surreptitiously to get a better lie. "Dean," I said, "these guys are cheating."

"I know."

"I see them moving the ball here and there."

"I know."

"What are you going to do about it?"

"Nothing. But Vic, lemmee tell you something. We're out here playing golf. I know what they're doing. But afterward they're going to have to come in and play gin with me."

Dean had been a dealer in his younger days, a master card player. He used to clean up.

"So fuck 'em, Vic. They'll be playing gin with me later."

Dean may have been the world's most relaxed human being. One day I was in the club with him, and the Capitol Records representative came to give him his royalty check. I knew the guy; he used to deliver my checks, too. It was a surprise to see him in the club, though. I asked him what he was doing there. "Dean asked us to drop the check off here. He said he'd be playing gin in the locker room."

"Oh, there he is," he said. "Hi, Dean!"

"Oh, yeah. Hi, man. Good to see you."

"Here's your check."

"Oh yeah, thanks for coming. I almost forgot about it."

Dean took the check, folded it, put it in his shirt pocket, and went back to playing gin. Didn't look at the check.

"Jesus Christ," I said to the guy. "Dean didn't even look at the check. Not one of his big ones, I guess. What was it, a couple of thousand?"

"No," the rep whispered. "It was over four hundred thousand dollars."

Dean didn't even glance at it. "Oh, yeah," he said. "Thanks a lot, man." Then he put it in his pocket and went back to his hand.

Dean did well. When he had his TV show he was getting paid eighty thousand a week—back then that was a lot of money. He took forty a week for personal expenses, agents' commissions, and so on. The other forty he invested in two stocks, Loews and RCA Victor. I knew about this. I was doing his summer shows for him, but Dean got paid that eighty thousand every single week, even when I was on in his place. They still used his name: *The Dean Martin Show.* So, for all the five years that his show ran, he put forty thousand a week into those two stocks. He got to be one of the biggest stockholders in both companies.

When Dean died he was quite a wealthy man. But with all his money he was simply one of the nicest, kindest people I've ever known. And an absolutely no bullshit guy. He wouldn't bullshit anyone, and he wouldn't take it from anyone, either. He was a fun guy, he loved life, which he used to live in his own laid-back manner. I used to ask him, "Jesus, Dean, how come you always look so damned good?" Which he did. He had a kind of ruddy, healthy aura to him.

"Nap," he said.

"What?"

"Take a nap!"

Every day after golf and gin Dean would go home and take an hour's nap. Then he'd have a rubdown. Take his shower. Get dressed for dinner. And he'd be in bed by ten-thirty. Asleep.

That was when he wasn't performing, of course. Onstage he never drank anything. It was only colored water, an act. I loved his line after his first song. He'd turn to his piano player and say, "How long have I been on?"

You know, all of us, the different singers, we all had different ways of warming up. I'd be in my dressing room going, "Hee hee, haa haa, hee hee." Loud. Hitting the vowels, elongating them. That was mine. Steve Lawrence would go, "Seebwah seebwah seebwah." Dean's warming up? He didn't bother to do it in his dressing room like everyone else. He'd do his warming up walking onto the stage to the microphone. He'd walk out there going, "Wha wha wha wha wha wha." That was how he warmed up. Why waste your energy in the dressing room? I'm telling you, Dean Martin was a relaxed man.

The warming up was partly warming up your vocal chords, but what I found, anyway, was that it was especially important for getting my diaphragm working, aspirating that "h"—*hee, hee, haa.* Pushing the diaphragm. I'd do breathing exercises at night, too—I still do. Breathing in deeply, not from the chest, but from the diaphragm, then letting the air out slowly between my teeth, slowly and evenly, as long as I can. Over time you increase your lung capacity and your breath control.

Breath control and lung capacity are essential, of course. And I think most audiences weren't aware of what a struggle it used to be for nightclub singers to keep their lungs healthy.

If it hadn't been for golf I'd probably be dead. With people like Dean and Frank and Tony Bennett and myself, Steve and Eydie—our entire lives we were working clubs. Theaters, too, of course, the Paramount and others, but the big thing was nightclubs, the Copacabana, the Riviera, the Mocambo, Vegas. And when we were singing in clubs, people smoked—not like today. You'd be onstage, and as you were singing you could see the smoke hovering over the audience and rolling up to where you were. It was almost something you could feel. The spotlights lit up the haze of smoke, sometimes a wall of smoke, hovering up over the audience and coming at you, like the fog rolling over the hills outside of San Francisco.

So every time you took a deep breath—exactly what you do when you are singing—you inhaled a cloud of secondhand smoke. That was true through all the years and all the shows we did.

I didn't smoke myself. On top of the secondhand smoke, that would have been an absolute killer. I never smoked because of my father. When I was thirteen my father asked me: "Do you smoke?"

"No, Pop, I don't."

"Come with me."

He took me into this little living room we had in Brooklyn and he closed the door.

"You know, the boys-a, you friends? They goin' to start-a you to smoke. No, no, no. *I'm* gonna start-a you. I teach you how to smoke."

"No kidding, Pop. Okay! Wow!"

So he gave me a cigarette, a Sir Walter Raleigh. He said, "Now. I'm gonna light-a the match here. When you take-a the drag. Mmmm, you suck in on the cigarette, you take-a the drag. I want you to take a deep-a, deep-a, deep-a drag."

"Okay, Pop."

He lit a match, put it to the cigarette. I took a deep drag. And, oh my God, it burned my throat. I started choking. Coughing. I said, "Pop, Pop!"

"What's-a matter?"

"Oh my God, that hurts, Pop. My throat!"

"No, no, no, no. One-a more drag. This time take a deep-a, deep-a, deep-a deep-a drag."

"Okay, Pop."

I took a deeper drag. "Oh, Jesus. Oh, my God!"

"What's-a matter?"

"That's it, Pop. That's it! No more!"

And that was the last cigarette I ever had. After that I never touched another one.

The postscript is that when my son, Perry, was sixteen, I thought I'd teach him how to smoke—like my pop taught me.

I said, "Perry, come here. I'm going to teach you how to smoke."

"You're going to what?"

"Teach you how to smoke."

"Okay, Pop."

I lit a cigarette for him, told him to take a deep, deep drag. He sucked it right in, blew it out, and went, "Aaaaaah."

"You sonofagun, you smoke don't you?"

"Yeah, sometimes, Pop."

So that didn't work out too well. But anyway, *I* didn't smoke.

When I was performing at night I was breathing in all of that secondhand smoke in those smoke-filled rooms. Then, the next day, I'd have my breakfast and go play golf. Out on the golf course I was in the fresh air, breathing in that good oxygen. My body needed it, my lungs needed it. I could feel it physically. So every day I was out on the golf course. Every single day. Not that I particularly thought about it in those terms; I just loved the game. But at the same time I was purifying myself.

In retrospect, golf gave me a lot more than healthy lungs. It was more than just an activity I enjoyed doing, too. I think golf gave me something a lot deeper.

Let me try to explain. If you ask a dozen golfers why they are so attracted to the game, you're likely to get a dozen answers. But at least some of them will talk about how challenging it is. Golf is a sport you play mainly against yourself; it's the ultimate nonteam sport. So the challenge is, likewise, mainly to yourself.

What I've found is that when you do this day after day after day, the business of challenging yourself becomes part of you; it becomes part of your character. You get into the habit of struggling against your limitations, of fighting to perfect yourself. Maybe the actual content of that struggle isn't the most important thing—though some golfers would probably disagree with that. Maybe you do the same thing if you are writing, or playing music, or involved with some other sport or profession. But it's the effect of the constant striving on your character that's significant. And golf, with its infinite challenges, is ideally suited. At least that's how I see it.

In golf each shot is different. Is it short, long? Is the course fast, slow? Where's the wind? How much wind? You feed it all into the computer in your head and you use different mechanics, depending on how the conditions lay themselves out. And you are by yourself in this, even when you're playing with others. It's just you and your swing. Putts, chips, drives. So many different aspects, so many different swings.

Mac O'Grady is one of the world's most talented golfers, a plus four when he plays right-handed—that is, he can be expected to shoot four under par—and a plus two or three left-handed. *Golf Digest* once published a series of photos of him swinging right-handed and underneath those a series of him swinging left-handed. You couldn't see a difference. That's just extraordinary. But Mac's real claim to fame is his teaching. He's widely acknowledged to be one of the top instructors in the game; he's especially known for his understanding of the biomechanics of hitting the ball. "You have to remember," he says, "you have thirteen joints in your body, and everything has to go together. Your ankles, knees, hips, shoulders, elbows, wrists, neck—that's thirteen. You have to get all of those joints working together, so when you take that club back every joint has to be doing its job properly."

It's that complexity that makes the challenge to better yourself, to perfect every element of your game, so intense. That's what's so absorbing. If you talk to Tiger Woods, he'll tell you, "I'm working on my game." He's always working on his game. He's won fourteen majors, but he hasn't perfected everything, or maybe anything. He'll never perfect everything. He's working on his game. So am I. That's what it's about.

13

September Song

Alan Drake was a very funny comedian who worked with me on occasion in Vegas and elsewhere. I'd known him for years, ever since my first performance after I got out of the army, the one at the Riviera with Joey Bishop and the Champions. Alan had been in the audience with his wife and mother-in-law, sitting at a table near the front. Before the show, I was backstage, when some kind of ruckus broke out in the club. "Oh, man," said the stage manager. "You should see what's going on out there."

What was going on was a brief encounter between Alan and the four guys sitting at the next table. Apparently the four men were talking loudly and using foul language. Tough guys. Very rude and out of place—the Riviera was an elegant club. Alan apparently asked them, nicely, to have some respect. To which the response was, "Go fuck yourself."

The background to this was that Alan had been a professional fighter before he became a comedian. His nickname was Mugsy, and he looked like a Mugsy. He had a rugged face and a boxer's broken nose. Now that I think of it, it's strange that various fighters I knew became comedians afterward, Rocky Graziano and Jake LaMotta, for instance. Alan had always been a tough fighter, and he took care of those four guys fast. Three actually, since after he decked the first three, the fourth said, "Wait, wait, I wasn't saying anything."

I mention Alan because we became good friends, partly through boxing. I enjoyed hanging out with guys who knew about fighting, the pugilistic kind of guys. Alan knew many of the fighters I knew—Graziano, Jake LaMotta, Sugar Ray, Rocky Marciano. Marciano, to digress a moment, had a little game he'd play on the golf course—with me and no doubt with others. At some point in the middle of the course he'd say, in that surprisingly soft, almost girl-like voice of his, "Okay, give me ten." That is, push-ups. He'd make you do ten push-ups right there and then. He wouldn't beat you up if you didn't do them, he just wouldn't go on until you did. So, if you wanted to finish the game, you got down and gave him ten. At least I did, and I'll bet I'm not the only one.

Anyway, Alan and I sparred together. I picked up some good tricks from him, too, tricks not covered by the Marquess of Queensbury rules.

I also mention Alan because he introduced me to my third wife, Becky Jones. This happened in Las Vegas a year after Judy and I were divorced. Becky would come to my shows. She was young and pretty, and very hip, a jet-setter. We liked each other, and went out, and eventually she became my girlfriend. After a couple of years we decided to get married.

We had actually just announced our plans when I got terrible news. Judy was found dead in her bedroom. Daniella, our youngest, had found her. What a trauma for her, and a huge shock for all the kids, and for me. The coroner ruled that she died as a result of an accidental overdose. She had been taking all those pain pills, a situation that had only worsened in the years since we broke up, and apparently she had just had some dental work, which involved even more painkillers.

This happened on March 28, 1974, three years after our divorce. Daniella was six; Andrea eight, Victoria nine. I had no idea what to do. I was living in Las Vegas, by myself, working nights. Half of each year I was on the road. I needed to keep perfoming as much as possible to get my finances back in order. It wasn't possible to bring the girls to Vegas; I knew there was no way in the world I would be able to handle that. The question was eating me up with anxiety. How in the world was I going to take care of my children?

Thank God, Joan Parnello came to the rescue. Joan was married to Joe Parnello, my piano player and conductor. The Parnellos had an older daughter. They lived in Los Angeles, in the Valley; Joanie and Judy had been friends, and the girls and Joanie knew each other well. "Don't worry, Vic," Joanie said. "They can live with me and go to school here. You and Joe work. I'll take care of the girls." I don't know that I have ever been more grateful for anything in my life.

We kept that arrangement going even after Becky and I got married. Becky was young, only twenty-six. She led an extremely active life. She was a champion rally driver and a top rodeo performer, a real rodeo queen. In the things she enjoyed doing she was highly accomplished. She lived fast, and she moved with a fast set. There was absolutely no way I could simply bring three little girls into her life and expect her to be their mother. Especially when I myself wouldn't be around nights, not to mention the six months a year I was on the road. Becky had no experience taking care of children, and she certainly hadn't bargained on becoming a mom to my three daughters when we decided to get married.

But things went well with Joan Parnello and the girls. She was like a mother to them, and I got down to Los Angeles regularly to see them. I'd fly down to spend afternoons or evenings with them whenever I possibly could, then I'd fly back to Vegas at night. It was far from ideal, but I did my absolute best and, as young as the girls were, I think they knew how much their father loved and cared for them.

The situation continued that way for two or two and a half years, until Joan and Joe decided they needed to get divorced. After that Joan became a lot less interested in being a surrogate mom to them. Suddenly the girls started missing school, and I realized they were not being taken care of properly.

The instant that was clear to us, Becky and I went down to get them. With my finances in better shape now, we moved from Las Vegas to Los Angeles, where we got an apartment. Since this happened in a hurry, and I couldn't get a place large enough, I rented the adjacent apartment as well, with bedrooms for the girls and for a babysitter. Becky or I drove them to school. We hung out with them. We had lunch and dinner together. We washed their hair and taught them how to take care of themselves. We spent as much time with them as we could. But living like that was a strain, and after a while we decided the best thing would be to move to Houston, Becky's hometown. Which is what we did. We bought a house there, and brought the girls down, so we could finally live like a family. And although I was a little apprehensive about how that might work out, Becky took to it; she got to be quite a mother.

Becky's father was a highly successful businessman. He was in real estate and a variety of other ventures. The whole town knew him as "Available" Jones, a nickname he had picked up during World War II, when consumer goods were tightly rationed. Apparently, when friends would ask if he might be able to get them something—tires or a kitchen appliance or nylons—his answer was usually, "I think it's available." He himself was a rally driver; he had taught Becky. He loved cars and knew everything about them. He had a house built next to his regular house for his collection of high-end and exotic automobiles. I say a house because, from the street, the garage for these cars was built to look exactly like a house. But on the side were large car-port doors, and inside the place was nothing but a vast garage space.

Becky and I were married in 1974. I was forty-six years old. In Houston life fell into a normal routine, to whatever extent an entertainer's life can be called normal. The girls were in school and growing up. Becky had her friends and carried on with the things she did, trying to balance that with being a mother, which was a tough job for her, but one she worked at conscientiously. I sang and traveled. I played Vegas a lot, and London, where I had developed a loyal following.

Ten years earlier the Beatles had made their appearance. Then the Rolling Stones came along, and Led Zeppelin. Rock music transformed the entertainment landscape. But it didn't transform everything. Despite the rock invasion, my bookings stayed strong. So did Frank's and Dean's and Sammy's and Ella's and Steve and Eydie's. The youth culture had changed, but our audiences had grown older with us. This was a generation that had made the great songwriters their own, Irving Berlin and Gershwin, Cole Porter, Hoagy Carmichael, Johnny Mercer, Jerome Kern, Richard Rodgers, Jule Styne, Sammy Cahn, and the others. We were part of that, the singers, myself and others. Just because rock had arrived didn't mean the American Songbook—the great standards of popular music and Broadway—was going anywhere. It wasn't.

So many hundreds and hundreds of those melodies and lyrics had become landmarks in people's minds, as they still are. Think about it. "I'm Dreaming of a White Christmas," "Embrace Me (My Sweet Embraceable You)," "You've Got to Accentuate the Positive," "Try a Little Tenderness," "On the Street Where You Live." These aren't song titles as much as phrases everyone knows by heart, that are part of their lives, even if they're not usually conscious of it. And the words aren't separable from the melodies. You can't think of one without instantly thinking of the other. So the melodies are part of people's lives, too. Nothing was going to change that, at least not for a long, long time.

So, just like the songbook wasn't going anywhere, the singers weren't going anywhere, either. No matter how popular the Beatles became, I didn't feel for a moment that I was being displaced or that I'd have to look in some other direction. I was doing pretty well, and I didn't think that was going to change anytime soon.

Just before Thanksgiving in 1984 I came home from a tour. Becky was waiting for me at the airport, along with a friend of her dad's, Eb Rose. Becky gave me a hug and a little kiss. I said hello to Eb, thinking he was flying off somewhere, or maybe just arriving. But he wasn't.

"I'm here representing Becky," he said.

"What do you mean? Representing her in what way?"

And Becky said, "I want a divorce."

"You want a *what*?" I said.

"I want a divorce."

Somehow the answer was right there. "Okay," I said.

"What?"

"Okay. I said okay."

I don't think she was prepared for the answer. That was all right; I wasn't prepared for what she was asking. I didn't want it. But I had my kids, who were ten years older now. I was singing all over, doing well. I felt pretty good about things. I had thought we had a decent marriage. But if she wanted a divorce, okay. Fine with me. You're not happy, fine. That probably means it's time to part.

In retrospect, I don't know what to say about all these marriages. I wasn't the Hollywood type who would go from one marriage to another to another as soon as somebody new and more beautiful came along. I had been in love with Anna—maybe a youthful and unconsidered love, but still love. I had had a deep affection for Judy, too, and strong feelings for Becky. Judy and I had been married eleven years, Becky and I, ten. These hadn't been thoughtless, temporary affairs. I loved women. I didn't like being by myself. Singing was as unsettled a life as you could get, always out at night, always on the road. I wanted the affection and stability of a good marriage. But things just hadn't worked out that way.

Not that I was quite ready to give it up. In 1986 I did a club date at the Breakers in Palm Beach, and Diahann Carroll was on the same bill. After the show we had dinner together and talked. Diahann was a great singer and an intense performer, both onstage and in the movies. She had been on Broadway and on television. She had performed in the film version of *Porgy and Bess* with Sidney Poitier, Dorothy Dandridge, and Sammy Davis. She had starred in Richard Rodgers's *No Strings.* I had been a fan of hers for a long time, and we had run into each other on occasion over the years. But this was the first time we had done more than say hello.

I think at that dinner we discovered that we liked each other. We respected each other's work, and we had a lot in common, both of us having had long careers by that time. Not long after that we met again in San Francisco, where we were both singing. We saw each other's shows and spent time together. Diahann was beautiful and dynamic. She had great stage presence and was equally engaging in person. We found ourselves talking more and more, mostly about work, about the business, but personally, too.

Diahann had been married several times herself. Her last husband, the editor of *Jet* magazine, had died in a car accident almost a decade earlier. Diahann had bought him a Ferrari, which he had been driving at high speed on Mulholland Drive. She showed me the spot where he had left the road at a hundred miles an hour and gone off the side.

Diahann and I started going out together. Next thing you know, we were getting married. I think we both needed it in our own ways. We seemed to be compatible. We were singers, each of whom enjoyed what the other was doing. It maybe wasn't the most thoughtful of decisions, but it seemed to make sense to us at the time. Not only did we get along personally, but our singing styles also seemed as if they might be compatible. And before long we formed a performing partnership as well as a personal one.

This wasn't the first time I collaborated with a great female singer. In 1978 I had done a CBS tribute to Richard Rodgers with Peggy Lee and Lena Horne. Shortly afterward, Lena had been looking for a male singer to do club and concert work with, and she and I had gotten together in a professional pairing that lasted three years. I had learned a great deal about stage work and duet singing from Lena, which I was able to put to good use when Diahann and I started working together.

Diahann and I performed all over—in Vegas, New York, Chicago, Los Angeles. We were in England at the Palladium. We sang at the Kennedy Center when Perry Como received the Kennedy Center award from Ronald Reagan. Ordinarily, we'd go out onstage together, do a number, then Diahann would go off. After intermission she'd come on and do her thirty-five or forty minutes, then bring me back out, and we'd do a big medley together.

Although our collaboration was a great success, after a while I began to feel unhappy with the way things were going. Diahann, of course, was a big star, and we always gave her first billing: "Diahann Carroll and Vic Damone." Along with that, Diahann, with her trunks full of gowns and other paraphernalia, always took the star dressing room—which she did need and certainly deserved. But performers spend their careers fighting for marquee prominence and headliner status. It's one of the ways they measure their success. And over time I began to feel less and less valued. I began losing the confidence a performer needs to perform well, to do his or her best.

When I talked about it with her, there wasn't any give. I wouldn't call our conflict a crisis, but it made me think, not just about Diahann, but about myself. It focused me. Diahann was a show business person first, last, and always. She said that about herself. Show business was her life. But I didn't think it was mine. I never really had thought so. So why was I so concerned about such things?

The situation brought home to me the truth of one of Baha'i's most important lessons about human psychology. Baha'is teach about the nature of the soul, and especially about the conflict between the soul and the ego. Baha'ullah, the Baha'i founder, wrote that we are all living in our second world. Our first world is the world of the womb, where we live for nine months. In our first world we receive our bodies—all of the physical necessities we need in order to survive. But if our first world is about our physical self, our second world, which we enter into at birth, is about our spirit. And the essence of our spiritual lives is the soul. To survive in this world our soul has to grow. Our first world is about the body; our second world is all about the soul.

What we become physically in the first world happens in order for us to have healthy souls in the second world. And the great obstacle to having a healthy soul is the ego, which is constantly at war with the soul. That is true for everyone, but it is especially true for show business people.

The reason for this is that show business glorifies the ego. Your need in show business is to attract attention to yourself and to keep attention on yourself. You succeed by feeding your ego with the admiration of others. And if you do make it in show business, the battle between your soul and your ego becomes much harder for the soul. Your soul is saying, Be gentle, be kind, be generous, be a person who thinks of others and helps others. Your soul wants you to direct yourself outward, toward your fellow human beings. But your ego is saying, No, no, I'm the star. Don't touch me; I'm the star. Your ego wants you to exalt yourself at the expense of your soul. Some entertainers do win this battle; the confidence they need never deteriorates into egotism. But many don't. Baha'ullah says that you better win this battle; you better listen to your soul. Because at bottom that's what life is really about.

All this helped me understand what I was going through with Diahann. But it was hardly just her. I had been in show business since I was seventeen. But after the excitement of those first years, ever since I had broken in and established myself, I had never been completely at home with what I was doing. I felt I didn't quite fit in. I didn't feel fulfilled. There was always a distance between me and real show people, as if I didn't quite know who I was.

I used to hang out a lot with Milton Berle. After I won on *Arthur Godfrey's Talent Scouts,* Milton had taken me under his wing. He had given me my start, which I was always grateful for, and we stayed friends until the day he died. Milton often said to me, "You've got to learn to smile more onstage. Smile, please."

"Why, Milton?"

"Because the audience likes to see a smiling face."

"But that's a fake smile, Milton. If I'm singing songs that are happy, I'll smile. But I'm not showbiz. I don't feel that way."

I'm probably the only person in show business who, when I got a call from my agent telling me I was going on the Johnny Carson show, said, "No, I'm not."

"What do you mean, no?" My agent was horrified.

"I mean no. Johnny's my friend. I love doing his show. But no, cancel it."

"Why? Are you nuts?"

"Because I've got nothing to talk about."

If I had a movie coming out, or a TV show I was starting, or a hit record, I'd want to go on Johnny Carson to talk about it. But if I had nothing like that, what would I do? I'd sing my song and go and sit there. Johnny would say, "Hey, Vic. Great song. What's new?" What would I say? "Nothing, Johnny. Nothing's new." The point was, I was just not motivated to get my face in front of people all the time, no matter what.

My agent used to say to me, "You know, you are definitely crazy."

"No, I'm not. You know, I'll go on the *Merv Griffin Show* any time. That's different. It's a different kind of interview. Merv's a singer. We can go over to the piano. We can talk about music. We can sing together. But I am not going to put myself out there to do nothing but shoot the breeze."

That attitude was detrimental to my career, I'm sure. But I just did not feel comfortable with what show business expected of me. I was not given a special talent as a show person. I'm thinking of people like Milton, or Sammy Davis, or Jerry Lewis. Berle was a funny man, Sammy had more talent than ten people, Jerry was and still is a great physical comedian. But they were all consummate showmen. I never thought of myself that way. That wasn't my particular gift.

My gift was singing. I had been given a voice and the ability to use it. That was actually one of the reasons the Baha'i faith attracted me. Baha'is talk about these things. God gives each of us talent, Baha'ullah says. And one of our purposes in living is to find what our talent is: business, music, carpentry, working with people, whatever. And when we find that out, then we are called on to follow it, to bring it to its full potential. That's our job, our duty; that's one of the things we are put here for.

I listen to recordings I made when I was seventeen. My voice was already mature. It had depth and reach; I could sustain notes. It wasn't normal. I don't know how I got that way. I still don't, after my whole career. I can only think that God gave that to me. That was His gift to me.

I always felt that. I always felt somehow that it was my obligation to use that gift I had been given. I don't think I could have, or maybe would have, articulated it like that in the earlier part of my career, but those were my feelings from the beginning. That's one of the reasons I never abused my voice—never drank or smoked—although many of the people I knew in entertainment smoked and drank a lot. Why should I abuse something that's God given, that in a sense doesn't even belong to me?

I took that feeling about singing with me onto the stage. When you are onstage and the spotlights are on, you can't see anybody or anything. The lights blind you. It's almost as if you're up there alone. You hear the music, you turn around and see your conductor, your musicians, but when you look at the audience, you can't see anything. Maybe the people right beneath you in front, but that's it. All the rest is lost in the glare.

When I did concerts I always liked to move back a bit. I wanted to be back toward the orchestra, where I could feel the music enveloping me. I wanted to feel that I was by myself onstage, just me and the music. And during certain songs, especially, I would feel not only that I was alone, I would feel that I was singing to God.

"On the Street Where You Live" is the best example of what I mean. John Williams picked that song out for me from the *My Fair Lady* score. "*This* is your song," he had said. Then Percy Faith had given it a big orchestral arrangement. I had recorded it that way, and it had been one of my biggest hits. But after years of singing it like that, one night I told my pianist, "Let's do it differently. I want to sing it with just piano, nothing else."

"Just the two of us?" He was a little shocked.

And that's how I started doing it onstage, softly, with just piano. "I have often walked on this street before . . . knowing I'm on the street where you live." I'm on the street where *You* live.

This is a romantic song, sung in the musical to Eliza Doolittle by her suitor, Freddie Eynsford-Hill. But when I sang it I felt I was singing not to a girl, but to God. I was on the street where He lived.

I was giving thanks, on the stage, where He had given me the main thing in my life. And I know my audiences could also feel that there was something unusual going on. When I sang that song, the room or the concert hall was always so quiet you could hear a pin drop.

I don't mean to make myself out a pious or especially religious person. I am not. And even though I never felt completely at home in show business, I have lived an entertainer's life, a singer's life. But I did have those other feelings. In one way or another I always had them. And they gave me a great feeling of comfort. To feel I was in contact like that. To feel that He was listening—to the gift that He had given to me. Which He gave to others also, of course, and to some of them a larger gift than to me. But this He did give to me.

Performing is a tough life. It puts strains on your marriage—which for entertainers often becomes your marriages, plural—on raising your children. But it has its compensations. It puts you together with the most interesting, talented people. If you're lucky, it gives you lasting friendships with those sorts of people. I was lucky.

I never felt that more than when Frank Sinatra died. I was at Frank's funeral with Rena—Rena Rowan, who became my wife in 1998. I'm saving Rena's story for last, because in these pages I'm summing up, and she is the person who has helped me sum up and understand some of the meaning in all the things that have happened to me. She has helped me put it all in perspective. But I'll tell you something about Rena's remarkable story shortly.

We went to Sinatra's funeral with Larry King and his wife, Shawn. Nancy Reagan was sitting behind us; Ron was already very ill then. I had known Nancy back at Metro, where she had been extremely kind to me. I knew Ron, too, from when he had been head of the Screen Actors' Guild. I had sung for him at his inauguration as California's governor and several times at the White House when he was president. His absence at the funeral just heightened the sense of loss that everyone there was feeling.

So many other friends were there, too: Don Rickles, Steve and Eydie, Bob Newhart, Johnny Carson, Milton Berle, Kirk Douglas. It seemed like the entire entertainment community was in the church. The funeral Mass was long, but beautiful. Frank Sinatra's son, Frank Junior, outdid himself; his eulogy moved everyone.

Maybe the most memorable moment for me, one that will stay with me for the rest of my life, came at the end of the funeral, when they played one of Frank's records. There he was, singing "Put Your Dreams Away": "Put your dreams away for another day, and I will take their place in your heart." That was his good-bye theme song, the one he always sang at the end of his television shows. And I was thinking, Oh my God, it's truly the end of Sinatra. It's his farewell song. And I got chills all over me. I couldn't believe he was gone. He was so big, in everything: singing, acting, Hollywood, Vegas. He was the king, and now he was dead.

Sinatra was a giant media presence, but in his case the public image wasn't an exaggeration. He was an oversized talent and an oversized personality—one of those rare people who really are larger than life. He was the leader: personally, musically, artistically. For me, he was my mentor, at the beginning of my career and all the way through. He was always there to discuss problems—singing problems and life problems, to give me advice and guidance. He had saved my life. He was a true friend.

I felt I could hear him at that funeral. Hear him and almost see him. Funny, everyone else called him Francis. But I could never do that. I always called him Frank. Just as he always called me Dago. "Hey, Dage." I could hear him. All those vivid memories that we all had of him, those of us still around. Sammy, of course, was gone, Dean. Dean didn't call him Francis, either. Dean used to call him

"Hey." Or "Listen." "Hey, listen, what time are we on?" They were the best of pals.

Being who he was to all of us wasn't always easy for him. Sometimes it exhausted him. He told me once—this was in Vegas—how tired he was. He was doing movies, shows, and everyone would call him, including myself, wanting to talk things over, wanting his advice. It was one of those afternoons when the two of us were sitting in the health club. Hanging up after some call, he said, "I'm tired of being the leader. Why don't you take over? Everybody calls me. Jesus, I'm just so tired of it."

"Sorry, Frank," I said. "What are you, kidding?"

But tired or not, he was always there. He was that kind of guy. And if he was your friend, you had a friend for life.

After the funeral some of us went out to eat: Jerry Vale and Jack Jones and their wives; Milton Berle and his wife; Rena and I. We talked about our memories, of course. The discussion continued later on the *Larry King Show.* Larry had invited several of Frank's friends and colleagues on to talk about Frank's life. Eartha Kitt was there, and me, Wayne Newton, Shirley Jones, George Schlatter, the producer. Joey Bishop wasn't at the studio, but he joined in by remote. Eartha talked about how Frank had opened so many doors for African American entertainers. Schlatterer, who had produced an eightieth birthday tribute for Frank and knew him well, said he had raised a billion dollars in his life for charity. The show was like a group of old friends sitting around trading stories.

Larry himself also went back many years with Frank. But Larry and I had known each other even longer. We had first met in the late fifties, when I was working at the Eden Roc in Miami. My manager at the time told me there was someone doing radio interviews on WIOD. The guy apparently lived on a houseboat anchored across from the Eden Roc in the Inland Waterway, which was where the show was broadcast from. He was interviewing all the name entertainers working the city.

"His name's Larry King," my manager said. "Everybody loves him. He's from Brooklyn."

Brooklyn, I thought. Can't be that bad if he's from Brooklyn. "Good," I said. "So book me."

When I sat down a few days later in Larry King's houseboat for the interview, the first thing he said was, "Vito Farinola!"

"What?"

"I said, 'Vito Farinola!' "

I was astonished.

"How do you know my name?"

"How do I know your name?" King said. "How do I know your name? I had to look at it for years."

"What?"

"I sat at the same desk you did at Lafayette High School. I must have been three or four years behind you. You carved your name in the desk. I sat and looked at it the whole time I was there. 'Vito Farinola.' For years I'm thinking, who the hell is Vito Farinola? Then I find out that Vito Farinola is Vic Damone. Oh my God, I can't believe it."

Every year I'd work the Eden Roc, and I'd always go back to see him. So we got to be friends. Once, years later, when we were discussing songs and songwriters, he came up with the idea of doing a music show. Monday through Friday, he'd do interviews and the news. Then on Saturday he'd have this music show.

Larry would invite singers on to sit around a piano and talk about songs and songwriters, and sing. I did three or four of these shows, most often together with my piano player, Norman Geller, who could play everything from jazz to classical. I was on once with Eartha Kitt and Barbara Cook. Robert Goulet was on. On one show Michael Feinstein sang and played piano for us. We'd sing individually or do duets, whatever struck our fancy. It was wonderful sitting around the piano, singing our favorite numbers from the songbook and talking about how best to interpret them, and the great talents who had written them. We had an evening of Gershwin and another of Cole Porter. Richard Rodgers and Jerome Kern. I loved it. We all loved it. It was our music.

The one aggravation was that Larry knew the lyrics better than we did. Of course, we knew them, the singers. But occasionally someone might forget a word, or a line. Larry knew, though, and he'd remind us. Larry knows the lyrics cold. All of them. He was passionate about this music, a true devote. He still is.

Over the years, Larry became one of my closest friends. Like Frank, he was one of the people I knew I could always count on. Of course, I tried to be there for him as well. I sang for him at a special concert he did in Washington. Another time there was a tribute for him at the Beverly Hills Hilton. I was going to be singing. Steve and Eydie were there, too, in the audience.

When Steve came backstage to say hello, I told him I had an idea.

"How about if you guys sing with me?" I said.

"Okay. How?"

"I'm going to be doing eight or nine songs. When I get to "It Had To Be You," here's what I'd like you to do. I'll start with the verse—"Why do I do, just as you say"—and so on. Then, when I get to the chorus, you start singing—while you're sitting at the table. We'll get mikes set up there. When you start singing, the spotlight will look for you, then it'll find you, and you stand up. Then Eydie will start singing. So now you're both up and singing, "It had to be you, it had to be you," and I'll join in—the three of us will be singing to Larry."

Steve's another of my best pals, Eydie, too. The three of us singing together to Larry was one of the high points of my career. There was such thunderous applause, it was unbelievable.

On one of Larry's shows Barbara Walters said, "You've interviewed presidents, kings, everyone. Of everyone you've interviewed, who would you most like to be?"

And Larry said, "Vic Damone!"

"Vic Damone?" Barbara said. "Why?"

"What do you mean, 'Why?' Have you ever heard him sing?"

This past year he had Queen Latifa on. And she, too, asked him who he'd like to be. And again he said, "Vic Damone!"

"Why?" she said. "What's the matter with you?"

There was nothing the matter with him. The fact is that for all Larry's success and fame, what he really wants is to be a singer. That's his secret desire. When the Songwriter's Hall of Fame gave me a lifetime achievement award, I asked if he would present it to me. That night he flew in for the ceremony and did his show from New York. As I say, the friendships I've had with Frank, with Larry, with Don Rickles and Dean and Steve and Eydie—these have gone a long way toward making up for the stresses and dissatisfactions that have come along with the long life I've lived in the business.

Finally, I want to tell you about Rena Rowan, the person who has allowed me to look back on it all with a sense of purpose, and of happiness. I met Rena after Diahann and I had separated. Our marriage had never been that easy, and now she was playing in a long-run revival of *Sunset Boulevard* in Toronto, while I was living by myself in Palm Springs. We had both agreed that it was over; we just hadn't gotten around to filing for a divorce.

Sometime in late February 1996 I got a call from Cissy Hurst, the wife of Ed Hurst, a Philadelphia DJ I knew well. I liked and respected Ed. He had brought a lot to the Philadelphia music scene. His shows on radio and television were the forerunners of Dick Clark's *American Bandstand,* and he had a long-running radio program that I had been on quite a few times. I considered him a friend.

Cissy told me she was working on a big charity gala, a fund-raiser for a project helping Philadelphia's homeless. The person behind this project was someone named Rena Rowan, a Philadelphia woman Cissy thought the world of. Might I possibly be available to sing at the event—on September 11?

I looked at my schedule. I had the date free. I told Cissy I'd be more than happy to talk to this Rena person, to please give her my phone number.

Eventually, after a couple of back-and-forths, we managed to get hold of each other. Rena introduced herself and described her project It sounded great, though I have to admit I didn't register all the details. Something about providing shelter and training for homeless women and children.

But it turned out she was calling from Palm Beach, Florida, where she had a home. I had an engagement in Palm Beach in a couple of weeks, at Donald Trump's Mar-A-Lago, coincidentally, another charity fund-raiser. "If you'd like," I told Rena, "I can put you on the guest list and we can take time to talk."

The night of the Mar-A-Lago performance it rained as if Palm Beach was going to be washed away. Bolts of lightning; thunder crashing. Absolutely torrential. Like a hurricane. But despite the weather we had a full house, which was hard to believe. You had to be crazy to go out in that. I didn't really expect Rena Rowan to be there. We were going to have dinner together the next night, anyway, so there was no point. But after I had finished singing, Donald Trump and the Mar-A-Lago events manager, Debra Cammarata, met me as I was coming down from the stage. Debra was the daughter of my old friends Lou and Marion Cammarata, whom I was staying with. "Vic," she said, "I'd like to introduce you to Rena Rowan."

Well, Rena Rowan was a big surprise. In my head I had a picture of some ninety-year-old dowager philanthropist. Instead, here was this petite, beautiful woman who looked to be about sixty. Dressed in some kind of chic black pantsuit. Obviously very shy. "Hello," she said, "I'm Rena Rowan." Softly. With all the noise I could barely hear her. I took her hand and said, "Look at you, will you." Which was probably a little bold, but all I really meant was, My goodness, you're not exactly who I thought you'd be.

The next night, Rena and her husband, Sidney Kimmel, had dinner with Lou and Marion Cammarata and me. At least, I thought Sidney Kimmel was her husband. When I asked how long they had been married, Sidney said, "We've been together almost thirty years." But before he had even gotten the sentence out, Rena said, "We're not married. July thirteenth we'll have been together thirty years. If we're not married by then, I've told Sidney I'm out of here."

That was a conversation stopper. "Uh, okay," I said. Lou and Marion just looked at her. Hmmm, I thought, sounds like some trouble in that relationship. But nothing else happened. Sidney looked uncomfortable, but Rena didn't say anything more, and the moment passed.

Instead, we talked about Rena's project, the one I had committed to sing for in September. Rena had apparently bought and was refitting a big old residential building in West Philadelphia, one of the city's most blighted neighborhoods. She was creating apartments for homeless women with children, mostly women who had suffered a lot of abuse in their lives. She was also arranging training and counseling programs, so that the women could learn job skills and become self-sufficient.

This was obviously a huge undertaking. The building she had bought was old enough that it was on the historical register. Gutting it and renovating it had already taken a couple of years, and very large sums of money. She had gotten support from Ed Rendell—Philadelphia's mayor at the time—and also from various fund-raisers she had organized. The one I was going to sing for was especially important, she said. They were in the last stages of getting the building ready and needed to make a big final push for funds.

All this was interesting, but what really impressed me was that Rena Rowan was so obviously in this thing heart and soul. And it wasn't as if she was just some person with money who wanted to do good. She and Sidney Kimmel had founded Jones New York, the big women's clothing company. Rena headed the design side of the business. Of course, she would never say such a thing, but I found out from friends that she was an extremely famous person in the fashion world. She designed not only for Jones, but for Ralph Lauren and Dior. She was right up there among the stars. And here she was, completely dedicated to her homeless project. I had never met anyone remotely like that.

I flew back to California a couple of days later, but in a few weeks I was booked for an extended engagement at the Rainbow and Stars, a beautiful, intimate club in New York at the top of Rockefeller Center. Rena and Sidney lived part-time in New York, and they were headed there, too, so I invited them to come as my guests.

I was at the Rainbow and Stars for four weeks, and I think Rena and Sidney must have come to five or six performances. We had dinner together and talked a lot. Sidney and I were getting to know each other and, if anything, my admiration for Rena only deepened. The two of them had started their company twenty-five years earlier without a cent between them. Over the years they had built it into one of the dominant players in women's clothing. Rena had taken high-fashion European design and transformed it into clothing for American professional women. She had changed the way American women dressed, almost single-handedly.

Not that you would ever know it from talking to her. Everything about her was understated and elegant. And—this is what really got me—completely modest. She was friends with Calvin Klein and Perry Ellis while he was alive, and with big European designers like Armani and Dior's Mark Bohan. These people were superstars, international celebrities. But she was as far from that as you could imagine. She was completely dedicated to doing good for other people. I had been living in a world of celebrities myself for most of my life—show business celebrities—and I knew a lot of good people, and charitable people. But no one I knew was anywhere near as motivated as she was, or as modest about their accomplishments.

Something in me really responded to that. I was happy that she was giving me the opportunity to help her raise the money she needed. I admired her and respected her tremendously for what she was doing. But I didn't allow my feelings to go any further than that. She and Sidney had been living together for thirty years, whatever problems they might be having. And even though Diahann and I were separated, we were still married. The last thing in my mind was entering into some complicated romantic arrangement with somebody. Who needed that, especially at my age? I was almost seventy.

That's what I thought, anyway, until a couple of days after I closed at the Rainbow and Stars. That evening I was going to have dinner with Rena and Sidney and Charlie Cumella, one of my oldest, closest friends. Charlie and Sidney and I were at the bar at Nanni's, an Italian restaurant near Rockefeller Center, waiting for Rena, who was driving into the city from Jones's headquarters outside of Philadelphia. Rena was late, held up in traffic, and the three of us were making idle talk at the bar, passing the time.

"So," Sidney said, "how's Diahann? How's your marriage going?"

"Well, it's not really. Diahann and I are separated. She's working up in Canada this year. We see each other, but only occasionally. It's been over for a while now. You know, Sidney, this is my fourth marriage. I'm tired of it. I've had it. I'm never getting married again. Who needs it?"

"I don't know," said Sidney. "But you know who you ought to marry?"

"What?" Maybe he hadn't heard what I said. "Who should I marry?"

"You ought to marry Rena."

"What? Are you nuts? You two are—"

"No," he interrupted. "No, it's been over for years. We're just in business together."

"But you live together."

"Means nothing, Vic. But I'm telling you. She's a great woman. She'd make a great catch. A great wife."

I was listening to this but hardly believing what I was hearing.

"I'll tell you what," Sidney said. "If you were to marry her—and I'm telling you, she'd be a truly wonderful wife—if you marry her, I'll pay for the wedding myself."

And just at that moment Rena walked into Nanni's.

When I told Rena about this conversation later, she was shocked that Sidney would say such a thing to me.

"Well," I told her. "That's what he said. That you'd make a great wife. And that he'd pay for the wedding. But forget that. Does this mean you're available?"

"Vic," she said. "I guess maybe it does."

From that moment on I looked at Rena in a different light, as something more than just an acquaintance I admired. I began to allow her into my head and into my heart.

That summer we talked a lot on the phone. We got to know each other. I couldn't believe what Rena had been through in her life. She had been born in Poland, though you couldn't tell; she didn't have an accent or anything. In World War II the Russians had deported her and her mother and younger sister to Siberia. They had been jammed into a boxcar for a month, then dumped out in the open with twenty or thirty other women and children—in the middle of nowhere, with no food or shelter, just left to die. But Rena and the others had been rescued by nomads who had a village around there. She was twelve years old when this happened. She had lived with the nomads for several years before she and her mother and sister escaped by walking hundreds of miles across Siberia.

I had never heard of anything like it. Rena looked young, but she and I were almost the same age. I hadn't even been all that aware of the war when I was growing up, other than that it was going on. And I thought we had had it pretty tough, living hand to mouth in Brooklyn when I was a kid. But what did I know about having it tough?

Rena and her family had finally ended up on an American army base in Iran. She was working in the mess hall there as a waitress when she met a young American officer. They had gotten married, even though she was only sixteen or seventeen. She had come to the United States as a war bride.

I was amazed to hear about this. I couldn't imagine how she had survived it all: the Russians; riding in a boxcar across a continent; the nomads; the Siberian winters. And then, how she had come here and built her career as a designer out of nothing, with no money and no one to help her. This was not like anybody's life I had ever heard of. To say that Rena had no similarity to any of my former wives was putting it mildly.

On September 10, I flew to Philadelphia with my musicians, ready to do the gala. Rena had made all the preparations: the room at the Rittenhouse Hotel; the dinner; the decorations; the light and sound—everything was perfect. I knew it was going to go well, and it did. My sense was that the two hundred or so guests loved it. Judging from the applause, I knew they liked the music. But I think they loved Rena more—most of them seemed to know her, and they enjoyed being part of what she was doing for the city. She was like a queen that evening.

I could feel where my own heart was going, too. Rena had said good-bye to Kimmel that summer—she had finally just kicked him out. So she really was available. Diahann and I were finished, too. It would take a while for the divorce to come through, but we had completely had it with each other. I felt like I was courting again. I thought, could I *possibly* be getting that warm, wonderful feeling for someone? Now? At this stage of my life? But there it was.

We kept in touch by phone after that. But it was a strain, me being out in California and she in Palm Beach. I think my friend Lou Cammarata was part of a conspiracy to get me to move to Florida, not that it took much conspiring. My father had died a number of years earlier, but my mother was still alive, though getting on in years. She was living near Miami in Hallandale, where I had bought her a condo. Florida would allow me to help take care of her. And, needless to say, that's where Rena was.

Once I did move—to Palm Beach Gardens—Rena and I were able to see each other all the time. She had been married twice, but both husbands had turned out to be alcoholics. Then she and Sidney Kimmel had gotten together as partners in business and personally. They had invented Jones out of ideas Rena had had about women's clothing. But it hadn't been a happy relationship, especially after Jones New York went public and Sidney ended up with nineteen million shares to Rena's one million—which made him one of the wealthiest people in the country. Rena had a lot of anger about that, and I didn't blame her. I thought, how could this individual have done such a thing to her, after she had built the business equally with him? Jones had been Rena's life's work every bit as much as his. That's why she had eventually gotten rid of him.

But she wasn't dragging him through the courts, which most

women in my acquaintance would have done in an instant. Instead, she was turning the money she did have to other uses. Jones was a Philadelphia company, and Philadelphia had a terrible homeless problem. Rena herself had been homeless with her mother and sister on the steppes of Siberia. They would have died there had not someone decided to help. She saw Philadelphia's homeless women with children, and her heart went out to them. That's what had motivated her to put all her energy into her charity. Now that she had the ability, she felt she needed to give back. And boy, was she ever giving back. Her efforts in West Philadelphia and in North Philadelphia, too, were helping turn the city from a place of shame into a national model.

I'm not sure what Rena saw in me, but at bottom what I saw in her was character. That's what drew me to her. And what I discovered was that she was yearning for a normal relationship, a normal marriage with someone who would take care of her the way a husband should take care of a wife. After suffering through everything she had suffered through with the men she had known, she was still looking for that. She was not ready to give herself up to loneliness.

Maybe she saw that what I really wanted was the same thing she did, a normal marriage with a woman who wanted to be taken care of and who wanted to take care of me. My parents had had that. In all their years together they had never exchanged a harsh word. Rena's parents had had it, too, before they were torn apart by the war. Neither Rena nor I had lived what I would call ordinary lives, but despite everything, we both wanted what I think most everybody wants: love with someone who loves you. That need doesn't leave you. It hadn't left us, and by the time we married we were both seventy. It still hasn't left us, ten years later.

When I was nineteen years old, doing my very first nightclub engagement, at New York's La Martinique, I had sung Kurt Weill's beautiful "September Song." Ever since then the song has been one of my favorites. I think I sang it with a lot of emotion back then. But the words do mean more now that I really am reaching toward December: "And these few precious days I'll spend with you." For me, at this stage, the lyrics are a lot more than just a coda to a song. Now they seem more like a coda to my life: "These precious days I'll spend with you." No one has to tell me how lucky I am that it's turned out the way it has.